D0701416

RECIPROCAL
SOVEREIGNTY

Resolving Conflict Respectfully

TONY ROFFERS, PHD

ISBN: 1-4392-6516-X
ISBN-13: 9781439265161

ACKNOWLEDGEMENTS

A group of eight attorney mediators met with me once a month for approximately six years to engage in one of the most enjoyable training experiences of my life. These attorneys intuitively sensed that once they left the adversarial way of resolving conflicts they entered a different world. The world of collaborative conflict resolution required a different perspective and new skills. The communication skills model delineated in this book evolved from our work together, and I want to acknowledge and thank each one of these highly skilled attorneys: Dana Curtis, Laura Farrow, Nancy Foster, Susan Keel, Arlene Kostant, Katherine Page Nowell, Maude Pervere, and Martina Reaves.

I have deep gratitude to my mentors Robert R. Carkhuff, who taught me that empathic responding is a trainable skill; John Gottman, who taught me that emotionally flooded people have a difficult time using their communication skills; and Asha Clinton, who taught me that trauma, the source of flooding, responds to effective treatment.

My heartfelt thanks to Tom Jackson, Ernie Baumgarten, Nancy Pearson, Martina Reaves, Nancy Foster, Stephanie Marohn, and Judi MacMurray for offering many valuable suggestions for the book.

CONTENTS

PREFACE

As a psychologist I have devoted the last forty-two years to helping my clients live more effective lives and have trained hundreds of therapists how to work more effectively with their clients. This book describes a communication skills process that gradually evolved to assist couples in resolving their conflicts more amicably and collaboratively. This process later evolved into a model for assisting mediators in working with couples that wanted to end their marriage but not go through the typically adversarial legal process. The process has also been used in organizations both to prevent and to resolve conflicts in the work environment. It has since been expanded into a model that can be used by anyone who wishes to gain clarity, if not resolution, in any kind of conflict or disagreement. The model is also useful when two or more people must make an important decision together.

I have often wondered why I have been so interested in helping others resolve their differences in a more respectful and less adversarial way. My first hunch is that I didn't learn how to do it very well myself in my own family. My parents never fought or argued in front of me or even made joint decisions in my presence. As a result, I never observed how they made joint decisions or resolved their disagreements. I later observed my peers and their families. Nobody seemed to deal directly and effectively with conflict. I observed that people either avoided conflict and hung onto their grudges while withdrawing from each other, or argued and blamed each other.

In a way, I developed an allergy to conflict. I avoided it like the plague and spent most of my life trying to prevent it by not being fully myself. Instead, I would try to assess in advance what others wanted and then either give it to them or hide my true feelings.

When I was in training to become a therapist, I realized this pattern was not effective and learned various ways to deal more effectively with disagreements and conflicts. Working as a couples' therapist was particularly challenging because I was often thrown into the middle of heated arguments in which I was expected to be the wise judge deciding who was right and how to get the other person to see the error of their ways. I soon learned that this was a trap and that my role was quite different from that of a judge. I realized that if I were to truly help these people I needed to redefine my role as a teacher who would instruct them on how to handle their differences on their own when they were not in my office. The conflict resolution model you are about to learn came from this transformation in my role with couples in conflict.

If you are part of a relationship or organization that is in conflict, reading this book can help you understand how to communicate in a way that maximizes your chances of reaching resolution. I can guarantee that you will gain clarity and that there will be fewer misunderstandings. Many conflicts are caused by misunderstandings and this model is particularly good at discovering them.

Conflict resolution is intrinsically an emotionally difficult process for many people. If you are one of those people this model can give you a structure that will make the process less mysterious and upsetting for you. Some will be able to implement the skills delineated in this model simply by reading the book and practicing them with the person or group with whom they are having difficulty. Others may need additional training or coaching. I periodically lead workshops to train people in these skills and coach those who need guidance as they are implementing the model. To learn about these options, you can contact me through my website (www.tonyroffers.com) or at the address given at the end of this book.

If you are a therapist, marriage counselor, mediator, relationship coach, or related professional, this book can give you a model for training your clients in resolving their differences either to improve their relationship or to end it. Organizational development consultants can use the model for training managers, supervisors, and employees to prevent or resolve conflicts. Productivity and job satisfaction can increase significantly if an entire organizational community is trained in these skills and agrees to use them when there are disagreements or conflicts.

The title of this book, Reciprocal Sovereignty, was chosen because it describes the kind of relationship that embodies the mutual respect needed between two or more people to resolve conflicts collaboratively. The model both requires and creates mutual respect between people. People can, of course, have the mutual respect that reciprocal sovereignty requires without using this model. If there is no conflict mutual respect can prevail quite naturally. Once there is conflict, however, the interpersonal ambiance of mutual respect all too often evaporates quickly. Though this is common and understandable, it does not help the conflict resolution process, which is why this model can be so useful and effective under those circumstances.

Because resolving disagreements and conflicts can be difficult and emotionally upsetting for many, this model provides a process you can follow that will make resolution more likely and easier to achieve. At a minimum, this model will help you gain clarity on the issues involved in your conflicts so you can make better decisions if resolution is not possible. It also has the added benefit of maintaining and possibly enhancing the rapport you have with the other person or group.

I have spent my entire adult life learning the attitudes, values, and skills espoused in this book. It has proven much easier to write about these skills and attitudes than to live them. Having the structure of this model to follow, however, has gradually healed my allergy to conflict, and although I still don't enjoy conflict, I find it much less intimidating and stressful.

INTRODUCTION

Traditionally, a sovereign person reigned superior over others, supreme in power, rank, or authority such as a ruler, chief, king, queen, or boss. Individuals, groups, and countries have fought for domination over each other from the beginning of human culture.

Relationships based on one person wielding power over another person, or one group over another, provides a major source of conflict. Because it takes a great deal of work and skill to conduct relationships any other way, and because the people who have power over others usually resist voluntarily giving it up, power relationships remain ubiquitous. While it takes considerable skill and patience to conduct egalitarian relationships in which people resolve differences collaboratively, such relationships yield enormous benefits of reduced interpersonal conflict, tension, and resentment. They also create more opportunities for individuals to grow and develop in ways unique to them, unfettered by the demands and expectations of others.

Power relationships emerge when one person or group has sovereignty over the other. This arrangement has short-term advantages of efficiency, control, and wealth for the person or group in power as well as less obvious short-term advantages, such as less responsibility and accountability, for those who yield power. However, in the long-term, power-oriented relationships usually spawn anger, resentment, and rebellion by those with less power, ultimately leading to conflict. While power relationships can last a lifetime for individuals and for generations among groups of peoples, they usually end in disaster and cause great turmoil and lost potential for many people along the way. If we seek to increase the quality of our personal relationships and the quality of our individual lives, we must find ways to relate to one another that free us to become more fully who we are, and to achieve our full potential while respecting the rights of others to do the same. I believe that if marriage partners, ethnic and religious groups, political parties, business and government institutions, as well as nations could learn to engage in egalitarian relationships, rather than power oriented hierarchical relationships, they would experience the long term advantages of reduced interpersonal and inter-group conflict, increased individual creativity and productivity, feelings of safety, enjoyment, personal growth, as well as reduced stress.

The opposite of power relationships are egalitarian relationships. This book focuses on how conflicts can be resolved within the context of two or more parties who respect each other as equals. Three components are involved:

- Having sovereignty over one's self
- Respecting others' sovereignty
- Reciprocal sovereignty

HAVING SOVEREIGNTY OVER YOURSELF

Having sovereignty over myself means exercising my independent will based on my own values – even when my choices and actions do not meet with others' approval. I have the freedom to choose for myself whether or not others like or approve of my choices. If my choice gives my life meaning or happiness without intentionally harming you or directly depriving you, I am exercising my sovereign power of choice. If I fail to exercise this priceless asset, I cannot advocate for myself in a disagreement, nor will I likely muster the courage to leave an unacceptable relationship.

Part One of this book explores ways of developing full sovereignty over one's self. If you never gain sovereignty over yourself, you will endlessly play slave or pawn in someone else's drama.

RESPECTING OTHERS' SOVEREIGNTY

Respecting your sovereignty means that I don't try to control your life through physical force, psychological manipulation or intimidation, and that I respect your right to make your own choices based on your own desires and value system, and I also respect your right to act on those choices even if I dislike or disagree with them.

Part Two of this book explores the attitudes and skills helpful in respecting others' sovereignty. Ironically, when one claims their own sovereignty, respecting others' sovereignty becomes easier. Part Two challenges the belief that we have the right to control how other people live.

RECIPROCAL SOVEREIGNTY

Resolving conflicts with reciprocal sovereignty means working together as equals to resolve differences through mutually acceptable solutions. This way of relating has its roots in a definition of the word sovereignty which describes one nation having independence from another nation, as when the United States declared independence from England.

Part Three of this book extends this definition to all levels of relationships, focusing on interpersonal relationships first and how honoring each others' sovereignty is a prerequisite for resolving conflict collaboratively.

If I honor my sovereignty as well as yours, and you honor your sovereignty as well as mine, we can relate with reciprocal sovereignty. Reciprocal sovereignty exists when I make decisions and act for my own welfare in a way that does not impinge on your right to decide and act for your welfare, and when you make decisions and act for your welfare in a way that does not impinge on my right to decide and act for my welfare.

When I make decisions and act for my own benefit without any intention of harming you, I behave "selftruistically" (being true to myself). Selftruistic behavior differs from selfishness. When I act selfishly, I make decisions and act for myself at your expense, or in a way that takes away your freedom to make choices and to act for yourself. It is not selfish to live my life as I see fit, as long as I do not intentionally intrude upon or harm you; it is selfish to insist that you live your life as I see fit. Conversely, it is not selfish for you to live your life as you see fit, as long as you do not intentionally intrude upon or harm me; it is selfish for you to insist that I live my life the way you want me to.

If I act selfishly, I impinge on your sovereignty while doing something for myself. If I act selftruistically, I honor your sovereignty while doing something for myself.

For example, Jack and Jane seek to divorce amicably and remain friends in the process. Jack moved out about two months ago. Jane really doesn't want the divorce but is going along with it. She calls Jack and after they greet each other she says:

Jane: "You never call me anymore. I thought you said we could still be friends. Friends call each other once in a while you know."

Jack: "I do call you once in a while. I've been incredibly busy with this report that's due next week."

Jane: "You're always busy. That's no excuse! If it weren't a report it would be something else. How about meeting this afternoon and taking a hike like we used to? You need to take a break anyway."

Jack: "I really can't. I'd like to, but I need to keep working if I'm going to make the deadline."

Jane: "You really don't want to spend any time with me do you? You just told me you want to be friends to make the divorce easier to do. (She starts crying.) I can't believe a thing you say anymore!"

Jack: "Oh shit!" (He hangs up)

This conversation demonstrates how not honoring someone's sovereignty can alienate. Jane wants Jack to spend more time with her, but she does it in a way that fails to respect Jack's sovereignty (i.e., his right to make decisions and act on them even if they do not please her).

With reciprocal sovereignty this conversation could have gone differently:

Jane: "Jack I really miss you these days. Even though we are getting divorced I still would like to spend time with you."

Jack: "Yeah I know. I've been really anxious about this report that's due next week."

Jane: "I know you feel pressured by that. Is there any way that you would be willing to take a break from it sometime when you're blitzed by it and maybe go for a hike."

Jack: "Yeah I could do that but I never know in advance when I'll feel like it. If you could just hang loose with it, I'd be willing to call you and let you know when I could use a break, and if you could do it we'd just go then."

Jane: "Sure, that would be fine as long as I'm not doing something that I need to do."

Jack: "No problem, that's only fair."

In this case Jack makes choices and acts for his own welfare while honoring Jane's sovereignty; Jane makes choices and acts on her welfare while honoring Jack's sovereignty.

FOUR STAGES OF DEVELOPMENT

Understanding the following four stages of personal development can assist the reader in learning how to develop not only their own sense of sovereignty over themselves but how to engage in the kind of reciprocal sovereignty that is necessary for resolving conflicts collaboratively. While these stages are not strictly linear, people usually develop from one stage to the next in the following order:

- Self-unawareness
- Submission/Aggression
- Sovereignty
- Service

Self-unawareness. The first stage of development, characterized by our inability to observe our thoughts, feelings, and sensations, occurs not because we don't experience them but because we lack awareness of ourselves experiencing them. Young children live in this state naturally, and adults stay in this state because their parents and teachers have not empathized with them as children. When not acknowledged as a separate being with independent thoughts and feelings, children cannot develop a truly autonomous sense of self or identity. When we do not learn to develop awareness of ourselves or to observe our thoughts, feelings, sensations, and actions, we lack the capacity to make true choices. We may feel that we choose, but these largely illusory "choices" turn out to be responses conditioned by cultural expectations and the expectations of authority figures, friends, and advertisers.

Submission/Aggression. Submissiveness and aggressiveness, two sides of the same coin, elicit each other. Submissiveness, that stage of our development when we defer to others, is largely appropriate for children and adolescents who must depend on adults for their survival and education. Children appropriately defer to more knowing and more skilled adults in regard to many important life tasks. Healthy adults in this stage can experience increasingly self-aware states and yet know when they need the help of others.

Less healthy adults who fixate at this stage of submissiveness stay dependent on others' assistance and approval beyond the time optimal for their growth and development. Typically, submissive people have low self esteem and remain overly compliant and dependent. They essentially do not know how to honor their own sovereignty and therefore often betray themselves unknowingly. Their boundaries remain weak or confused and they mistake love with needing or being needed by someone. Excessive concern with the approval of others becomes a prison.

The other side of submissiveness is aggressiveness. Aggressive people demand or force others to act the way they think others should and do not honor their right to choose and act independently. Aggressive people attempt to have sovereignty over others and feel entitled to control or dominate others in terms of how they live and what they do. Aggressive people usually have grown up in a power-oriented family structure where reciprocal sovereignty did not exist. Instead, they experienced an environment characterized by a pecking order of power and dominance among family members with someone at the top ruling the others. Forced into submissiveness, some children grow up to become aggressive once they escape the parent in power.

People who become aggressive tend to make decisions for others and dominate or manipulate them. Aggression can take overt and belligerent forms, as in a physical fight, or it can operate more covertly through psychological or verbal domination and manipulation.

For example, George, a landscape architect in his early forties, and Ruth, an elementary school teacher in her late thirties, have been married for five years and live in a middle class neighborhood in the Midwest. Ruth currently drives an eleven-year-old Toyota station wagon with four-wheel drive. It is losing power, and it blows dark colored exhaust when she starts it up in the morning. She opens a conversation with George by saying:

Ruth: I'm beginning to get worried about the Toyota, George. It just crawls up the hill in the morning. It seems to take longer to wake up than you do."

George: "I've told you a hundred times to get rid of it and get a Camry. Consumer Reports rates them as high as anything except a

Lexus, which has almost the same engine. You're stupid to keep driving that old clunker."

Ruth: "Well it's been a good car until now and I don't want to give it up, but maybe you're right. I've been thinking of getting a Volvo. I had one years ago and I loved…"

George: "You don't want a dinosaur like that!! They drive like tanks and they don't look much better. Get a clue Rootie."

Ruth: "But I <u>like</u> how it looks, and it's…"

George: "Looks! It's like an upside down bathtub! No, worse! It's more like a dilapidated milk carton on its side. God, I swear I can't understand how that pea brain of yours works."

Ruth: "But all those new cars look the same. I can't tell one from the other. They're too curvy for me and besides…"

George: "They have curves because they have been tested in wind tunnels for wind resistance. They make them aerodynamically now like an airplane so you'll get better gas mileage. Volvos get about ten miles to the gallon if they're going down hill. Camry's get decent mileage and they have very sophisticated engines, brakes, the whole works. They're light years ahead of Volvos!"

Ruth: "But Volvos are safe! You gotta admit that!"

George: "Yeah they're safe like a Sherman tank is safe and they have so much heavy Swedish steel that it takes a gallon of gas just to get it started up from a stop light. You don't know shit about cars, Ruth, admit it."

Ruth: (tears in her eyes) "Maybe not. I just want a safe car that…"

George: "Okay, so we'll go down to that Toyota dealership on Lake Street Saturday and I'll show you what you should get."

The above dialogue illustrates how Ruth's submissiveness colludes with George's aggressiveness. George dishonors Ruth's sovereignty by failing to respect Ruth's right to have her own preferences about cars, let alone her right to choose a car she wants. George repeatedly interrupts her and ultimately assumes she'll capitulate when he makes a unilateral decision to take her to the Toyota dealership.

Ruth's submissiveness illustrates how she does not honor her sovereignty. She fails to exercise her right to make her own decision and thereby reinforces George's behavior by allowing him to interrupt her and verbally coerce her into going to the Toyota dealership.

This power relationship may work for a while longer if Ruth continues to defer and remains ignorant of her sovereignty. However, Ruth ultimately will feel increasing resentment toward George whether she understands the reasons or not. That resentment will usually become expressed indirectly or passively through withheld affection, sexual problems, or complaints.

The submissiveness and aggressiveness syndrome leads to a combination of compliance and defiance that we will discuss later. It does not lead to an egalitarian intimacy between Ruth and George. Sadly, as long as neither of them understands the possibilities of reciprocal sovereignty, their disintegrating relationship will continue to puzzle and frustrate both of them.

Sovereignty. Using Ruth as an example reveals the process of developing sovereignty over herself. As she grows more aware of herself and her right to have her own opinions and feelings and then exercises her will independent of George's approval, she will increasingly make decisions for herself based on her own values and welfare, and she will differentiate between being true to herself and being selfish. She will learn how to be *proactive* in regard to her values, interests, and preferences instead of *reactive* to others' demands or expectations. While remaining open to George's requests and preferences, she will not feel obligated to follow them to maintain his acceptance or approval. If she agrees with him or thinks he has a valid point, she will go along with him, but she will not betray herself or her own viewpoint in order to gain his approval or to maintain a false harmony with him.

When Ruth attains sovereignty over herself, she sits on her own supreme court. She assumes dominion over herself. She exercises independent will over other people's demands or expectations of her. She may also learn to have more control over her thoughts, feelings, and actions. She constructs a more authentic and congruent core within herself.

More specifically, Ruth will take George's viewpoint on Volvos and Camry's seriously. However, she will still buy a Volvo if she values safety and her own aesthetic preferences over lower frequency of repair and higher gas mileage.

Using George as an example illustrates the process of developing respect for the other person's sovereignty. As he grows more aware of Ruth's right to make her own independent decisions when it does not adversely effect him directly, he will learn to respect those decisions even if he does not agree with them. He will learn how to respect her wishes, needs, feelings and viewpoints without necessarily liking them. He will directly express his opinions to her without assuming his view as the only right one. He will recognize that his demands and expectations (i.e., unspoken demands) fail to respect Ruth's sovereignty by crushing her differing viewpoints and values with his dogmatism. He also will understand how forcing his point of view on Ruth alienates her, causing her to withdraw from him. He will no longer see her as a recalcitrant and uncooperative ingrate, but as someone who has the right to buy a car with a proven safety record in spite of its lower gas mileage. He will also accept that Ruth has different but not wrong aesthetic values.

Metaphorically, life fits almost everyone with custom tinted lenses. Those with blue lenses see the world as blue; those with green see green. Although few can ever discard the lenses entirely, learning to peep around the edges reveals a world of more fully aware adults capable of reciprocal sovereignty: a world of mutual understanding and acceptance. When George and Ruth learn to peep around their lenses, they will more clearly see, and thus better understand, each other.

When George learns how to honor Ruth's sovereignty, he will move a long way toward his own sovereignty. He will no longer need to control Ruth as a way of shoring up his own sense of self and security. He will see that he doesn't have to dominate her or keep her under his control in order to feel secure in his relationship with her. Rather, by respecting her right to her own preferences and choices, even when they differ from his own, he will find her much more open to him and less resentful.

For both Ruth and George this level of acceptance will require a lot of awareness and work. Reciprocal sovereignty requires conscious development. The developmental distance between the stages of submissiveness/aggressiveness and sovereignty stretches as wide as the distance between a rock and a plant, or a plant and an animal, or an animal and a human.

If George fails to learn how to honor Ruth's sovereignty and if Ruth increasingly achieves sovereignty over her self, she may begin to question why she stays with someone who disrespects her sovereignty. If not reciprocated, acquisition of sovereignty may lead to separation.

Let's replay the example of George and Ruth after they have awakened to the possibility of treating themselves and each other with the skills of reciprocal sovereignty:

Ruth: "I'm beginning to get worried about the Toyota, George. It just crawls up the hill in the morning and I see a big black cloud of exhaust in my rear view mirror."

George: "I know what you mean, I've seen the smoke myself. You sound pretty worried about it."

Ruth: "Yeah, I really love that car. But I know it's got to go soon and I'm not sure what to do."

George: "Do you want to talk about it?"

Ruth: "Yeah I do…but I'm afraid you won't like what I'm thinking."

George: "Well, I know I have strong opinions about cars, but I'll try to control myself and listen to you."

Ruth: "I would really appreciate that. I've been thinking about a Volvo. I used to have a station wagon years ago and I really loved it!"

George: "What was so special about it?"

Ruth: "Well, I like how I used to sit up high in the driver's seat, and I particularly like how it's got more of a squared shape and not like all these new cars now. I can't tell one from the other. They all look so curvy and the same."

George: "So it's the shape and the way the front seat is that makes you want to own another one?"

Ruth: "Yeah, I think so. But I also like how safe they are. I don't think you can buy a safer car, do you?"

George: "I agree, I think they are very safe and I do think that's an important point. I do have some opinions about Volvos that are not so positive. Would you be willing to hear them?"

Ruth: "Sure, that's why I wanted to bring it up."

George: "Well, one reason I think they're so safe is that they have a lot of heavy Swedish steel in them but that also makes them very heavy so they don't get very good gas mileage. That means extra costs to our transportation budget that I don't like. Because it does burn more gas, it also doesn't fit with our attempt to buy more ecologically oriented things."

Ruth: "What kind of gas mileage does it actually get?"

George: "I'm not sure but we could look it up in Consumer Reports. Which reminds me that the last time I looked they didn't have a very good frequency of repair rating which could also add to our costs and the hassle of bringing it into the shop a lot. You know how that screws up our day when we have to take each other back and forth."

Ruth: "Well, it's true I want something reliable as well as safe. But it sounds like you really think the gas mileage and repair costs are more important."

George: "I' guess I do, at least I'd like you to think about them along with the ecological considerations. I also have to admit that I don't particularly like how Volvos look. It's not that I hate how they look; I just prefer the aerodynamic look of other cars, particularly the Camry, which also is pretty safe and gets better gas mileage. It also has a very low frequency of repair record."

Ruth: "I know you like the Camry and it's true we have different tastes about cars. I'd be willing to test drive one given all the advantages you think it has. But I can't promise I would buy one because I really like Volvos. I guess I would just like to test drive each of them on the same day and then make up my mind."

George: "I like that idea. Would it be okay with you if I go along if I try not to sell you on the Camry?"

This dialogue illustrates how both Ruth and George can listen to each other, demonstrate their understanding of one another, and then come from their own perspectives in a direct and respectful way. They can respect each other's point of view without necessarily agreeing with it. This frees them both to learn from each other's viewpoints and come up with a potentially better decision. More importantly, they can live together without the usual tensions and resentments that can accrue when the stress of buying a car germinates the additional stress of a power struggle. The example above briefly illustrates a number of the skills in the conflict resolution model described in this book.

Service. A fourth stage of development deserves description. Only after reaching and solidifying our own sovereignty can we attain the developmental stage of service. True service to others (or to plants, animals, and the earth) implies that we assist out of conscious choice, that we have enough autonomy of will to make the conscious choice to help others because we choose to, because we care, and because we experience the interconnectedness of all things and all beings.

Before we achieve sovereignty, much of our helping arises from submissiveness, or a sense of duty and obligation. We need other people to like us, or we depend upon them for approval. Service before sovereignty often promotes servility.

HOW TO READ THIS BOOK

This book includes four parts: Part One explores methods of developing sovereignty over ourselves; Part Two illuminates ways to respect other people's sovereignty; Part Three focuses on how to resolve conflicts collaboratively; and Part Four demonstrates how a professional therapist and an attorney mediator can use the conflict resolution model in a couples counseling session and a divorce mediation respectively.

In the first two parts, we learn that achieving sovereignty over ourselves is important for our healthy development as human beings, and is a prerequisite for effectively engaging in a conflict resolution dialogue with others; and resolving conflicts in a collaborative manner requires us to respect other people's right to differ from us by acknowledging their sovereignty.

In Part Three, we look at two different types of conflicts: a conflict of values and a conflict of needs. We explore how to resolve each type. This section provides a structure for anyone who finds him or herself in conflict with someone and wants to know how to deal with it more effectively. It also provides therapists and mediators with a model for how to conduct a couples counseling or mediation session for resolving conflict.

As a professional therapist, coach, or mediator, you may be able to apply the model with your clients after reading the book. If you would like further instruction in how to use the model, however, this training is available by the author (see www.tonyroffers.com). Please refer to the Conclusion for further information.

Part Four gives examples of how the conflict resolution process can apply in a couples counseling session and in a divorce mediation. This part is written particularly for professional therapists, coaches, and mediators but may also be useful for anyone who wishes to get a realistic picture of how the model can work when there is a professional present to facilitate the process.

Professional therapists and mediators may choose to start with Part Three, which describes the collaborative conflict resolution model, and then read that section of Part Four that parallels your professional expertise.

If you are not a professional therapist or mediator, you can use this book in two ways. Those interested primarily in learning how to resolve conflicts collaboratively may want to shortcut to Part Three, Reciprocal Sovereignty, and read that section first to get an initial feeling for how the collaborative process works to resolve conflict constructively. Then, after trying the process with someone and having difficulty implementing the skills required, you can go back to Part One, Part Two, or both, depending on your assessment of what you need.

For example, if you have difficulty standing up for yourself or for your own point of view, Part One will provide a good overview of what you may need to learn before engaging in the conflict resolution process effectively. If you sense your domination or control of others hinders your success, Part Two suggests how best to change your attitudes and ways of approaching those who differ from you.

You can also read this book from beginning to end to get an overview of all the components of effective conflict resolution before trying to implement them. This method gives a broad perspective on what is involved in collaborative conflict resolution.

PART ONE
SOVEREIGNTY OVER YOURSELF

Carl Jung, the famous Swiss analyst, wrote in his book *Memories, Dreams, Reflections* about the individuation process as a stage during which we grow more independent of others' views of us. How differentiated we become from others, particularly significant others, bears heavily on how well we can hold our own in negotiations with others. Disagreements and conflicts often test the degree of individuation or differentiation in our development.

Having sovereignty over yourself proves important if you want to engage in relationships with others and not lose yourself or your point of view in the process, particularly if you have a conflict with someone or are vulnerable to the manipulative or controlling tactics of others.

People who have sovereignty over themselves can take responsibility for their actions. They can admit how they may have contributed to a misunderstanding or conflict. They can also calm themselves down without counting on others to do that for them. They may want, but not *need,* others to understand them or agree with them.

Learning to have sovereignty over yourself remains important not only in your life generally, but particularly in your conflicts with others. Honoring your own sovereignty goes hand in hand with respecting others' sovereignty. Learning to honor your own right to live your life as you see fit will enable you to respect other peoples' right to do the same.

I believe the journey to the land of reciprocal sovereignty can take place at any stage of life. Let's first look at how parents can help their children develop sovereignty over themselves and then how we as adults can claim it for ourselves.

CHAPTER ONE
HOW TO HELP CHILDREN DEVELOP SOVEREIGNTY

Far and away, it is best to develop a sense of sovereignty over one self as a child. This requires, however, conscious and skilled parenting and teaching. Although in this chapter I emphasize the role of parenting, everything I say is relevant to school teachers, child-care workers, grandparents, aunts, uncles, religious leaders, and anyone who frequently comes in contact with children.

How can parents raise their children to grow up with a sense of sovereignty over themselves? How can parents teach their children the limits necessary for social living and concurrently help them maintain their sense of individuality, uniqueness, and independence so they can make decisions for themselves?

The answer to these questions lies in a passage from *The Prophet* by Kahill Gibran:

Your children are not your children.
They are the sons and daughters of Life's longing for itself.
They come through you but not from you,
And though they are with you yet they belong not to you.
You may give them your love but not your thoughts,
For they have their own thoughts.
You may house their bodies but not their souls,
For their souls dwell in the house of tomorrow, which you cannot
*   visit, not even in your dreams.*
You may strive to be like them, but seek not to make them like you.

It all begins with parents' respect for their children as unique human beings, beings they have brought into the world but do not believe they own. They have leased their children for a finite period with the privilege of feeding, clothing, and nurturing them and then setting them free to go into the world with their own unique style, direction, and values. Parents can influence their children's development in profound ways, but ultimately they do not have sovereignty over them. Parents must understand this if they want their children to have sovereignty over themselves.

Many parents find this difficult to understand or to do because they sincerely believe that they should mold their children into their own image, or more commonly, their own idealized image of themselves. This often causes psychological damage to children and creates a significant barrier to their development of sovereignty over themselves.

Parents can best teach their children to have sovereignty over themselves by responding to their needs, wants, and feelings with understanding. Parents need to empathize with their children, reflect back to them what they communicate verbally or nonverbally so that the children feel understood and validated as separate and unique beings. This does not mean that parents have to give their children everything they want, or that they must always agree with them. It does mean, however, that parents need to communicate that they understand what their children want or need and that their children have the right to their own unique wants, feelings, and opinions.

For example, if Patty wants an ice cream cone, her parents should avoid telling Patty that she really doesn't want the ice cream cone (discounting Patty's feelings and desires), or that Patty shouldn't want the ice cream cone (criticizing Patty's feelings and desires), or that Patty is bad for wanting an ice cream cone (judging Patty as a person). Instead, her parents can let Patty know that they understand her desire for an ice cream cone (i.e., they empathize with her) and then explain to Patty that it is too close to dinnertime or that ice cream has an unhealthy amount of sugar in it. Her parents can empathize with Patty's tears or anger for not getting the ice cream cone rather than telling her she shouldn't feel sad or angry.

This respect for Patty's right to her own feelings and opinions establishes an important foundation for her to develop her own unique identity, her sense of who she is separate from her parents, how she feels, what she does or does not want, and her right to those feelings and desires. This ultimately paves the way for her to begin to make her own choices once she finds herself on her own. In short, she will feel entitled to her own sovereignty, her right to make choices on her own and act on those choices even if people disagree with her.

DEMONSTRATING UNDERSTANDING TO CHILDREN

For children to develop a sense of sovereignty over themselves, parents must learn how to empathize with them. If you want your child to "have a mind of her own," you will need not only to listen to her, but also to demonstrate that you understand what she communicates by putting into words what you sense she feels and why she feels that way. In other words, paraphrasing the content of what she says and describing in words what you sense she feels are both crucial in helping her know you have heard her accurately. This will prove to her that you actually heard her, help her identify her feeling more accurately, help her explore the meaning of what she says, and give her a sense of individual identity. You will help her know who she is as a separate person. She will feel respected by you and she will know that you consider her important enough to have paid attention to her, listened to her, noticed how she felt, and accurately understood what she tried to tell you. It will also give her a chance to clarify any inaccuracies for you in your perception of what she is feeling.

I can't overemphasize what an important role demonstrating understanding plays in helping your child develop sovereignty over herself and to grasp her identity as a separate person who has the right to her own feelings and point of view, even if they differ from yours. You have to experience it to believe it. Many parents neither grasp the importance of this nor have the skill to do it. The benefits only accrue after months and years, so it takes a great deal of patience and trust. It takes even longer if you start later in your child's life after years of the absence of empathy in your relationship. But it remains worth doing. It will just take longer for your child to trust you and believe that you really do care about what she has to say and about her sense of self.

Most parents don't even think about trying to demonstrate understanding to their children because their own parents seldom understood them. Even when parents learn about the importance of empathizing with their children, they often resist because parents often confuse empathy with agreement. They think if they demonstrate that they have accurately heard what their child has said to them, their child will think they have agreed with them and thus misbehave. This is not true. You can demonstrate that you accurately understand your child and then make it very clear that you disagree. You can also exert your parental power and refuse to give approval of what your child wants. I repeat, just because you listen to what your child wants, understand what your child wants, and demonstrate your accurate understanding of what your child wants, it does not mean that you have to agree or yield to her.

You really will not lose power or control over your child if you empathize with her! You have simply demonstrated to your child that you consider her important enough as a human being to be listened to and understood. Even if you refuse to give her the ice cream cone (or the family car on Saturday night), you have given her something incredibly important whether she knows it in the moment or not. You have respected the child as a separate person who has feelings and desires worthy of attention and an honest, direct response. You have given the child a sense of self-worth and value as a human being. You have facilitated her sense of self-awareness and autonomy. You have respected her sovereignty as a separate individual who has the right to her own feelings, opinions, and desires.

I will define and describe empathy in more detail later, and you will learn how to demonstrate your understanding of someone accurately even if you are in disagreement or conflict. Many people need training in empathic responding before they can do it effectively. Knowing its importance, however, can help to motivate you to learn how to do it better. Just the effort to listen to what your child says and the attempt to put into your own words what she has said to you in order to check if you have understood accurately will help. What you say may sound strange at first, and your child may not respond well to it immediately. This underscores the importance of training because the unpracticed can sound artificial. You have to develop a whole different mindset to empathize genuinely. You also have to learn when empathy is not appropriate. Paying attention to your child, listening to her, demonstrating your understanding, and getting corroboration from her that, indeed, you do understand her accurately, remains the single most important thing you can do as a parent to support your child's sense of self-worth, self-awareness, and sovereignty.

Everything I have said about how parents can facilitate the development of sovereignty in their children can be said to teachers, childcare workers, grandparents, and anyone who works with children.

MODELING SOVEREIGNTY OVER YOURSELF

In addition to demonstrating understanding of your children, the next best way to help them develop sovereignty over themselves is to model sovereignty over yourself. Being self-responsible, that is, making your own decisions without undo consideration as to whether others will accept those decisions and not needing everyone's approval, will teach your child through your behavior to be his or her own person. This modeling in conjunction with empathy for your children and respect for their boundaries serves as a powerful combination for facilitating their sovereignty over themselves.

SUMMARY

- Parents do not own their children.
- Parents, grandparents, teachers, and other child-care workers need to learn how to demonstrate accurate understanding (empathize) with children to facilitate their self-esteem and sovereignty over themselves.
- Parents who model having sovereignty over themselves will also facilitate their children's sovereignty.

CHAPTER TWO

DEVELOPING SOVEREIGNTY OVER
YOURSELF AS AN ADULT

If your parents did not follow Gibran's philosophy and raised you as though they owned you, they unwittingly forced you into what I call the "compliant/defiant syndrome." This syndrome traps you into a maze of reactivity. Hypnotized into believing that others have the right to dictate how you live, you can only react to them by complying or defying. Many people have work to do in claiming their proactivity, selftruism, and sovereignty. How can you as an adult develop sovereignty over yourself, particularly if your parents did not know how to respect and nurture your sovereignty as a child?

- Rather than following the dictates of your parents and doing what others think you should, you can learn how to become more aware of yourself, your preferences, your values, and begin making decisions based on them.
- Rather than surround yourself with people who want to control or dominate you, you can surround yourself with partners, friends, bosses, and work associates who respect your right to make choices for yourself. In those instances in which you have no choice, for example, with your parents, you can learn to immunize yourself from needing their approval. In some cases, you may even choose to limit your contact with them.
- Rather than depending on others' acceptance, understanding, appreciation, or support, you can learn to depend on and comfort yourself.
- Even if others don't agree or approve of you or your actions, you can learn to be true to yourself and to the values important to you.

- Rather than reacting to what others want you to do, you can become more proactive in your life by following what has heart and meaning to you.
- Rather than denying those actions that may have been mistakes or harmful to others, you can take responsibility for your actions.
- Rather than remaining unaware of your intentions and motivations, you can learn to inquire into yourself and explore what drives you so you can continue to grow and develop in your effectiveness with others.
- Rather than succumbing to ill health and debt, you can build your physical and financial independence in a way that allows you to engage in the difficult process of making decisions and resolving differences with others in an interdependent and collaborative manner.

This chapter explores each of these so you can prepare yourself for relating to others more effectively, particularly when you have important mutual decisions to make or conflicts to resolve. Resolving conflicts collaboratively takes two people who not only honor their own sovereignty, but who also can engage in the communication skills required to process their differences with mutual respect. The skills described in this chapter serve as important prerequisites for engaging in collaborative conflict resolution.

DEVELOP AWARENESS OF YOURSELF

Sovereignty over one's self begins with self-awareness. Awareness of your sensory inputs such as seeing, hearing, and touching serve as building blocks for constructing your awareness of yourself and your experiences. Rather than looking to others for the basis of your decisions, you can learn to trust your own thoughts, feelings, perceptions, desires, and intuitions.

If your parents poorly demonstrated their understanding of you, you will most likely have some difficulty knowing your own mind, trusting your intuitions and perceptions, or knowing what you want. If they tried to teach you that you didn't want the ice cream cone (when you really did), told you that you were "bad" for wanting the ice cream cone (which you weren't), labeled you a "bad" person for wanting it (which you weren't), or called you rebellious or selfish (untrue), then they were probably the type of parents that believed it was their job to make you be like them or what they thought you should be. Anytime you had a thought or desire different from theirs they felt they must correct you, punish you, or criticize you so they could control you into being more like their vision of what you should be. They probably did not do this maliciously, but thought their job required nipping any autonomy in the bud to retain their control so you would turn out like they thought you should. For the sake of obedience and conformity to their expectations, they did not encourage your autonomy, individuality, and uniqueness.

If you were the child of parents who "under-parented," you received the distorted impression that you were not worth understanding or spending time with. They may have given you the impression that you bothered them or got in their way. This did not lead to you feeling good about yourself or to feeling that you had the right to live your life as you saw fit. You might now feel like you have to earn your right to exist by complying with others' wishes in the hope that they will approve of you; or you might feel like rebelling to create the illusion of autonomy from others, not caring or needing others.

Under-parenting or over-parenting leaves the child, and later the adult, in an endless maze of reactivity. To get out of this reactivity maze, you must become aware of the deep, but false, hypnotic induction that you do not have the right to live your own life as you see fit. This maze leaves only two choices: to comply with others or to defy others. In order to dehypnotize yourself, you need to become conscious of this deep hypnotic conditioning and become more aware of yourself, your thoughts, your feelings, and your opinions.

Self-awareness, crucial for developing sovereignty over ourselves, differentiates us from rocks, plants, and animals. Self-awareness makes us unique as humans. Many of us, however, have a hard time being truly aware of ourselves. Behavioral psychologists assert that we harbor a set of conditioned responses that leaves free will an illusion for most of us. Many spiritual traditions view us as essentially "asleep," unconscious of our conditioning by our history and surroundings. We live out of habit and are so hypnotized by our language, families of origin, cultural customs, and advertising that our very consciousness reflects those trances. Until we wake up to this realization, we will remain victims of these hypnotic inductions and have little hope of developing enough self-awareness to have sovereignty over ourselves.

If you had parents who respected your sovereignty, you may have grown up understanding your right to make decisions for yourself based on the data you got from your senses or intuition, and to act on those decisions even though others may not agree with you. If you did not have those kinds of parents, you likely grew up feeling you did not have the right to make your own decisions or to act on them. When you no longer give other peoples' opinions, judgments, demands, or expectations final say over what you do, you attain sovereignty over yourself. You remain open to others' input, but in the final analysis you decide and act on your own awareness and experiences. Likewise, you take responsibility for those decisions and actions. You assume the right to make your own mistakes as well, so it remains important not to let others convince you that you should be perfect (i.e., not make mistakes). Mistakes constitute an important part of learning and your fallibility as a human being requires you to make errors of judgment periodically.

MEDITATE

Although having others empathically reflect back to you what you experience and feel can help you learn to know yourself better from without, meditation helps you learn awareness of yourself from within. Meditation helps you pay attention to yourself and to your experience. It provides a way to rehabilitate yourself from having grown up without empathetic understanding by your parents and significant others.

Since lack of self-awareness is so pervasive, most of us could benefit from meditation. Having greater awareness of yourself and your experiences can help you gain sovereignty over yourself. Developing more awareness of your thoughts, feeling, and intuitions helps you better honor your choices, and your right to act on those choices even if important people disagree with those choices. You must know yourself to honor yourself.

If you would like to learn more about self-awareness, I recommend Eckhart Tolle's *The Power of Now* and *A New Earth*. After you read these books, I further recommend getting some kind of experiential training in meditation. Most beginners find a guide helpful.

SURROUND YOURSELF WITH PEOPLE WHO HONOR YOUR SOVEREIGNTY

If your parents listened and demonstrated their understanding of you poorly, and if they failed to respect you as a separate person and your boundaries, you will find it particularly important to surround yourself with people who do so now. If you develop relationships with people who can listen to you and honor your right to make your own decisions, those relationships can help to heal your earlier relationships with your parents and other family members who could not listen respectfully to you.

To determine if someone in your current life respects your sovereignty, see how the person responds when you have a decision to make or a problem to solve. Does he try to make your decision for you or tell you how to solve your problem before listening to you? Can he let you explore the decision or problem on your own? Does he demonstrate that he has accurately heard what you have said after letting you talk about it without a lot of interruptions? Can he understand how you feel about the situation or does he just tell you what he thinks you should do or how he feels about your situation?

If you try this and fail to get a good response, ask the person if he would willingly listen to you and put into his own words what he understands you to be saying before offering his opinions or suggestions. Let him know clearly that you would like him to do this to help you explore your problem or situation more fully for yourself to see if you can reach your own resolution. Tell him you might want his ideas or suggestions later, but not until you have more fully explored things on your own. Do not expect another person to understand you accurately right away, but encourage him to keep trying. If he can willingly demonstrate reasonable accuracy before coming from his own frame of reference, you have the potential for creating a healthy relationship. Otherwise, it does not bode well. You cannot develop a reciprocally sovereign relationship with someone who cannot willingly listen to you and demonstrate understanding of you with reasonable accuracy. This particularly holds true when the person disagrees with you, which is usually harder for most people.

Those able to honor your sovereignty usually try to hear you out without a lot of interruptions, and they try to put into their own words what you have said to see if they understood you accurately before they speak from their own frame of reference. They attempt to help you come to your own decision or explore alternative courses of action to resolve the problem before giving advice or doing it for you. They do not assume you want them to decide for you or to solve your problem for you. Instead, they will ask if you want their input after they have heard you out, or they will offer their suggestions in an open-ended rather than in an autocratic way (i.e., imply their way is the only right way).

Seek people who request things of you rather than demand or expect things of you. Instead of assuming things about you, they respect your right to have a point of view that differs from theirs. They believe you have the right to think, feel, and act differently from them even if they do not particularly like it. They may get disappointed and even frustrated when you do things differently, but they do not get righteously indignant, angry, or withdraw to punish you. They can demonstrate that they understand your point of view even if it differs from theirs. These kinds of people not only respect your sovereignty, but will also help you heal the wounds of your childhood.

COMFORT YOURSELF

The ability to comfort yourself without depending on others to do that for you will assist you in having sovereignty over yourself. Ultimately, seek the ability to handle relationships with people who do not respect your sovereignty and to shed their rejection, criticisms, and judgments while holding to your own values and perceptions. You may prefer to have others understand and comfort you, but you must avoid dependency on others to comfort you. If you need others to understand and comfort you, you grow too dependent on them and are unlikely to have the autonomy needed to make your own decisions or negotiate your differences effectively.

When resolving conflicts with others, you need the ability to manage your emotional temperature when things get really stressful. This capacity to soothe yourself, extremely important in holding your own in conflict situations, also leads to more self-sufficiency in your life generally. The goal is to be able to protect and maintain your sovereignty with those who try to control or invade you. We will discuss ways to comfort or soothe yourself later in the book.

BE SELFTRUISTIC

To develop sovereignty over yourself you must also learn to trust your own experiences, perceptions, feelings, thoughts, and intuitions. I have coined the term "selftruistic" to describe people who remain true to themselves. A selftruistic person honors his own health, welfare, conscience, and values (i.e., what is important to him). Such people do not betray themselves in their interactions with others. They are genuine, honest, and authentic with others, allowing their outward behavior to reflect their inner thoughts and feelings, although they understand that situations may arise when this kind of honesty may not always prove beneficial, productive, or wise.

You must learn to differentiate between selftruism, altruism, selfishness, and martyrdom as you develop sovereignty over yourself.

Altruistic persons consciously and unselfishly do things for others out of the goodness of their hearts but without sacrificing their own health and welfare. Altruistic behavior remains quite compatible with selftruistic behavior. In fact, being selftruistic (the hallmark of sovereignty) is the prerequisite of true altruism (the hallmark of service). Selftruism and altruism bloom like flowers on the healthy stalk of sovereignty.

Martyrdom, a kind of extreme unselfishness in which someone suffers greatly or dies for a cause or another's welfare, is either pathological or a conscious choice to sacrifice one self. We may see this as either foolhardy or heroic depending on our point of view.

Selfishness is acting on one's own interests and needs without regard for the interests and needs of others, keeping good things for oneself and not sharing, or insisting that others live their lives the way one thinks they should. Selfishness is sovereignty gone awry.

Selftruism is often confused with selfishness. When we behave selftruistically, others may accuse us of selfishness when in fact we are merely doing something congruent with our own health and welfare and not taking anything away from others, harming them, disrespecting them, or limiting their freedom to act for themselves. In particular, people who believe they have the right to tell us how to live distort selftruism as selfishness. Whenever someone does something with which they don't agree they project their own selfishness onto the other person (i.e., the belief they have the right to tell others how to live). They act affronted, when in fact no one has done anything against them or harmed them. The selftruistic person seeks only to have the freedom to act on his or her own behalf without taking anything away from anybody.

Unfortunately, people who think they have the right to tell others how to live cannot see that you are acting selftruistically for your own welfare and not to defy or disrespect them. To live free requires you to trust your own perceptions and not need others to like or approve of you. People who feel entitled to tell you how to live endanger your sovereignty. If they do not accept your selftruistic behaviors, they will not promote healthy living for you. In my view, such people should be avoided if possible.

Someone who wants sovereignty over you will accuse you of selfishness if you act independently and stop being compliant or deferential. This conscious or unconscious manipulation works very well with those who linger in the submissive stage of development, because they need others' approval. You must understand the difference between selftruism and selfishness if you are to emerge from the stage of submissiveness to the stage of sovereignty.

Once you understand that selftruism does not mean selfishness, you free yourself to pursue your own growth and development without succumbing to the accusations of selfishness by those who feel entitled to control your life.

BE PROACTIVE

To achieve the selftruistic life, and thereby acquire sovereignty over yourself, you must also understand the difference between reactive and proactive behavior. You react when you respond to someone's demands or expectations without realizing you have a choice not to respond. You feel you have no choice but to react, either in compliance or defiance of the person who makes the demand or who holds the expectation. I define expectations as silent, unspoken demands.

Reactivity characterizes the submissive or aggressive stage. You either depend on the acceptance and approval of others or rebel against that dependence. Either route leads to control by outside expectations or demands. You tend to think you need to, ought to, have to, must, or should do what outside forces want you to do (or not do).

Proactivity characterizes the stage of sovereignty. You behave proactively when you act from your own frame of reference, your own point of view, your own wishes, needs, values, feelings, or intuitions. Rather than reacting to someone else, you initiate from within yourself. You behave congruently with your core being, independent of someone else's wishes, demands, or expectations of you.

In order to behave more proactively, you need to understand the compliant/defiant syndrome. Both compliance (doing what others demand or expect) and defiance (doing the opposite of what they demand or expect) leads to reactivity and grants the other person sovereignty over you. This form of reactivity causes many problems. People trapped in these compliant or defiant conundrums usually develop psychological problems and spend much of their lives in the submissive or aggressive stage of development.

Thinking that others have the right to make decisions for you commonly causes you to feel trapped in the emotions of guilt or resentment. If you do what someone expects or demands of you when you don't want to, you feel resentment; if you don't do what they expect or demand of you, you feel guilty.

When you believe that others have the right to make choices for you, you allow their expectations and demands to have sovereignty over you. This belief will entrap you in the submission or aggression stage of development, engulf you in the compliant/defiant syndrome, and consume you with guilt or resentment or both. You will trap yourself in a no-win reactive maze. Whenever you find yourself in conflict over what others think you *should* do and what you *want* to do, you will alternate between resentment and guilt, depending on whether you do what they want or what you want.

Being proactive emancipates you from this maze. To behave proactively you need to understand that other people do not have the right to have sovereignty over you. They do not have the right to make decisions for you. They do not have the right to demand or expect things of you that you do not want to do. Hypnotized into the opposite beliefs (that people *do* have the right) as a child, many people have never awakened from the trance.

Others have the right to request things of you, but not demand them. That does not mean they won't try. You, however, do not have to grant this power to them. In order to break out of the prison of compliance or defiance, you must renounce your need for the acceptance or approval of others. You may desire and prefer their acceptance, but you do not *need* it. You can learn to live independently without others' acceptance or approval. They may accuse you of selfishness, try to manipulate you, or withdraw their love. They may even disown you, divorce you, or write you out of their will. You have a choice between owning your own soul and giving it away. You can choose for yourself or let others choose for you. You must declare and defend your own selftruism in order to achieve sovereignty over yourself.

Being proactive means asserting your sovereignty and protecting your personal boundaries, knowing that you have the right to make decisions for yourself. Spite, revenge, vindictiveness, or selfishness will not fuel your drive toward sovereignty. Sovereignty comes from your own sense of worth, value, conscience, and character. Proactive people live on an entirely different plane from those who live reactively. Sovereign people may sometimes, in fact, do exactly what others expect or demand, but they do so out of choice. People who have sovereignty over themselves *prefer* acceptance and approval from others, but they do not *need* it. Once you understand this, you can embark upon the road to sovereignty.

As an exercise to foster your own proactivity, consciously make realistic commitments to yourself and then meet them whether other people approve of you or not. Decide on something you clearly and specifically want to do for yourself that does not harm others in any way. Schedule it on your calendar if doing it immediately is not feasible. What you decide to do does not matter as much as making a reasonable commitment to yourself and then carrying it out.

Instead of starting with something you think you should do, start with something you want to do. Be sure to choose something realistic. Choose a time when you can enjoy it and not rush. Do it whether others like it or not. Observe how you handle it if others don't approve of you or agree with you. Each time you make and meet a realistic commitment with yourself for your own health, welfare, or enjoyment (whether others approve or not) you build your proactivity, integrity, and self-trust, as well as your ability to be selftruistic.

As an example, one of my clients chose to put tires on his racing bike over the weekend so he could join a friend for a ride on Sunday afternoon even though his girlfriend did not approve. Since he had no intention of alienating his girlfriend he made plans to be with her at another time over the weekend but persisted in his desire for the bike ride.

TAKE SELF-RESPONSIBILITY

We come now to one of the major components of having sovereignty over your self. Can you take responsibility for your actions when those actions have caused others harm? Acknowledging your contribution to a conflict or misunderstanding, or simply owning your mistakes, tests the degree to which you have sovereignty over yourself. Mostly, you learn this if your parents were able to do it. A parent apologizing to a child for making a mistake or doing something carelessly that physically or emotionally hurt the child is a truly wondrous thing. Acknowledging your actions that contributed to a conflict reveals a highly developed human being and significantly contributes to resolving conflicts.

It is equally important not to take over-responsibility for circumstances beyond your control just to appease the other person. Balancing between taking under- or over-responsibility in their affairs with others marks those who have sovereignty over themselves.

INQUIRE INTO YOURSELF

Taking appropriate self-responsibility requires the willingness and ability to inquire into yourself, into what causes you to behave the way you do. You need to delve into how you feel and why you feel as you do. You need the ability to tell yourself the truth about your situation and yourself. You need to confront your self-justifications, rationalizations, and projections. This goes beyond the skill of self-awareness described earlier. If you develop the skill to look beneath and beyond the easy excuses and own what really goes on within you that causes you to behave in less than optimal ways, you can engage in the kind of collaborative conflict resolution process described in this book.

BUILD PHYSICAL AND FINANCIAL HEALTH

I believe that paying attention to your physical health facilitates sovereignty over yourself. Eating whole foods, keeping sugar and other toxins out of your body, treating allergies, exercising properly, getting enough rest and relaxation, overcoming addictions, healing past traumas, and transforming negative or dysfunctional beliefs all prove to put you into a stronger position to advocate for yourself when in conflict.

Reducing debt also has a very empowering effect on many people. Having some level of financial independence can be crucial in developing sovereignty over yourself. I have been amazed at how empowering it has been for my clients to achieve financial sovereignty. When they do, they are able to advocate much more effectively for themselves.

FIND A THERAPIST

If some of the described qualities of a truly sovereign individual sound foreign or too difficult for you to achieve, you might consider finding a therapist. Good therapists know how to demonstrate, without judgment, understanding of how you feel and why you feel that way. They can help you explore what you think, believe, value, and what you want in your life without telling you what you should want or how you should act.

If you had very controlling parents or parents who did not pay much attention to you, I recommend going into therapy to understand better how that damaged your sovereignty over yourself as well as to experience a respectful, non-dominating, non-judgmental, accepting, and empathic relationship with someone who has no vested interest in molding you in any particular way. A good therapist wants to help you find out who you want to become and how to achieve that goal.

So many professional groups do therapy today that you might find it confusing to choose the best approach for you. The theoretical orientation does not matter much, but it does matter that you like and respect your therapist, and that you sense he or she really cares about you, listens carefully to you, and empowers you to make your own decisions rather than allowing you to depend on him or her to decide for you.

How do you find such a person? Ask your friends and work associates if they know a therapist they like and found helpful. You can call a local college or university and ask to speak with someone in the counseling center or in a department that trains psychotherapists, counselors, or clinical social workers. Get three names and call each of them to find out more about them. Try to find a therapist who has difficulty finding time to schedule you. A full practice increases the likelihood that other people like the therapist.

In summary, if you do not feel that your parents' philosophy sought to set you free in the world as your own being, if they were autocratic, domineering, manipulative, martyr-like, needy, or, on the other hand, if they were neglectful, abusive, seldom knew what you did or felt, seeing a therapist might help you. In the context of this book, it might help you communicate and advocate for yourself better in relationships, particularly when there is conflict.

If you have difficulty finding someone, you could log on to the Advanced Integrative Therapy (AIT) website (www.aitherapy.com) and click on the Directory of Practitioners. I have practiced this form of therapy for many years and found it to be one of the most effective. AIT (formerly known as Seemorg Matrix Work) uses the body's electromagnetic energy to treat traumas and dysfunctional beliefs through the use of energy centers in the body. It integrates a wide variety of more traditional "talking" therapies such as Jungian analysis and Cognitive Behavior Therapy with energy psychology and transpersonal work. See the Advanced Integrative Therapy website for further information or contact me at tonyroffers@earthlink.net.

SUMMARY

Develop sovereignty over your-self in the following ways:

- Make decisions based on awareness of your own values and preferences.
- Meditate to increase your self-awareness.
- Surround yourself with people who respect your right to make your own decisions.
- Comfort and soothe yourself rather than depending on others to do so.
- Be true to yourself.
- Be proactive about what you want and in maintaining your boundaries.
- Take appropriate responsibility for your actions.

- Inquire into yourself so you can know yourself accurately without self-justifying.
- Maintain your physical health.
- Stay out of debt.
- Get help if needed.

PART TWO
RESPECTING OTHERS' SOVEREIGNTY

Although my mother frequently criticized our next-door neighbor, who came from Houston, Texas, Mrs. Hanson had a way of making me feel very special as a little boy and would always treat me with respect and affection. I liked her a lot.

Thinking back, I now believe my mother was jealous of Mrs. Hanson, although I had no idea of that at the time. At any rate, my mother would frequently criticize something Mrs. Hanson would do. For example, she never wore overshoes. Even when snow piled high on the sidewalks, Mrs. Hanson would wear only her high-heels as she walked down the steps and across the sidewalk to get into a taxi. My mother vehemently judged this as highly irresponsible behavior.

Mrs. Hanson worked part-time for a real estate agent showing homes for the realtor and successfully charming potential buyers, so she could afford taking a taxi on winter days. Besides, in her seventies, she didn't trust her driving anymore. Mother could not imagine taking a taxi to work. She criticized Mrs. Hanson for being a "spendthrift" and not wearing overshoes in the snow. Worst of all, Mrs. Hanson started inviting "John Honey" over to watch television, and they would stay up through the news talking and laughing. My mother couldn't stand John Honey, a loud man who smoked cigars and kept Mrs. Hanson up "way too late for her health."

As the years went by and I got older, it began to annoy me how frequently my mother would say something critical about Mrs. Hanson. I would listen to my mother's criticism and then start to defend whatever Mrs. Hanson had done. I began to say to my mother "To each her own!" every time she would criticize Mrs. Hanson. I would ask my mother "What difference does it make?" or "How does it affect you?" My mother could never answer those questions, and it only made her increase her critical remarks or give more reasons for Mrs. Hanson to wear overshoes, or not to spend money for a taxi, or get to sleep earlier and tell John Honey to go home.

This is an example of my mother not honoring Mrs. Hanson's sovereignty, her right live her life as she saw fit as long as it did not harm my mother in a tangible way. My comment "To each her own!" was the beginning of my seeing how important it was to respect someone else's right to be different from me. I did worry about Mrs. Hanson slipping on the ice in her high heels because I cared about her. But somehow I just knew it was not my business.

Honoring another person's right to think, feel, or behave differently from us is an important prerequisite for collaborative conflict resolution.

CHAPTER THREE
RESPECTING OTHERS' RIGHT
TO BE HOW THEY ARE

CIVIL LIBERTIES

We still have some civil rights left in this country, rights to personal liberty established by the Thirteenth and Fourteenth Amendments to the U.S. Constitution. Our civil laws give individuals permission to exercise those rights freely. Exercising our civil liberties provides one of the cornerstones of our democratic society. As long as you do not break a law or harm others, you have the right to live your life as you see fit.

For example, Mrs. Hanson's living room was close to my parents' bedroom. On hot summer nights, with all the windows open in both houses, it might have been disruptive of my parents' sleep to have cigar smoke and John Honey's boisterous laughter floating into the bedroom at night. On the other hand, if my mother's sleep suffered no adverse effect, it was none of my mother's business if Mrs. Hanson wanted to watch TV with John Honey in the evening. She broke no law and did not adversely affect my mother in any tangible way. In fact, I slept in a room above my parents, and I only heard them once after going to bed in the nine years John Honey visited Mrs. Hanson.

VIVA-LA-DIFFÉRENCE

Respecting the right of someone else to differ from you or behave differently from you does not mean you have to like or approve of what they do. It just means they have a right to do it if it does not harm or adversely affect you in some way. My mother would never have gone out in the snow without her overshoes on, and I understand her concern that Mrs. Hanson did. My mother cared about Mrs. Hanson and I think my mother feared that Mrs. Hanson would get sick if she got her feet wet or might fall on the ice in her high heels. Many reasons argued against high heels in the ice and snow. Mrs. Hanson had the right not to wear overshoes, however, even if she fell and injured herself or got sick from getting wet. Maybe she considered how she looked more important than the dangers of falling or getting wet. Her reasons do not really matter; she was not breaking any laws, and she was not harming anyone.

CONFLICT OF VALUES

Mrs. Hanson and my mother essentially had a conflict of values. Having come from different parts of the country and from different cultures, they differed in some of their aesthetic and life style preferences. If you cannot identify how the other person's behavior adversely affects you in a tangible way, you have a conflict of values. If Mrs. Hanson and John Honey stayed up late at night talking loudly and laughing so my mother could not sleep, it would be a different matter. But since Mrs. Hanson and John Honey usually ended their evening before my parents went to bed, their behavior did not adversely affect my mother's sleep.

Just because a conflict of values does not physically impact the other person does not mean that value differences are insignificant. Wars have been waged because of differences in religious beliefs that had no tangible adverse effect on those holding the different religious beliefs. My mother spent large amounts of her time stewing about Mrs. Hanson's not wearing overshoes, having John Honey over, and other behaviors that caused my mother no harm. Parents expend great energy in trying to get their children to wear the kind of clothes the parents think they should, or to have their rooms the way they think the children should.

If you really seek to respect the sovereignty of others (your children, spouses, friends, or whomever), you must stop pushing them to follow your values and your aesthetic and lifestyle preferences. When you disagree with someone's values, there are four options that exhibit respect for their sovereignty: (1) model the behaviors you want others to emulate, (2) serve as their consultant rather than a preacher, (3) accept that others have the right to their own ideas and behaviors as long as they do not adversely affect you in some tangible way, and (4) modify your own values or views of the situation.

Modeling. You can best influence others to value what you value by living congruently with your values. If you value being on time and want others to do likewise, you need to be on time yourself as often as you can. You need to practice what you value. If you want others to value what you value, you must live by example rather than verbally cajole or use your authority by making demands on others.

Consulting. You may influence someone else's values by sharing your ideas, knowledge, and way of doing things rather than preaching to them. It is usually best if you ask if they want your input, and if they say yes, you can offer your suggestions without imposing or demanding they do as you do. You must share your values, not impose them, because others have the right to do as they see fit as long as they do not harm you. If they say no to your offer to give them your input, it is best to refrain from sharing it at that point. Doing otherwise invades their boundaries. In addition, it usually works best to offer your input only once rather than over and over again. Offering your recommendations more than once, or without permission from the other, invades their sovereignty.

Accepting. Respecting others' right to their own ideas and behaviors requires not so much a skill as an attitude of acceptance that often culminates in not saying or doing anything. You just leave them alone. As I would say to my mother, "To each her own!" Some people find this easy to do. Others, who make other people's lives their main passion and concern, find it very difficult. For some of us, helping or criticizing others constitutes a pervasive life activity.

I know that I have spent much of my life thinking I knew how other people should live and have gone out of my way to educate them. I unconsciously considered everyone my client and felt entitled to "help" them, not realizing they had not asked me for that help, let alone hired me as their therapist. I would then internally criticize them for not following my advice, suggestions, help, and insights. Finally, I became conscious of this presumptuous belief and am working on accepting other people's right to live differently from the way I live.

Modifying self. Finally, to deal with value conflicts, you can change your own values or attitudes. When others behave in ways that you don't like or respect, but do not tangibly affect you, you can try a number of things to get resolution without trying to change the other person. You can work on reducing your perfectionistic or unrealistic expectations of others (and yourself); you can question your right/wrong, black/white, all or nothing thinking; you can work on your own self-acceptance and self-esteem, which almost always increases your acceptance of others; you can seek greater understanding of why others behave as they do or seek more information about them or about the situation.

For example, when I asked Mrs. Hanson why she took a taxi rather than drive herself, she laughed and said, "Oh, I stopped driving in the winter a long time ago, after I slid into a telephone pole." When I told my mother what Mrs. Hanson had said, she stopped criticizing her for taking a taxi. Mother had not known about the accident, and it changed her perspective.

UNSOLICITED HELPING

You also invade other people's sovereignty when you help them without their indicating any need or desire for help. Giving unsolicited help is not necessarily "bad." It can, however, invade and demean if the recipient does not want or need it. If I see someone who seems in difficulty, pain, or confusion, I will now ask if that person wants my assistance before jumping in with advice or help. I try to respect their first answer without double- or triple-checking. I used to think this a cold and distant way of relating, but I now realize I am respecting other people's sovereignty and do not assume everyone wants or needs my help.

GOOD INTENTIONS

When helping others out of genuine caring or altruism, you freely give of your time, resources, and expertise. It feels good and you experience giving as a true gift to yourself as well as to the other. If you help out of a sense of duty or obligation, however, or a "need" to feel better than others, or to feel more powerful or superior to others, or to shore up your self-esteem, you fail to consider the other person's sovereignty and use other people to meet your own needs or desires under a socially acceptable guise.

Helping others, while often a very "good" thing, has a shadow side. It can intrude, invade, control, usurp, demean, and disempower the recipient unless the recipient wants or needs your help. Otherwise, you invade their sovereignty, no matter how altruistic your intentions.

If the other person neither wants your help nor asks for it, try not to give it. If you find this difficult, you may have grown addicted to helping others. This often indicates that you have been doing it for reasons other than genuine altruism. You may have been giving unsolicited help in order to feel good about yourself, to demonstrate to yourself your own knowledge, and to shore up your sense of self-worth.

For example, I now monitor my unsolicited helping behaviors and watch for what drives me to do it. I also watch the effect it has on others. Some people seem to like my help whether they ask for it or not. These people probably would have said yes if I had thought to ask if they wanted my help before I gave it. Some polite ones seem to respond favorably, but I soon see they really didn't want the help and hesitated to tell me no directly. I have also noticed that some people became dependent on me in ways that I resented later.

For example, I had observed that my friend Joe seemed naive about how to invest the money in his retirement plan, so I suggested that he follow the method I use. He agreed, but when I started to show him how to implement the plan, which took about fifteen minutes of monitoring each weekend, he balked and said he wasn't sure he could do that. I said I could do it for him and call whenever he needed to buy or sell. He agreed, and we proceeded for the next few months with this understanding.

The problem came when I called to tell him he needed to sell a certain mutual fund and later found out he hadn't. He waited a week or so and then called to ask why he should sell. I began to realize that even though I had tried to explain the theory underlying the investment method, he really did not understand it, nor did he realize the consequences of not selling promptly when I recommended it. I also realized he was not emotionally simpatico with how the plan worked, and my doing it for him only made matters worse. Doing his investing for him made him dependent on me. When he didn't follow my buy or sell signals, I became resentful.

This example demonstrates a number of points. First, I did not explicitly ask Joe if he wanted my investment help. I made suggestions, assuming he needed my help. Second, rather than empowering him to learn how to implement the plan himself, I did it for him. This fostered his dependency on me and set up a hierarchical relationship, with me controlling his investments. None of this helped our friendship. Third, by taking over the work, I set myself up to resent his not following my recommendations.

I now wish I had either waited for him to ask me for my help or that I had asked him if he wanted my help. If the other person asks for help, I can feel confident he really wants it. Even so, I may not always choose to give it.

Even if Joe had asked me for my help, I might better have taught him how to implement the plan on his own rather than doing it for him. Once I started helping him and realized his unwillingness to implement it on his own (and unwillingness to learn), I might better have dropped it. If those who need help are not willing to learn how to do something for themselves, helping only reinforces their dependency. If they truly cannot do it for themselves, or learn how to do it themselves, then that may be a different matter. I can help them if they truly want it and only if I truly want to, realizing that I am now doing something for someone who truly cannot do it for himself or herself, and I willingly take that on as a gift to that person.

CHECK IT OUT

One thing you can do after becoming conscious of a compulsive need to help someone is to ask the other person if they would like your help before you give it. If they decline your help in a clear way, trust their response and refrain from helping. What is particularly interesting is when you take time to reflect on your motivation for offering help.

For example, I eventually realized that in addition to genuinely wanting to help Joe invest his retirement money, I also wanted to share with him my method because I really enjoy doing it and take pride in it. Upon reflection, I think I wanted someone I could share my investment plan with because I find it a little lonely to do it just by myself. Unwittingly, I was also meeting my own needs by offering to help Joe. (For more about the example of Joe and the empowering way to help, see Appendix A.)

HELPING KIDS

What about giving unsolicited help to kids and adolescents? Very young children need many things done for them simply because they can't do many things for themselves yet and are not developed enough yet to learn. The art of parenting requires you to discern when the child reaches the developmental stage when he can begin to learn how to do a particular task for himself rather than have you do it for him. Adolescent years seem difficult for many parents because knowing when to do something for adolescents and when to help them learn to do it for themselves can be difficult.

Consider whatever you do for your child or adolescent a demonstration of how you want them to do it later in life. Then, as soon as he can begin learning how to do it for himself, begin to let him do it in a graduated way, giving supportive feedback. After showing a child how to do something and teaching the child how to do it in a step-by-step fashion, try to leave the child some room to make mistakes and then learn how to rectify them on his own, perhaps using you as a consultant.

It is also good to tell children why it is important to learn something, and to help them understand the underlying purpose, reason, or benefit to them. Unless they understand what it will do for them in a positive way, they may not be motivated to learn it. I remember asking my trigonometry teacher in high school how I would use it later in my life. He couldn't answer me. Despite the intrigue of trigonometry, it really deflated my mathematics sail when I could not see where or how I would ever use it.

For parents who wish to explore this topic further, Thomas Gordon's classic *Parent Effectiveness Training* can be a good start.

SOLICITED HELP

Help proves most effective when others ask for it. This does not imply an obligation to help them. It simply means the recipient remains more open to help when feeling no sovereignty invasion. It also does not mean that you need to help in whatever way the person wants. For example, if my friend Joe asks me to teach him the method I use to invest, I would be more than happy to do so. If he asks me to do it for him without teaching him how to do it himself, I would decline.

Helping works best when done by choice. If we help out of a sense of duty or obligation, we often experience it as a burden. Helping someone out of obligation can lead to resentment on the giver's part and guilt or resentment on the receiver's part. Saying yes to someone who wants help is only a true choice when you feel free to say no, without guilt. That means you clearly understand that you have no responsibility to help. This obviously does not always apply, particularly in parent-child relationships. In many adult-adult relationships, it does apply, however, and the more we realize we have no duty to help, the more we can consciously choose to help. This usually leads to a better outcome for everyone.

If you wish to learn more about helping others effectively and in a way that both respects their sovereignty and empowers them to become more self-reliant, refer to Appendix A: Helping to Empower Others.

WHY ARE PEOPLE SO INCOMPETENT?

We all are fallible human beings, but some of us have more difficult histories than others. I don't deny its frustrating when others make mistakes and don't seem to care when they do. But be careful that you are not using your assessment of other people's incompetence as a cover for your negative judgment that they are not doing it your way. If you find that people often resist you or fail to appreciate your advice or directives, it could mean that you are unwittingly trying to manage their lives, and they are trying to tell you that you are not honoring their sovereignty.

HONORING OTHERS' SOVEREIGNTY IN CONFLICT

It is probably most difficult to honor another's sovereignty when you are in conflict with them. We have already discussed how to handle it when it is a conflict of values. Even when someone's behavior is not adversely affecting you, it proves difficult to use the methods described earlier. But what if the conflict involves a situation in which the other person's behavior does affect you tangibly and adversely? How can you communicate with someone you are in conflict with around an issue that is negatively impacting you and still honor that person's sovereignty?

Before answering these important questions and describing the communication skills needed to do this, let's explore the kind of attitudes it takes to be willing to use these skills in the first place. The first attitude is that other people have the right to disagree with you and act differently from you. If you don't hold that attitude, you will unlikely be willing to use the skills in the model about to be described.

Second, the age-old golden rule can apply here, but with an important adaptation. Rather than just following the usual "Do unto others as you would have them do unto you," I recommend following the new golden rule: "Do unto others as they would have you do unto them." The difference here can be profound. While the old golden rule can work, it assumes the other person is like you. If they are, it can work quite well. But what if they are different from you? What if they would like to be treated differently from the way you want to be treated? The new golden rule then applies, as long as treating them in the way they would like to be treated is not harmful to you or against your values.

The new golden rule requires a new set of skills in addition to the right attitude. Where the old golden rule just required you to project onto others the way you want to be treated, the new golden rule requires that you be able to understand how the other person may differ from you. This frequently proves more difficult but is usually more effective. The communication skills model described in this book, called the B-E-A-R Process, is for those willing to learn how to implement this new golden rule.

Exhibiting these attitudes comes down to whether you can respect others' right to have an opinion, position, value, or set of behaviors different from yours, particularly when the other person's behavior has some adverse tangible effect on you. Typically we behave in many dysfunctional ways when this occurs.

One typical pattern is when I assume that you know (or should know) that what you are doing harms or bothers me. A second pattern is when I infer that you are consciously and intentionally doing (or not doing) something that harms or annoys me. A third pattern is when I project onto you that you are (or should be) like me and therefore should do as I do, feel as I feel, or think as I think. These patterns are often unconscious and therefore difficult to change.

To use the skills described later in this book (e.g. making a direct request that the other person change his behavior, or informing the other person how his behavior is adversely affecting you) takes a high degree of emotional control as well as respect for the other person's right to be different from you. We usually move very quickly into judgment, anger, hurt, disdain, or a variety of negative and dysfunctional attitudes and behaviors when someone else is impacting us negatively. We often project onto others that they will be unhelpful or uncooperative in reaction to us.

These projections usually come from our past experiences with members of our family of origin or past significant relationships with bosses, friends, lovers, and ex-spouses. These unconscious projections are like conditioned responses that we don't have control over and lead us to behave in dysfunctional or destructive ways. If you find yourself assuming the other person will respond badly if you bring up an issue but have no real evidence or negative experience with that person, you can be pretty sure you are projecting earlier negative interactions onto him or her.

These unconscious projections need to be made conscious and monitored so they do not become self-fulfilling prophesies. How do you do that? First of all you need to be suspicious if you react intensely to someone or something that, upon reflection, did not warrant that intensity. Reacting stronger than what the situation warrants is often a cue that some past event or relationship has triggered you. When this happens, you need to reflect on what past experience is getting triggered by the current situation.

For example, Jane gets incredibly anxious every time she begins to get sexual with a man. She actually goes into a panic and gets so upset she cannot continue the sexual interaction. Her reaction is so intense that it has become obvious to her that she is reacting to more than the person she is with currently. With her therapist's help, she has uncovered a number of experiences in her past that may account for her overly intense reaction. Her father sexually abused her when she was around eight years old and then her mother's boyfriend did when she was thirteen. These experiences were never treated and resolved and were adversely influencing her relationships with men once they became sexual.

She developed a belief that all men are sexual predators and that she needed to protect herself from them. She had come to fear men and got extremely anxious the closer she got to them. This is an example of projection. This projection blocked her from being open to those men who were genuinely interested in her. Sometimes becoming aware of this pattern can help ameliorate it. However, it often takes therapeutically working through these earlier experiences to end the projection and, in this example, to begin involving oneself in a less fearful and healthy way with men sexually.

Perhaps more commonly than not, behavior that results in not honoring another person's sovereignty comes from a history of being abused by one or both parents, an older sibling, or extended family member. Sometimes the abuse comes from a neighbor, teacher, or a religious authority figure. Victims of this abuse often become perpetrators later in life. Since their sovereignty was invaded in a traumatic and humiliating way, they engage in that behavior with others if they are unable to get help in healing those experiences.

For example, Stan grew up under a very self-centered and defensive mother who dominated her relationships with her three husbands. Stan witnessed his father and two stepfathers being intimidated and rendered powerless by her criticisms and judgments. He worked hard all his life to avoid her judgments and became quite docile in her presence. He used his above-average intelligence, however, to dominate his friends and girl friends. He married a woman who was quite dependent and proceeded to criticize her in a manner similar to how his mother criticized her three husbands as a means to maintain control in the relationships.

When he and his wife came in for therapy, he was totally unaware of how demeaning and damaging his way of behaving with his wife was. It took great skill and tact on the therapist's part to help him see what he was doing to his wife and how the pattern got established, particularly since he also exhibited extreme defensiveness, like his mother, in acknowledging anything less than perfect about himself.

The example of Stan is just one of many in terms of how difficult it is for someone with his background to see what he is doing and then take responsibility for changing in a way that begins to honor his wife's sovereignty. This pattern is often lived out in more physically abusive ways in marriages or in the development of criminal behavior. Since people with this pattern were not treated with dignity or respect, they neither feel obligated nor willing to treat others with dignity or respect.

Not all victims of physical or psychological abuse take the route of perpetrating abuse on others, but if this sounds at all familiar to you, it behooves you to seek help in healing the wounds that occurred in your abuse as a way to prevent you from turning those wounds into abusive behavior toward others and thereby not honoring their sovereignty.

Conflict of needs. The attitudes I've described are all important when trying to resolve differences while in conflict with someone who is adversely affecting you. The skills of how to resolve those differences while honoring the sovereignty of others is what Part III: Reciprocal Sovereignty is all about.

SUMMARY

- Respect the right of others to be different from you.
- If someone's behavior does not adversely and tangibly affect you, realize you have a conflict of values, not a conflict of needs.
- If you want to change someone else's values, model the value yourself in your actions, ask if the other is open to hearing your recommendations, change your own values, or expand the range of your acceptance.
- Try not to help others unless they have asked for it or you have checked whether or not they want it.
- Help others, particularly children, in a way that empowers them to learn how to help themselves when they are developmentally ready.
- Make sure your help is not a way of managing other's lives or of making yourself feel more powerful.
- Do unto others, as they would have you do unto them.
- Observe how you tend to project things onto others from your past.
- When in conflict with someone who is adversely impacting you, use the B-E-A-R conflict resolution model delineated in Part Three so as to respect their sovereignty.

PART THREE
RECIPROCAL SOVEREIGNTY

We come now to the heart of this book. If you have learned to honor your own sovereignty as well as the sovereignty of others, you have the prerequisites for making decisions or resolving conflicts with others in a mutually respectful and collaborative manner.

Whereas most of us do not enjoy conflict, some people like a good argument, and a few even thrive on conflict, using it to intimidate others and to get their way. The conflict resolution process presented here will appeal to those who do not enjoy conflict and who wish to prevent or resolve it as effectively as possible. Rather than arguing or fighting about disagreements, you will learn how to talk about them so that conflicts either do not develop or can move to resolution in a less adversarial manner.

Most of us have learned to argue by having that behavior modeled for us, or we have learned to withdraw, avoid, or over-accommodate when we have disagreements. Many of us alternate between arguing, avoiding, and over-accommodating. If we argue or fight, we often end up polarizing the disagreement and making the situation worse. If we avoid the disagreement, we end up feeling alienated from the other person and do not give ourselves or the other person the chance to resolve things. If we over-accommodate, we end up feeling usurped, disempowered, or resentful. Usually these "fight, flight, or freeze" methods work poorly and the conflict remains or intensifies, leaving us feeling frustrated and helpless. Sometimes this frustration and helplessness endures for a long time at great expense to our health and peace of mind.

The following method of resolving conflicts (and making difficult decisions that could lead to conflict) addresses the realm of conflicting needs: conflicts that concretely or tangibly affect you rather than situations in which the conflict concerns values, beliefs, aesthetic preferences, stylistic differences, or your philosophy of life. These "conflicts of values" do not involve an adverse "tangible effect" on you. For example, in a parent-adolescent relationship, conflicts of values may occur over how the adolescent wears her hair, how she wants to dress, how she decorates her room, how she spends her allowance. These behaviors do not tangibly affect the parent, although the parent may have an aesthetic preference or value that differs from that of the adolescent.

Examples of "conflicts of needs" in this situation might include the adolescent not cleaning up after himself in the kitchen, thereby leaving it up to the parent, or playing music loudly in the living room and thereby interrupting the parent's concentration while working at her desk.

The method described below best suits "conflict of needs" situations but can sometimes help to resolve "conflict of values" situations as well. This distinction between a conflict of needs and a conflict of values is important because many people mistake their values for needs, although sometimes a conflict can include both. For a more detailed description of a conflict of values, refer back to Chapter Three.

CHAPTER FOUR
COLLABORATIVE CONFLICT RESOLUTION: THE B-E-A-R PROCESS

The B-E-A-R Process, a way to resolve conflicts directly, collaboratively, and respectfully, helps you to live your life and your relationships with less frustration, anxiety, and resentment. The acronym B-E-A-R stands for Breathe, Empathize, Acknowledge, and Respond. These are the phases of responding to someone who is raising a potential conflict (see Figure 1).

In addition to greater effectiveness in resolving conflict, you will usually feel less stress and anxiety during the B-E-A-R Process, particularly after you have practiced the method over a period of time with another person who also willingly learns it. Gradually, each person learns that discussing a difference does not have to be so anxiety producing. When you feel more self-confident and empowered to resolve differences, you deepen the trust and intimacy in your personal relationships as well as in your working relationships. Ultimately, this process leads to a more productive life, improved health, increased enjoyment in living, and better relationships.

OVERVIEW OF THE B-E-A-R PROCESS

The B-E-A-R Process takes us through three stages of conflict resolution:

- Mutual understanding
- Mutual agreement
- Mutual action

Mutual understanding. The mutual understanding phase emphasizes a dialogue between two or more people in an attempt to understand the other person's point of view and feelings, your own point of view and feelings, and what each of you finds personally important in regard to your disagreement. Trying to reach an agreement before fully understanding the real issues for each of you often proves frustrating and ineffective. Only when you understand what each of you considers important, and why each of you finds it important, can you find a truly creative resolution. Mutual understanding can create an atmosphere of respect and a collaborative process that optimizes your chances of reaching a mutual agreement.

Mutual agreement. Once you accurately understand each other, not only in regard to your differing positions but also the underlying meaning and importance the issue has for each of you, you can then more readily reach a mutual agreement. Trying to reach mutual agreement before parties achieve this deeper level of mutual understanding proves frustrating and sometimes futile.

You may not always achieve mutual agreement. Good communication can bring clarity but not always agreement. Even very skilled and respectful communication does not always guarantee resolution. In fact, sometimes a really good dialogue can lead you to agree to disagree and continue your relationship after deciding you can live with the disagreement or to end your relationship more amicably.

Mutual action. After reaching mutual agreement, accepting the disagreement, or finding a compromise, you can move toward mutual action. Often the first action step, delineating the resolution in writing, encourages the kind of specific detail that complex or legally binding agreements require. For example, if a mediator has facilitated your dispute, the next step would be for each of you to have your consulting attorneys review the agreement. This review might then lead to a more refined version that could ultimately work better. Sometimes new information might require you to repeat the whole process.

In less formal negotiations, you might not need to put anything in writing, but I recommend that you each put into your own words who does what by when. I find that very few people think of doing this, but taking the extra time either to write the agreement down or to review the agreement verbally can prevent a lot of trouble later. You might also find it useful to agree to a trial period of implementing the resolution

ASSERT

- Contract & Clarify intentions
- Speak respectfully
- Give I-messages
- Make direct requests

BREATHE

- Listen
- Observe
- Manage emotions
- Take time out

RESPOND

- Elicit specificity
- Respond directly
- Apologize
- Make amends

EMPATHIZE

- Understand intention
- Understand viewpoint
- Understand importance
- Understand feelings

ACKNOWLEDGE

- Areas of agreement
- Take responsibility
- Express appreciation
- Accept disagreement

RESOLVE

- Brainstorm options
- Evaluate options
- Delineate agreement
- Implement agreement

Figure 1. The B-E-A-R Process for Resolving Conflict

Figure 2: How to Use the B-E-A-R Process

MUTUAL UNDERSTANDING STAGE

- Person 1 Asserts by using the skills under the Assert part of the model:
  - Contract & Clarify intentions
  - Speak respectfully
  - Give I-messages
  - Make direct Requests.

- Person 2 Responds with the B-E-A-R Process using the skills listed under each phase:
  - Breathe
  - Empathize
  - Acknowledge
  - Respond

- Person 2 Asserts by using the skills under the Assert part of the model (see above).

- Person 1 Responds by going through the B-E-A-R Process (see above).

- Person 1 and 2 keep alternating between Asserting and Responding with the B-E-A-R Process until they understand each other's points-of-view, positions, feelings, needs, and important issues.

MUTUAL AGREEMENT STAGE

- Once Mutual Understanding is reached Person 1 and Person 2 engage in the Resolve part of the model until they reach Mutual Agreement:
  - Brainstorm options
  - Evaluate options
  - Delineate agreements

MUTUAL ACTION STAGE

- Once Mutual Agreement is reached Person 1 and Person 2 implement their agreements and continue to evaluate the effectiveness of those agreements:
  - Implement agreements

during which you each evaluate its effectiveness and appropriateness. Setting up a follow-up meeting after a reasonable period of time to discuss progress and to make further revisions can be helpful as well.

THE PHASES OF THE B-E-A-R PROCESS

As illustrated in Figure 1, this conflict resolution process involves a series of phases or stages: The first phase is labeled Assert. This involves one person initiating the dialogue around a potentially conflictual situation or difficult decision. The next four phases delineates how the recipient can best respond to the person initiating the dialogue. These phases are labeled Breathe, Empathize, Acknowledge, and Respond. This series of steps has the acronym B-E-A-R for which this communication skills model is named. If the parties to the conflict or decision can alternate between the Assert and the B-E-A-R phases of the process (that is, one asserts and the other practices the B-E-A-R skills, then they reverse roles), they can achieve the mutual understanding that is so important for preventing or resolving conflicts collaboratively.

The Resolve stage of the model emphasizes skills that facilitate mutual agreement that leads to more effective mutual action.

Figures 1 will become more understandable once all the skills in the B-E-A-R Process are delineated and described. See Figure 2 for a sequential description of how the Mutual understanding, Mutual agreement, and Mutual action stages of the B-E-A-R Process works in a two person dialogue. More than two people can use this process, however, for description purposes it is best to think in terms of a two-person dialogue.

I recommend that you review Figures 1 and 2 as you read each phase of the model. That will assist you in keeping a conceptual perspective on the whole process as you go along. Learning any new skill usually feels awkward at first.

Once learned and practiced, however, it becomes more comfortable and fluid.

You cannot resolve all conflict with this method, particularly in situations in which parties have hardened in their adversarial positions or have come to dislike or disrespect each other intensely. Even in those difficult situations, however, you will have a better chance of breaking through the barriers with the B-E-A-R Process than with the old argue, avoid, or accommodate methods.

In more formal mediation contexts, the mediator describes the components of the B-E-A-R Process in advance to the parties, who then agree to use the process before the mediation begins. The parties learn what the mediation requires of them in successive approximations throughout the process. In less formal conflict resolution settings, such as marriage or work relationships, it helps if all the people involved understand the basic sequence of the skills in the model before proceeding.

I know of no way to take away all the anxiety in conflict situations, but you can learn a dialogue process that engages you in a more collaborative and cooperative way to resolve your differences. Over time, you can trust this process to get you closer to the kind of work and personal relationships you want to have. The most important shift you need to make is to move from an adversarial position (i.e., me against you) to a collaborative position (i.e., me with you) which means you work together (i.e., co-labor) to understand the underlying meaning the conflict holds for each of you and what each of you holds most important in regard to your differences.

I might best summarize this shift as a move from "furious to curious." You can gain much if you can instill the attitude of curiosity into the conflict resolution process. Rather than getting angry for not having your way, you might better get curious about why the other person wants something different from what you want. Many people find this difficult because they retain a kind of "primary narcissism" that children have during the developmental stage when everything seems to revolve around them or be caused by them. In children, we find this kind of perception of the world understandable, given their developmental stage. I have observed, however, that many people have not evolved out of this kind of early, primary narcissism, particularly when we do not get our way.

The attitude shift from furious to curious can be very challenging. When you have a temper tantrum and your emotions flare, you might find it very difficult to get interested in what someone else considers important and to become curious about it. This is exactly what you need to do, however, in order to resolve your differences in a way that does not polarize the situation further.

You need to get out of your early childhood strateies of throwing a temper tantrum, withdrawing, or over-accommodating. You can develop a more mature attitude that understands that other people have different histories, values, and desires and that when you differ with them, you can come to understand their point of view–what they consider important and why–and take these understandings into consideration in trying to work out a resolution.

This process takes a different perspective and set of skills that I call "dialogue skills." Rather than fight, debate, or argue about who is right and who is wrong, who is to blame and who is not, you become curious about what the other person wants and why he or she wants it, as well as clarify what you want and why you want it. The curious attitude leads to a dialogue process rather than the "fight, flight, or freeze" mode of conflict resolution. The B-E-A-R Process structures the dialogue for people who want to resolve their differences collaboratively rather than adversarially.

WHICH BRAIN DRIVES YOU?

Before proceeding with a more detailed description of the B-E-A-R Process, I want to explain why it might feel difficult at first, and why only humans can do it. To better understand the nature of the challenge, you need to understand the three major parts of the human brain: the reptilian brain, the mammalian brain, and the human brain.

Reptilian brain. I will call the part of your brain that evolved first the reptilian brain, often referred to as the brain stem. This part of the brain sits directly on top of your spinal column and oversees involuntary activities such as breathing, digestion, and excretion. It also processes sensory stimuli (sights, sounds, smells, tastes, and touches). This part of your brain functions all the time and stimulates you to approach the pleasurable and avoid the painful. You can sometimes override the brain stem (e.g., not eat the piece of chocolate, or sit in the dentist's chair), but it takes real motivation, which comes from a different part of your brain. To overcome addictions, you must address the reptilian brain.

Mammalian brain. The part of your brain that evolved next, the mammalian brain or limbic system, is the large middle part of the brain that consists of the amygdala, cingulate gyrus, cerebellum, hippocampus, thalamus, hypothalamus, and pituitary gland. This part of your brain synthesizes external sensory perceptions and images as well as internal emotions and makes associations or connections between these. This part of your brain constantly monitors your safety and survival. If anything threatens your safety, it responds by reviewing previously associated images and emotions, and you react *(unthinkingly)*, based on your previous conditioning. For example, if a lover abandoned you in the past, you tend to project that your next lover will abandon you. Given the history of your previous ways of dealing with this trauma, you would fight (accuse your current lover of planning to leave you), flee (withdraw from your current lover to avoid being left first), or freeze (become immobilized). This area of the brain reacts in ways that seem irrational in the present situation but reveals much about your history.

Since conflict can trigger both pain (reptilian brain) and lack of safety (mammalian brain) you must somehow deal with these parts of your brain during the B-E-A-R Process.

Human brain. The cortex (cerebral cortex, prefrontal cortex)–the uniquely human part of your brain capable of abstract reasoning, rational thought, language, problem solving, making choices, and self-awareness–focuses on increasing your cognitive control of your world by discerning what is reliable, valid, true, and useful, and how you can make it so. You need to access this part of your brain if you have any hope of using the B-E-A-R Process when you become emotionally upset.

Implications. When you become frightened, anxious, threatened, or angry, the reptilian and mammalian parts of your brain dominate and the cortex loses control. When this happens, one or more of the fight, flight, or freeze responses takes over and you can neither think straight nor use the listening and communication skills in the B-E-A-R Process.

For this reason some people do not believe learning a communication skills model is very useful (Gottman and Silver, 1994). They claim that when you really need it, you can't use it. All your skills go out the window when emotional upset triggers the reptilian and mammalian parts of the brain to become dominant. Why learn it if you can't use it when you need it?

I agree that we lose much of our capacity to listen accurately and to communicate clearly and respectfully when we become emotionally flooded and the more primitive parts of the brain dominate. My experience suggests, however, that humans, with practice, can monitor their emotional temperature so that when anger, fear, or frustration invoke the primitive parts of the brain, they can engage in various cooling-down, self-comforting, and centering techniques to regain control of these emotions and thereby reestablish cortex dominance. Once the emotional temperature lowers enough, the cortex can predominate again and more constructive listening and communication can resume.

I consider it a serious mistake to throw out communication skill models just because we use them poorly when emotions run high and the primitive parts of the brain dominate. As humans, we have the ability to realize when this happens and, with practice, can deal with it in a way that gives us access again to our cortex. Although not easy, you can learn to do this. You can train yourself to monitor and then control your emotional temperature, and allow your cortex to maintain or reestablish dominance. As your cortex begins losing control, you can engage in various techniques to assist in reestablishing control while refraining from engaging in destructive speech and other behaviors.

Learning the specific communication skills in the B-E-A-R Process takes time and motivation. As you learn, not only how to use the skills when your cortex retains control, but also to sense when you are "losing it," you can implement the B-E-A-R Process more and more effectively. People who have spent the time and energy to learn this process develop greater and greater confidence in themselves and trust in their partners to do just that. Although almost no one can do the B-E-A-R Process perfectly, increasing approximations reap incredible benefits that accumulate exponentially. Each conflict resolved in this manner paves the way to approaching future conflicts similarly. Although resolution of all conflict cannot be guaranteed, greater clarity of the issues almost always evolves and the parties to the dispute grow in the process.

SUMMARY

- There are three stages in the B-E-A-R Process for resolving conflict: Mutual Understanding, Mutual Agreement, and Mutual Action.

- The B-E-A-R Process is initiated by someone asserting his or her point of view respectfully.
- There are four stages of responding to the person asserting: Breathe, Empathize, Acknowledge, and Respond.
- The B-E-A-R Process requires our human (prefrontal cortex) brain to be dominant, and does not work well when the reptilian or mammalian part of the brain is dominant.
- Keeping your emotional temperature under control is an important prerequisite for using the B-E-A-R Process effectively.

CHAPTER FIVE

PREPARE

Before I describe each component in the B-E-A-R Process, let's discuss how to prepare for engaging in this dialogue process.

Preparing for the B-E-A-R Process involves three steps:

- Prepare yourself.
- Prepare the physical setting.
- Prepare others.

PREPARE YOURSELF

You have already prepared yourself for engaging in the B-E-A-R Process if you have read the first two parts of this book and have incorporated the skills and attitudes covered there. To engage in the B-E-A-R Process skillfully, you must be able to honor your own sovereignty and the sovereignty of others. You can do a number of additional things to prepare for the dialogue. If you can begin reasonably relaxed, well fed, rested, and clear about your positive intention for the dialogue, you are much more likely to achieve a satisfactory resolution.

First, you must understand how you feel about the communication: Angry? Frightened? Anxious? Upset? Recognizing feelings helps manage the primitive parts of your brain (see previous chapter) so you can listen accurately and speak respectfully. Next, calm yourself sufficiently to approach the other person in a respectful way. In other words, operate from the cerebral cortex as much as you can.

You can consciously tighten and then relax one set of muscles after the other, or visualize a peaceful, soothing scene or memory. I recommend a particular method of focusing and preparing for the dialogue that has surprising effectiveness in calming your negative emotions and preventing you from slipping into your reptilian brain. This method involves holding your hand over your heart and moving your other hand slowly down the energy centers *(chakras)* of the body, holding the center of the palm sequentially over the top of your head, on your forehead, at the base of your throat, over your heart, solar plexus, navel, pelvis, and then sitting gently on your hand at the base of the tail bone. While thinking of the upcoming communication, hold each of these energy centers for about ten to fifteen seconds (without counting). This method will help you center yourself for the coming interchange.

After composing yourself, you will find it useful to clarify your positive intention for the dialogue before approaching the other person. An example of a positive intention is telling your landlord that you cannot meet the rent increase and ask for a reconsideration of the amount so you can stay in the apartment (rather than threaten to get a lawyer to exercise the cost-of-living increase restriction in the lease agreement). Another example is telling your spouse that you would like to talk about your disagreement so you can feel closer to him or her (rather than proving to your spouse that you are "right"). This prepares the other person for why you wish to have a talk and gives them a positive motivation to listen to you. Clarifying the purpose or intention for the talk within yourself first can help you clarify your intention to the other person at the beginning of the dialogue.

In summary, preparing yourself for a successful dialogue includes beginning well rested and well fed. Fatigue or hunger can severely compromise listening and communicating skills. The combination of weariness, inadequate nutrition, and emotional volatility disrupts effective conflict resolution or decision-making because it sets you up for the primitive parts of your brain to dominate.

PREPARE THE PHYSICAL SETTING

Preparing the physical environment for the dialogue can also facilitate the resolution process. For example, it could prove important for a married couple to delay their talk until after the children go to bed so they can have privacy. Finding a quiet room to avoid interruptions or taking a walk may really help the B-E-A-R Process. Discerning the best physical setting for the dialogue and proposing it to the other person can go a long way toward a good start. For example, "How about taking a walk Sunday after we drop the kids off at your folks so we can talk about our plans to move this summer without upsetting them just yet?"

PREPARE OTHERS

After preparing yourself and the physical setting, you must prepare the other person or persons for the dialogue if it is to succeed. Informing the other person of your desire to have a talk, revealing your positive intentions, and perhaps suggesting when and where to meet expedites beginning a dialogue because it shows respect for and consideration of the other person. Arranging a place and time conducive for the other person increases the chances of having a fruitful talk. For example, if I want to talk to my office mate about leaving the space heater on all night, it would be better to ask him if he has a few minutes to talk about a problem before just launching into my feelings about his behavior. He could have an important meeting coming up, or he might have to leave the office soon for a troubling medical appointment. I will discuss more about preparing the other person when we get to the contracting and clarifying intentions skills in the Assert part of the B-E-A-R Process.

SUMMARY

- Prepare yourself for the dialogue by being as relaxed, rested, well fed, and clear about your positive intention as possible.
- Find a quiet setting where you will not be interrupted.
- Prepare the other person by letting them know in advance that you want to have a talk rather than launching into it without their agreement.

CHAPTER SIX
ASSERT

The B-E-A-R Process begins when you respectfully Assert your point of view, request, or proposal. This means avoiding disrespectful words, phrases, or labels as well as disrespectful tones of voice or facial gestures (e.g., rolling the eyes). Should these verbal and nonverbal forms of communication arise in the dialogue, the other person in the dispute or the mediator should point them out as not helping the process. If you use a mediator to assist you, he or she should encourage you to phrase things respectfully and monitor facial and other nonverbal gestures that can derail the dialogue process. Thus, you need to agree ahead of time to avoid any form of disrespectful communication. Ideally, you should agree ahead of time that if either party (or the mediator) experiences disrespectful communication, they should point it out so the dialogue can continue in a more respectful manner.

Examples of disrespectful communication include judging, criticizing, name-calling, diagnosing, moralizing, interpreting, ordering, threatening, advising, diverting, arguing, interrogating, and similar behaviors. These forms of communication trigger the more primitive parts of the brain and cause people to move into competitive and disrespectful rather than collaborative and respectful feelings and behaviors. Particularly important for establishing a mutually respectful ambiance, all must accept the perspective that there may be more than one "right" point of view or solution. The right/wrong mentality will sabotage any attempt to resolve differences constructively. The same holds true when the participants focus on blaming the other person for the problem or asserting something in a judgmental way.

Venting in a conflict resolution process tends to weaken and delay the resolution process. In this context, venting is when a person gives free expression to a strong negative emotion such as anger or rage in order to relieve the pressure built up inside them rather than resolving what gave rise to the emotion. Although venting might feel good, it often triggers disrespectful forms of communication and ultimately exacerbates the conflict. Whereas it is possible to express anger and frustration in a respectful way, venting anger in disrespectful ways seldom serves the resolution process. Often we later wish to retract venting statements because they have been so hurtful. At worst, some venting statements cause such harm that the relationship never recovers. At minimum, it causes harm to the rapport between you and the other person and derails the collaborative process, requiring much soothing and healing before a constructive dialogue can continue.

If you truly need to vent, find a good friend or therapist willing to help you give uninhibited expression to your anger, resentment, or other negative emotions in preparation for entering the B-E-A-R Process where these emotions will be channeled into a more respectful dialogue.

Many people need help in expressing their anger constructively and respectfully. When you have held your anger for a long time or need to voice strong feelings in order to make yourself heard and participate equally in the process, you might wish to employ a mediator or therapist who can coach you in how to express anger respectfully.

BENEFITS

Asserting initiates the B-E-A-R process. When you assert respectfully, you gain at least four benefits:

1. Reduced emotional upset triggering the more primitive parts of your brain and the brain of the other person with whom you are in conflict.
2. Increased ability to listen and be receptive to each other's point of view.
3. Better mutual understanding.
4. Improved rapport and mutual respect.

SKILLS NEEDED

Asserting respectfully requires at least four skills. In initiating a dialogue, you can use them individually or in any combination to maximize the other person's willingness and ability to listen to and understand you:

- Contract and clarify intention.
- Speak respectfully.
- Give I-messages.
- Make direct requests.

CONTRACT AND CLARIFY INTENTIONS

Preparing the other person for a dialogue involves two skills: contracting and clarifying intentions. Contracting involves asking the other person if he or she is willing to talk about a particular issue, set a time and place, and agree to use the B-E-A-R Process. Clarifying intentions involves both letting the other person know why you want to have a talk and revealing your positive intention for the dialogue.

Contracting. Getting an agreement from the other person to have a dialogue using the B-E-A-R Process sets the stage for a more successful interaction. You ask for trouble if you assume the other person is ready and willing to talk about a potentially conflictual topic whenever you want to do so. This fails to take the other person's wishes, time, circumstances, or readiness to talk about something potentially difficult into consideration. The other person may have an important meeting or phone call to make, not feel well, or feel too tired or preoccupied to give you and your issue full consideration. If you force a discussion under less than optimal conditions, you can expect less than optimal results.

Therefore, contracting for when, where, and how you would like to talk about your issue proves extremely important if you want to set the stage for a constructive dialogue. For example, rather than Jim jumping on Emily in anger at how she just treated him in front of their daughter, he might better wait until they put their daughter to bed before even trying to have the dialogue. After the daughter has fallen asleep Jim could say to Emily, "I'm feeling upset by something that just happened before we put Jill to bed and I'd like to talk about it. Would you be willing to sit on the couch and talk about it using the B-E-A-R Process?"

Notice that he clarifies when *(now)*, where (on the couch) and how (the B-E-A-R Process). Emily might say, "No, I'm just too exhausted tonight and I have an early meeting tomorrow that I'm very preoccupied about. Could we do it tomorrow night?" Or she could say, "Yeah, I guess so, but I need to go to the bathroom first." Either way, Jim has paved the way for a more successful interchange by not just assuming Emily is both ready and willing to talk. Jim may also need to clarify what he wants to talk about and why. The next section covers this issue.

To contract for a dialogue about complaints, criticisms, or requests, you might wish to set a time each week when both parties agree to discuss these more difficult issues. Having a set time each week to air problems in the relationship can serve as a safety valve for people who tend to erupt into negative criticism. This gives them time to cool down so they can voice the complaint with less negative energy. A set time can also help people who tend to avoid conflict because the structure of the weekly meeting assures that they will be listened to, heard, and responded to with some understanding by their partner before hearing the partner's reactions. Over time, the B-E-A-R Process can reduce some of the anxiety that avoiders have in discussing difficult issues.

You may benefit by writing down any issues you wish to bring up as they arise during the week, and then reviewing them before the meeting to decide which items to bring up. Some of the issues may have evaporated already. Some may have grown even more important or urgent. It can also help for each person to jot down things that he or she has appreciated about what the other person has done in the past week.

The structure of these weekly meetings can remain quite simple. One person goes first and mentions the things that he has appreciated over the past week. The other person then follows with her appreciations, the more the better, as long as they are genuine. They have agreed that they don't have to have an equal number of appreciations. If one partner has more appreciations than the other, that partner should let them all come out. If a partner has no appreciations one week, he should not seek to fabricate but should keep the exchange genuine and sincere. Following this, the partners go through the B-E-A-R Process (delineated as follows) as consciously as possible. Each person should set priorities on issues to avoid overloading the other person. Perhaps each person can handle only one issue, particularly in the beginning. It can also help to limit the time or number of issues brought up to avoid exhaustion.

This format can also be used in the work setting with two people or a group of people in a work team.

Clarifying intentions. The second part of preparing the other person lets him know why you want to have the dialogue in the first place. All too often a discussion about a difference begins without participants revealing the underlying intention for the dialogue. This often results in an emotional roller coaster no one can control and can lead to destructive interchanges. People often assume that others know their intentions, priorities, or why they do or say something. At the same time, many people don't know their own intentions, or why they do what they do. We seldom consciously reflect on the motivations for why we want to bring up an issue, let alone recognize our positive intention for the outcome.

For example, toward the end of a particularly difficult couples counseling session, the husband invited his wife to take a walk in the rose garden before going over to her parents' house to pick up their children. She very abruptly said, "No way," and stalked out of the room. He showed visible frustration and confusion. Processing this episode the next week revealed that he had wanted to spend some time with his wife to calm down from the difficult session and to rebuild their rapport before going over to her parents' house. When she found out his intention, she asked, "Why didn't you tell me? I just didn't want to go to the rose garden because it was so hot outside, and I hate to walk in the heat with all those bugs around." She might just as well have assumed that her husband wanted to keep on the stressful topic during the session rather than cool things down before going over to her parents' house.

Without the husband clarifying his intentions, or the wife asking him to clarify his intentions, they leave open a major gap in their communication where misunderstandings and misinterpretations can thrive. Because he did not tell her why he invited her to the rose garden (i.e., his positive intention), she totally misunderstood, and they missed an opportunity that they both wanted. It really didn't matter to the husband where they spent the time together; he was perfectly happy to sit in the car with the air conditioner on and talk for a while to cool down literally and figuratively. He inaccurately assumed his wife knew his positive intention.

This common and sometimes tragic phenomenon provides one of the primary reasons for misunderstanding between people, particularly during a disagreement or conflict. When in conflict, the brain stem and limbic system tend to take over because we often experience anxiety and threat. This often leads to negative inferences and predictions about the other's behavior or words. These negative assumptions and inferences very easily get translated into blaming, accusations, or criticisms, creating defensiveness.

The solution, seldom easy, requires that you remain aware of your positive intention in any given communication and remember that the other person may not know your intention. You must then communicate your positive intention preferably before, or at least during, your main communication.

On the other hand, you also must remember that your sensing negativity does not necessarily mean the other person intends to have that effect on you. You must remain vigilant about how frequently you make negative inferences about someone else's intentions, particularly in conflict situations. You must try to discover what the other person intends by asking rather than just assuming. You need to treat your inferences as hunches, not facts.

Thus, in the example of the couple, the husband would need to stay aware of why he wanted to spend some time with his wife before going to pick up the kids, aware that she might not feel the same way and certainly not know why he would want to spend some time with her right then. He would then need to share his intention or motivation before inviting her to the rose garden. It might go like this: "Jane, this has been a good but very rough session for me. I'm not quite up to seeing your folks and the kids just yet. I'd like for us to spend just a little time together to regroup and cool down before seeing everybody. How about taking a walk in the rose garden for a few minutes before going over to your parents?"

Jane could then say: "No way do I want to go to the rose garden today in this heat! But I would like to calm down a bit too. How about just sitting in the car for a while with the air conditioner on?"

Alternatively, if the husband does not remember to clarify his intention ahead of time, Jane could ask her husband why he wants to go to the rose garden (as opposed to inferring, for example, that he wants to continue the stressful discussion started in the session). We just as frequently make negative inferences of others' intentions as we fail to clarify our own to them, particularly in conflict situations.

Discovering and clarifying your underlying intentions is extremely important in preventing the negative inferences and interpretations ubiquitous in conflict situations.

By thinking of the other person at this stage of the process, you pave the way for a more collaborative process. Rather than just trying to get your own needs met or having your own way, you take the other person into consideration. This proves not only respectful to the other person, but also more optimal for you because it keeps you in your cerebral cortex, a much more effective place to be in a dialogue that involves conflict.

SPEAK RESPECTFULLY

In an effective dialogue process, expressing your viewpoint respectfully becomes very important. To communicate respectfully, you do not imply that you have the only right answer or solution. Rather, you express your personal viewpoint. Sharing your point of view connotes a very personal and subjective way of talking to others. The term "viewpoint" suggests that you have just one among many possible perspectives on an issue, which may not have an objective truth, or a "right" or a "wrong." This can be illustrated in the story of the three blind men exploring an elephant by touch. One blind man declares it feels like a tree *(leg)*, the other a rug *(ear)*, the other a rope *(tail)*, each adamantly defending his perspective as the "right" one.

Accusing the other person of wrongdoing and blaming him or her for the conflict can lead only to defensiveness, hostility, or withdrawal. It also deflects the process into fighting over whom to blame rather than assessing what really happened, how each person could have contributed to the problem, and moving on to what it will take to resolve the issue and prevent it from happening again.

Our egos make speaking respectfully difficult. Our emotions and those primitive parts of our brain often dominate. It takes a mature, psychologically healthy person to communicate subjectively, taking full responsibility for perspectives and behaviors. Essentially, speaking respectfully comes from your attitude toward yourself and the other person. If you have an attitude of self-respect and respect for the other person's sovereignty, even when you disagree, you can usually speak in a tone of voice and behave in a way that will demonstrate that respect.

Voice tone. Probably the most important thing to do when in a conflict, particularly if you are angry, is to speak in a respectful tone of voice. This takes a high degree of self-awareness and a conscious intention for a positive outcome to the dialogue. When you talk with someone about something that upsets you, you need to hear how your voice sounds to the other. If it comes across in any way that might sound dismissive, demeaning, or belittling, you will create a defensiveness that will more than likely get in the way of the other person hearing you accurately, let alone sympathetically.

Facial gestures. How we look at someone can create the same feelings as a tone of voice. We can look at someone with love and affection or hatred and frustration and the other person will read it accurately no matter what the content of the words.

Rolling your eyes, looking out from the corner of your eye, squinting, raising one side of your lip, raising your eyebrows, looking away, and many other facial gestures can communicate disrespectful or disruptive messages to the other person. You should avoid these in the B-E-A-R Process.

In summary, people intuitively trust more what they hear in your tone of voice or see in your facial expression than the content of your words. Speaking respectfully means getting yourself to look at the other person respectfully and to speak with a respectful tone of voice. This takes conscious intention, self-awareness, and practice. Awareness of which brain controls you can help. The more you can do this, the more effective your communication will be.

Stating opinion as fact. One particular method of communicating requires amplification because it illustrates not only the importance of speaking respectfully but also subjectively, that is, having the attitude that your point of view is your personal truth and not objective or universal truth. An example of this would be someone speaking with autocratic authority. Stating your opinion as a fact is the opposite of speaking subjectively and usually works poorly because it implies there is only one "right" answer or solution. Collaborative conflict resolution escapes people who see their view as the only "right" one. People who voice their opinions as facts often poorly identify how they have contributed to the conflict and loathe taking responsibility for that contribution. Healthy dialogue and effective conflict resolution require both skills.

For example, Jane says to her husband, "Look you just did it again! That's not the way to clean the silverware. You have to use soap! And wash both the front and the back of the forks and spoons as well as both sides of the handle." Jake reacts defensively by saying, "Well, aren't you the obsessive one! What's the big deal?"

Although Jane's way of doing the silverware may very well clean the silverware more effectively, she comes across to Jake as the Queen of Dishwashing when she issues her edict on how to do it, and he resents it. It unnecessarily invokes a right/wrong frame to the interaction, which works against a resolution.

If Jane says something like, "Would you be open to hearing some feedback on how you wash the silverware?" it gives Jake a chance to say, "Not right now, honey. I'm really preoccupied with my presentation at work today." If he says okay, however, she can then say, "Well, I've noticed egg yolk stuck on the forks and other food stuck on the handles of the knives and spoons, which has annoyed me. Would you be willing to wash more carefully all parts of the silverware? It would make eating more enjoyable for me."

Jake still might not like to hear what Jane says, but at least Jane speaks more subjectively and does not set herself up as the dishwashing police. Jake might more likely respond, "Yeah, when I'm washing the dishes, my mind sometimes just starts to wander on to what I'm going to do next, and I don't always pay much attention to what I'm doing. I don't feel it's that big a deal since it's not poison I'm leaving on the silverware, but I'll try to be more careful."

Speaking respectfully and subjectively allows for other potentially valid perspectives. For example, if the blind man holding the leg of an elephant could listen to his colleagues, he might learn that an elephant can also feel like a rug (ear) or a rope (trunk) and thereby ultimately come to a fuller, more accurate understanding of an elephant. This metaphor aptly illustrates creative conflict resolution because two or more heads often brainstorm better than one for win-win or "both gain" solutions that might outshine any one idea that either party could produce alone.

In summary, expressing your point of view respectfully and subjectively usually leads to a more fruitful dialogue because it allows for other viewpoints that might also have validity, because it might communicate a fuller reality, and because it doesn't create as much defensiveness. Therefore, people are more likely to hear what you say and more willingly cooperate. Perhaps no one has said it better than Rumi:

> *Out beyond ideas of wrongdoing and rightdoing,*
> *there is a field. I'll meet you there.*

GIVE I-MESSAGES

Often, when in a dispute, we withdraw in silence, over-accommodate, prematurely compromise, blame, judge, or accuse the other in an adversarial manner. Although none of these methods prove effective, we often don't know what else to do.

Alternatively, reporting the feelings, personal meanings, and importance underlying our point of view promotes the decision-making or conflict resolution process. We can usually behave more constructively when we understand why we feel as we do and why others feel as they do.

Few of us think of sharing our underlying feelings and meanings when we try to make a joint decision or have a disagreement. Some of us have trouble confiding in others when not in conflict, let alone when in conflict. If, however, you can learn to share with others your feelings and the underlying meaning of why you are feeling that way, you can literally transform arguments into intimate conversations. Stepping outside the fight to explore what really goes on within you and sharing it with the other sets an entirely different tone to the interaction and pierces to the heart of what really matters.

When intimate partners or friends face a conflict or important decision, this deeper level of sharing true feelings and the real underlying importance of an issue expands in importance for the maintenance of the relationship. If this level of sharing does not take place, the conversation can very quickly turn into a power struggle. Parties in a divorce or commercial mediation in which they will have a continuing relationship (e.g., to co-parent children or to continue a business relationship) will find it particularly beneficial to get to this deeper level.

You may wonder, "What if the other person uses my disclosures against me?" This can, of course, happen, but I propose that most situations make it worth risking. If the other person does use your disclosures against you, you might need to question if the other person really wants or can have a mutually respectful relationship. If not, then sharing deeper feelings and the underlying importance may not serve; in fact, you may need to seriously evaluate continuing the dialogue or even the relationship itself.

Thomas Gordon, in his book *Parent Effectiveness Training*, used the term "I-message" in contrast to "You-message." You-messages describe all the ways one person tells another person how to live. I-messages provide a structure for sharing feelings and underlying meanings in the subjective way I describe.

A complete I-message has three parts:

- A non-inflammatory description of the other person's unacceptable behavior
- One or more accurate feeling words
- An unexaggerated description of the adverse tangible effect the other person's behavior has on you personally

An I-message works best when it includes all three parts succinctly. For example, "I get annoyed when you don't clean off the counter because I then need to clean it." A generic format for giving an I-message could be "I feel _____ when you _____ because I _____." The order of the three parts does not matter. For example, "When you don't clean off the counter, I feel annoyed because then I need to clean it, " serves just as well.

I-messages might sound awkward at first, but you can communicate this way more effectively, particularly when using a non-accusatory tone of voice. I-messages also provide more useful information to the other person. Although there is no guarantee that the other person will change their behavior, I-messages often reduce resistance or defensiveness compared to You-messages.

Examples of You-messages include: "Get into that kitchen and clean that counter top right now!" "God you're a slob!" "When was the last time you cleaned up after yourself?"

You-messages, usually much more emotionally inflammatory than I-messages, obstruct the communication process significantly because they use blaming ("You make me angry!"); use "war" words ("You *never* clean up after yourself"); imply you have the right to tell others what to do or how to live their lives by giving them orders ("Stop that!") or making demands ("Clean up that kitchen now!"); or use name-calling ("You're such a slob"), just to identify a few examples.

I-messages inform others about the adverse impact their behavior has on you, yet do not tell them what to do about it, leaving them with the decision of whether to change their behavior and, if so, how. An I-message educates and informs the recipient, giving him information he needs if he wants to cooperate with you. Some recipients of an I-message will change their behavior immediately and others won't. Either way, I-messages often provide a good way to initiate a dialogue at times of potential conflict because this kind of message does not imply that you have the right to dictate to others how they should behave. In other words, I-messages do not imply you have sovereignty over the other person, whereas You-messages do. Since this is such an important skill for initiating a dialogue about a problem, let us look more closely at the three parts of an I-message.

Describe behaviors. This part informs the other person specifically what he does or fails to do that bothers you without unnecessarily inflaming him by exaggerating or distorting his behavior, or making inferences about or interpretations of his behavior with which he could take exception. You describe the behavior as objectively and neutrally as possible in words and in tone of voice.

For example, "When you raise your voice and interrupt me..." rather than "When you constantly bully me..." The first phrasing attempts to describe behavior as accurately as possible whereas the second hurls an accusation that includes an exaggeration (assuming the interrupter has listened to the speaker all the way through at least once) and an inference ("bullying" infers or interprets the interrupter's behavior). It doesn't matter if the interpretation or inference is correct or not. An inference or interpretation will most likely spark argument by the other person: "What do you mean 'bully' you? I haven't laid a hand on you!" The less behaviorally descriptive one gets, the more room it leaves the other person to defend or take exception, and the fight gets derailed onto your exaggeration or inference rather than how you feel, why you feel that way, and how to resolve the issue.

Describe feelings. How you feel about the other person's behavior often proves central to resolving conflict. You cannot avoid emotions, even though they often get quite messy. To resolve conflict, you must learn that experiencing feelings and expressing feelings constitute a necessary part of the resolution process, no matter what the setting. If you fail to express your feelings, you will not give the other person what he needs to understand you fully, and you may find yourself unable to listen to him very well.

Knowing how to express your feelings provides the key. For example, when Ginny came back from a week away at a professional conference in her field of chemical engineering, Matt started interrogating her about what she did and who she spent time with during the conference, particularly during the evenings. He even made snide remarks about her tendency to socialize at meetings rather than go to the meetings to learn. Ginny got defensive and they ended up in silence the rest of the way home. The next day, Matt's counselor asked him why he behaved as he did. After considerable digging, Matt finally said, "Well, she's an engineer and surrounded by men all the time!" He felt threatened and jealous. So rather than saying, "Ginny, I know this is unfair to you but I started having all kinds of fantasies about you at the conference with all those men and I started feeling threatened that you'd find someone more interesting than me. I even started feeling jealous. I guess I would like some reassurance that nothing happened over the week."

By sharing his feelings directly rather than going into interrogation and criticism, he might feel vulnerable, but he avoids creating an unnecessary and harmful distance. Matt creates a barrier by not sharing that he felt threatened and jealous. Not communicating feelings can sometimes cause just as many problems as turning the feelings into blame or accusations.

To avoid slipping into blame, criticism, or judgment, you must express feelings directly and use an actual feeling word after the words " I feel _____." For example, "I feel impatient..." rather than "I feel like you don't value my time as much as your own," or " I feel as if I don't exist when you don't call and let me know you're going to be late," or "I feel you're an irresponsible ingrate!" You can easily get into judgments or accusations when you think you're expressing feelings.

You must also avoid blaming others for your feelings. Others' behaviors do not cause your feelings. Rather, the meaning and interpretation you place on events or other people's behavior causes your feelings. Feelings grow from your interpretations, perceptions, and inferences. Therefore, when giving an I-message, take responsibility for your feelings by saying, "I feel frustrated because I was expecting you to come home sooner," rather than blaming the other person for your feelings as in "You make me feel frustrated when you come home later than you said you would."

It helps if you can get to the primary feeling rather than the secondary or derivative feeling. For example, a secondary or derivative feeling such as anger may morph from an underlying hurt, worry, or jealousy. Expressing the primary feeling, such as jealousy, might prove more difficult because it often feels more vulnerable, but it usually works better. You might find it hard to identify what you actually feel because feelings come in ways that often confuse and contradict. For example, Matt felt both excited and eager for Ginny to come home, but at the same time, he felt threatened, jealous, and even a bit angry.

Feelings can also confuse you because you may have learned not to have certain feelings. As a result, if you feel scared, and scared is not an acceptable feeling for you to have, you not only won't admit that you feel scared, you might not even recognize that you're feeling scared. The fear somehow turns into belligerence or righteous indignation. As a result, it is often necessary to prepare yourself before giving an I-message. You might need to explore within your-self what you feel and why before the I-message becomes clear.

You need to include an honest disclosure of your primary feelings to prevent a complex set of barriers from developing and lessening the intimacy in a personal relationship or lessening the effectiveness in a working relationship. You cannot ignore feelings if you want enjoyable and productive relationships.

Describe the tangible effect. When you let another person know how his behavior impacts you, you accomplish a number of things at the same time. You educate the other person about the impact his behavior has on you, you assert that you value and honor yourself, and you make yourself vulnerable to the other person because they may or may not care.

Expressing even a small adverse tangible effect may prove useful because the other person might not know how his behavior impacts you. For example, "I feel frustrated when you came later than you said you would because I ended up waiting for you rather than finishing my application." If you don't share that information, the other person has no way of knowing why you felt frustrated.

Sharing the adverse tangible effect or impact on you lets the other person know what you consider important and what you value. This sharing might make you feel vulnerable because it lies at the heart of your image of yourself. You might also find it difficult because you might not know what upsets you because you rarely take your own needs or desires seriously.

Stating explicitly the adverse tangible effect someone's behavior has on you truly tests whether you value yourself and honor your sovereignty. If you cannot state this part of the I-message, resentment eventually builds up. You have not only betrayed yourself, but you have also not given the other person a chance to change or respond to your concerns.

It might also be hard for you to share the adverse tangible effect because you confuse feelings with tangible effects. Remember, your feelings come from how we interpret others' behavior. For example, "I'm upset when you come home late because I ended up worrying about you." This blames the other person for your feeling worried and will usually get a negative reaction. This is an example of what is commonly called a "guilt trip." A better example of a tangible effect is "... because then I had to take care of the children and was late for the PTA meeting and missed my agenda item."

Do not speak for someone else when bringing in the adverse tangible effect. For example, do not say "... because Mother will be angry if we're late." This speaks for your mother and not for yourself. To be optimally effective, the tangible effect needs to point to "you." Speaking for other people will dilute the I-message and make it arguable again ("Your mother didn't seem to mind!").

Finally, if you can't find an adverse tangible effect for the I-message, it means the other person engages in a behavior that you don't like, but it does not directly affect you in a tangible way. For example, "I feel disgust when you have your nose pierced because..." This conflict involves your personal values or aesthetic preferences regarding something the other person has chosen that you do not agree with but that has no real adverse tangible effect on you. You might place a very negative aesthetic value on pierced noses, you might even believe it physically unhealthy for the other to pierce his nose, but it does not affect your health or have any other adverse tangible effect on you. You still might want to communicate your disagreement with someone piercing his nose, but you need to recognize this as a "conflict of values," as discussed earlier. For a more detailed description of how to deal with a "conflict of values" situation, consult Thomas Gordon's *Teacher Effectiveness Training*.

Sharing the adverse tangible effect takes a great deal of self-awareness, vulnerability, self-honoring, and skill, but it works powerfully when communicated clearly and concisely. It takes practice. The more you honor your sovereignty and the more you are willing and able to be vulnerable, the better you will be able to do it.

MAKE DIRECT REQUESTS (OR PROPOSALS)

Many people find making direct requests difficult because to do so requires openness and vulnerability. This deceptively simple skill requires expressing what you want directly in specific, positive terms. The phrase "Would you be willing to..." is one good way to begin a direct request. Sometimes it helps to add an explanation so the other person understands the underlying purpose of the request (i.e., "Would you be willing to _____ because _____?"). For example, "Would you be willing to rub my back tonight because I'm really tight in my left shoulder and can't get to sleep?" Sometimes it also helps to add how you would like it done so the other person does not have to guess (e.g., "It really helps when you use your elbow to press down just to the right of my left shoulder blade.").

The more vulnerable you feel in making a direct request, the more difficult you will find it to communicate in direct, specific language. The less direct and less specific your language, however, the more potentially confusing the message is. Lack of specificity frequently leads to misunderstanding. Misunderstanding frequently leads to unnecessary conflict.

Why do many people find such a simple thing like making a direct request such a difficult and vulnerable thing to do? First of all, they may not have a history of having simple, direct requests listened to attentively and considered seriously. Those who do not honor themselves or their desires have a particularly difficult time asking others for something because they do not feel they deserve to get what they want. Some believe it selfish to ask for what they want, confusing selfishness (consciously taking something from someone else either against their will or to their detriment), with self-honoring (asking for or taking something for themselves for their own health or welfare without taking anything away from others). Others don't ask for what they want because they anticipate the other person will say no, or take offense, or they fear what other people will think, or they dread embarrassing refusals.

Not everyone has difficulty making direct requests. Some people actually feel entitled to get whatever they want. This presents a different problem: to distinguish between a direct request and an indirect demand. A request respects the other person's right to say no. You should not disguise requirements as requests. An example of this is asking, "Would you like to get this to me by Friday?" rather than stating the true requirement, "I need you to get this report to me by Friday so I can look it over before my meeting Monday morning."

If your request is a true request and not an indirect demand, you will be able to accept a no and even empathize with the person's reasons for not doing what you ask. If your request if a hidden demand, you will likely feel critical of the person and possibly guilt trip them in some way.

Making a proposal, a variation on making a direct request, leaves more room for negotiation regarding the specifics and often proves useful in negotiating differences or making important decisions. It implies that the person who has made the original proposal understands that the other person may want to change or adapt it. More formal negotiations often use proposals.

Making direct requests provides a courageous, self-honoring, respectful, clear, and empowering way of relating to others. Detaching yourself from the other person's response through a willingness to hear a "no" also takes considerable self-esteem. Understanding the ineffectiveness of demanding things from others and the appropriateness of asking things of others, as long as we accept their right to say no, provides an empowering way to live and reduces misunderstandings and conflict.

ADDED BENEFIT

I have not mentioned one of the positive by-products of asserting respectfully. Effective use of the assertion skills described here substantially reduces the recipient's emotional temperature from rising to levels that trigger the more primitive parts of the brain. In other words, it reduces the chances you will trigger the other person to fight, flee, freeze, or get defensive. Instead, that person will hear you better and respond from a more "reasonable" part of his or her brain.

The asserter assumes responsibility to initiate the dialogue in a respectful way so as to minimize the recipient's defensiveness and maximize the recipient's ability to listen and respond effectively. The listener *(recipient)* must accept responsibility to manage his or her own emotional temperature. The next phase of the B-E-A-R Process explores these responsibilities.

SUMMARY

- Clarify your positive intentions for initiating a dialogue.
- Get an agreement or contract from the other person affirming his or her willingness to discuss the issue.
- Use respectful language, tone of voice, and facial gestures.
- Give I-messages rather than You-messages.
- Make direct and specific requests or proposals.
- All these actions contribute substantially to launching a productive and collaborative dialogue for settling conflicts or making important decisions.

CHAPTER SEVEN

BREATHE

While Asserting initiates the B-E-A-R Process and deals with how best to begin the dialogue, the second phase, Breathe, deals with how best to receive and respond to the speakers' message. This second phase provides a series of skills to improve your ability to monitor and manage your emotional temperature so you can pay attention to the person speaking and hear their communications accurately. These skills will enable you to better demonstrate accurate understanding to the speaker in the next phase of the model.

BENEFITS

The Breathe phase involves paying attention when the other person asserts their point of view by listening not only to the content of their words but also to their tone of voice and observing their facial gestures as well as managing your emotional temperature throughout the dialogue process. The Breathe phase imparts at least four benefits:

1. Reduces the likelihood that the primitive parts of your brain will activate overwhelming emotions.
2. Improves your ability to listen.
3. Increases your ability to empathize with others.
4. Enables you to respond more respectfully.

SKILLS NEEDED

The Breathe phase of the B-E-A-R Process requires you to use four skills:

- Listen
- Observe

- Manage emotions
- Take time out

LISTEN

You must pay very close attention to the other person in a dialogue if you want to resolve an issue or make an important joint decision. You cannot afford to miss anything about another's tone of voice, facial gestures, and body posture because they carry most of the information you need to assess accurately the other person's feelings and meanings. You must discern another's meanings and feelings to demonstrate that you understand them in ways that will help the other person not only feel understood but also respected, both of which are important in reaching a mutually satisfying resolution.

Listening to both the content of another's words and their tone of voice is an important skill in conflict resolution. Without careful attention, your internal conflicts and anxieties can overpower hearing accurately what others really say.

Between what I think,
What I want to say,
What I believe I am saying,
What I say,
What you want to hear,
What you hear,
What you believe you understand,
What you want to understand
And what you understood,
There are at least nine possibilities for misunderstanding.
    François Garagnon

Listening more consciously to the tone of voice, inflection, and volume changes in another's voice gives clues to how the person feels and what has the most meaning or importance for him. To hear one simple example of how powerful the tone of voice, pace, or emphasis can make a difference, say, "I love you" out loud with the emphasis on "you." Now say, "I love you" with the emphasis on "I." Notice how the latter sounds defensive while the former sounds more genuine. These subtle changes in emphasis can make all the difference in how we interpret what others say.

OBSERVE

Paying attention to the facial expressions, body posture, hand gestures, appearance, grooming, and energy level of others helps to interpret accurately their feelings and meanings as well. First, speaker and listener should face each other directly. Sometimes this is not possible when walking with the person, but insofar as possible orient your body toward the speaker. If the speaker sits, you should sit. If the speaker stands, you should stand. You should find a distance from the speaker that suits you both, observing but not staring, while looking for indications of feelings in facial expressions, body posture, gestures, and other visual indicators. Making inferences from observations of how others communicate provides a major way to respond accurately to others' feelings. How you place your body in relation to others and how you look at them reveal to them whether you respect them or not.

MANAGE EMOTIONS

Recall our discussion of the three parts of the brain: the reptilian, mammalian, and human brain. While the other person asserts, you have the responsibility in the B-E-A-R Process to manage your emotions so the reptilian and mammalian brains do not gain dominance. There are ways to monitor and manage these parts of your brain so you can respond from your cortex and thereby have better access to the skills in the B-E-A-R Process.

In *Why Marriages Succeed or Fail* and *The Seven Principles of Making Marriage Work*, John Gottman, Ph.D., who has researched marriage for more than 30 years writes of his discovery that if a person's heart rate increases by only 10 percent above normal, it precipitously lowers their ability to listen to and understand accurately what someone says or to communicate constructively. Gottman refers to this phenomenon as "flooding."

Two steps help to manage our emotions so we don't trigger our reptilian and mammalian brains: monitoring emotional temperature and managing emotional temperature.

Monitoring emotional temperature.   Monitoring emotional blocks to listening or speaking constructively requires elevated self-awareness at a time when you are least likely to have it. On the other hand, you have to recognize your flooding before you can do anything about it. Some people get loud and agitated when they flood. Others appear very calm and withdraw physically or emotionally.

Recognizing when you flood takes practice. Becoming angry, agitated, or frustrated, or experiencing any strong negative emotion provides a major cue. Breathing rapidly and more shallowly from your chest, feeling your palms sweating, and speaking louder and with a higher pitch also indicate flooding. Some people become steely cold and start speaking very slowly and unemotionally or super-rationally. Measuring your pulse rate is a reasonably accurate method of assessing your level of flooding. Based on years of research with couples in conflict, John Gottman recommends cooling down if your pulse rate goes 10 percent above what it is normally. Spotting the upset that signals in you that you are approaching a flooded state or recognizing that you have already flooded can prevent the escalation of conflict.

If you proceed in spite of flooding, you court disaster. Gottman discovered that most people quickly lose their ability to listen accurately or communicate respectfully when they flood. Most of the real damage in relationships occurs when one or more participants flood, because conflict usually escalates under these conditions. You must monitor your emotional temperature if you wish to prevent escalation, which can derail the conflict resolution process and ultimately damage the relationship. You must know when you flood in order to manage your emotional temperature, but practice paves the way for preventing your primitive brain from gaining control of you.

Managing emotional temperature. In addition to recognizing your agitation, you must know how to calm yourself. Both of these steps help prevent the escalation of destructive conflict, which is when the primitive brain becomes dominant.

Conflict frequently stimulates strong negative emotions (e.g., anger, impatience, frustration), and Gottman's research demonstrates how important it is to manage your emotions when you seek to resolve a conflict collaboratively. Always cool down before trying to negotiate a conflict or disagreement.

Three things help relieve flooding: closing your eyes, breathing deeply from the abdomen, and putting one hand over your heart and the other hand over your forehead. You can do all three at the same time. Placing one hand on your chest at the heart level and the other on your forehead while your eyes are closed and while you breathe slowly and deeply from your belly will help you calm down quite effectively. It does not matter which hand rests on which body part. The sooner you catch yourself flooding and the sooner you start breathing deeply with your eyes closed and hands on your forehead and heart, the more likely you will prevent the primitive parts of your brain from taking control.

You may not have to do all three. Just breathing deeply and closing your eyes can help, but placing your hands on the two centers as well helps even more. It is not fully known why these three methods work so well, however, I believe each of them helps the nervous system to calm down.

While cooling down, remind yourself of your positive intention for the dialogue. Most people get off track in a conflict by throwing in peripheral details, shifting the focus to another issue, or making counter-attacks. These mistakes most often occur during flooding. Stay focused on the issue at hand and resume the dialogue when calmness returns. If these methods of calming yourself fail, and you still feel too emotionally upset to use the skills delineated in this model, or the other person is too upset, take a time-out.

TAKE TIME-OUT

When all the techniques mentioned previously fail, you will find it better to take a time-out than to continue talking. If you keep trying to talk while flooded, you run the risk of making resolution impossible and also of damaging the relationship.

Taking a bathroom break and washing your face and hands, or taking a walk outside and breathing deeply can help you cool down and gain access to your cortex again. Not thinking about the dialogue for a few moments while engaging in deep breathing, walking, and/

or creating relaxing mental images, can do wonders in a fairly short period of time. Once your emotions cool down, your cortex can regain control over your brain stem (reptilian brain) and limbic system (mammalian brain).

Gottman recommends a break no shorter than twenty minutes because it takes at least that long for most people's heart rate to return to normal. When we are upset enough to need a time-out, we need enough time to calm down more thoroughly. This could mean taking much longer than twenty minutes. You might need to wait one or more hours or days before resuming the dialogue.

This leads to an important aspect of taking a time-out. If you call the time-out, you need to give the other person a reasonable estimate of when you will resume the dialogue, be it twenty minutes or two days, and hold to that estimate, initiating the dialogue when the estimated time has elapsed. If you still have not calmed down enough to engage respectfully, make sure to communicate that after the time has elapsed and make another estimate as to when you will return to the dialogue. Unless you follow these steps, time-outs might not work in the future. The person left on hold has to trust that you will take responsibility for returning to the dialogue at a later time and not use the time-out as a way to avoid the dialogue.

Take time-outs only when you really need to. Often the person who does not want the time out finds it quite difficult to stop the dialogue. It is disrespectful to the other person to take a time-out and not let her know when the dialogue can resume. It is also disrespectful to make the other person have to reinitiate the dialogue. Thus, it is essential that the person who initiated the time-out initiate the dialogue again when the estimated time has elapsed.

If you use time-outs as a way to avoid resolving issues directly rather than as a way to reduce emotional flooding, the other person will lose patience and no longer respect the time-out option. If you choose to avoid dealing with a conflict, tell the other person directly that you are not willing to discuss the issue.

I recommend that the flooded person call the time-out to show he is taking responsibility for his emotional temperature. But if the flooded person cannot do it, the other person, even if not flooded, should have the right to take the time-out as well. Taking a time-out serves the conflict resolution process only when one or both people cannot listen or talk respectfully and responsibly because of emotional upset.

This means that each participant can call a time-out unilaterally. It works best if both can agree to a time-out, but this won't always happen, so you should agree ahead of time that either person can call the time-out unilaterally and the other person will honor it. Time-outs help prevent further damage to the relationship, acting like a fuse or circuit breaker in an electrical system.

Sometimes we so emotionally flood that continuing a dialogue becomes too difficult even after taking a time-out. If you find yourself unable to have eye contact with the other person, unable speak in a respectful tone of voice, or becoming emotionally volatile soon after resuming the dialogue, a past traumatic experience might be triggering you. When this occurs, returning to the dialogue can prove fruitless until you resolve the emotional issues around the past traumatic experiences.

Even if the other person has said or done something that warrants your anger and stimulates you to flood, you still need to take responsibility for your flooding and explore your past for what is getting triggered. It often takes a professionally trained therapist to help you identify historical issues and to resolve them. I recommend looking for a practitioner in your area that specializes in finding and treating past traumas (see www.aitherapy.org to find a therapist in your area who uses Advanced Integrative Therapy).

PUTTING THE BREATHE PHASE TOGETHER

Once you have learned to listen, observe, and manage your emotions, you have accomplished a great deal. Let's look at how the Breathe phase of the B-E-A-R Process might work in real life. Let's say you have an issue with me and you initiate a dialogue. I listen best if I can generate interest in what you have to say and remind myself to pay attention to you with my eyes as well as my ears, so I can attend to the content of your words, your tone of voice, and your facial gestures as well. This will help me later to demonstrate that I understand you accurately before responding from my perspective. This sequence of listening first to understand you before I respond from my frame of reference is challenging, particularly if you bring up an issue that upsets me. I may consciously have to breathe deeply as I listen to you, so I can manage any emotional upset I experience, thus keeping my cortex dominant.

When I am listening to your I-message or direct request (or to a criticism of or complaint about me), it helps to make a commitment to myself NEVER to criticize or complain back to you until I have demonstrated my understanding of your criticism or complaint FIRST! This means accurately paraphrasing what you have said until you are sure that I have understood you accurately. We will cover this skill in the next phase of the B-E-A-R Process, which is Empathize.

In order to do all of this, I need to calm and center myself emotionally because when I get angry or upset I usually get emotionally attached to my own message and have difficulty listening to others and hearing them accurately. I also tend to lose my ability to speak respectfully.

The Breathe phase of the B-E-A-R Process occurs while you are receiving someone's assertion. As the only component in the process in which you do not speak, it focuses primarily on how to conduct yourself as the listener and observer of the person with whom you have conflict. Your silence does not mean you have no work to do. In fact, you may find this the most difficult part of the entire process because it requires you not only to pay close attention to the other person while possibly hearing upsetting things, but also to monitor and manage your emotional temperature to prevent the reptilian and mammalian parts of your brain from gaining control over your human brain. If you fail to keep your cortex dominant, you might not have available all the skills that follow the Breathe phase in the B-E-A-R Process, making it more likely that you will fall back into the fight, flight, or freeze modes of responding.

SUMMARY

- Listen carefully to the content of the other person's words as well as their tone of voice, inflection, and volume changes to discern their feelings and what is most important to them.

- Observe the other person's facial expressions, posture, gestures, appearance, and energy level as well to aid you in discerning their feelings and what is most important to them.
- Monitor you emotional temperature by sensing when you are getting too angry, upset, frustrated, or impatient to listen well.
- Manage you emotional "flooding" by closing your eyes, breathing slowly and deeply, and placing your hands on you heart and forehead.
- If you can't calm down take a break; you need to continue operating from your cortex to listen well and respond respectfully.
- Let the other person know when you think you can return to the dialogue.
- If you continue to get triggered beyond what the situation warrants, consider seeking help in uncovering what occurred earlier in your life that is being triggered.

CHAPTER EIGHT

EMPATHIZE

All the effort you put into listening to the content of another person's message and their tone of voice and inflections as well as observing their facial expressions, hand gestures, and posture serves to gather as much data as you can about what he considers important, how he feels, and what he wants to tell you. If you have managed your emotional temperature well enough, even if the content somewhat upsets you, you can use the next phase of the B-E-A-R Process called Empathy to demonstrate to the other person you heard his message accurately.

To empathize with another means putting into your own words the content and feeling the other person communicates. Demonstrating accurate understanding of another human being, definitely a cerebral cortex activity, takes practice. It takes even more practice when you try to demonstrate your understanding of someone with whom you disagree or have conflict. Putting into your own words what someone else says when we disagree with them seems quite unnatural to most of us.

We seldom need empathy in normal conversations or when understanding someone accurately is not important. In conflict situations, however, it can prove very important because we tend not to hear very well and distort what people say to us, which can lead to needless misunderstandings.

BENEFITS

Empathy during a conflict resolution dialogue offers at least four benefits:

1. Empathy demonstrates understanding. If you do not feel understood when in a conflict, you tend to talk louder, faster, and

get more upset, triggering the reptilian and mammalian brains. When not understood, you tend to feel little inclination to listen to the other person and keep repeating your own message or just fall silent and withdraw. Empathy means more than just telling someone you understand him. It means actually demonstrating that understanding by putting into your own words the other person's point of view and feelings. At its best, empathy includes the underlying meaning and importance of what someone says. This paraphrasing of what others say and feel proves to the other person that you have heard him accurately. This increases the likelihood that he can stay in his cortex rather than get triggered into operating from his primitive brains and can better listen to you and work more collaboratively toward a resolution.

2. Empathy prevents misunderstandings. If you put into your own words what someone has communicated to you, it gives her the opportunity to let you know that you have not heard her accurately and can repeat what she said until you understand fully. A surprising number of conflicts evaporate when people explicitly demonstrate accurate understanding of each other because often what you heard was not what the other person said.

3. Empathy demonstrates respect. When you go to the trouble of demonstrating that you accurately understand another person, she usually feels respected by you. This improves her ability to listen and respond to you. When that occurs, something happens in the relationship that makes each person more willing to approach a resolution from the perspective of how they can optimize meeting both people's underlying needs and interests. In other words, when each person understands the other's underlying desires and why those desires are personally important to them, they grow more willing to explore mutual gain solutions with each other. Mutual understanding on a deeper level creates the mutual respect necessary for a more collaborative and less competitive interpersonal ambiance.

4. Empathy increases receptivity. When you demonstrate understanding of the other, particularly on the deeper level of underlying intentions, desires, feelings, and meanings, it paves the way for the other person to open more to your point of view. This is a prerequisite for establishing a collaborative problem solving process. This mutual interest in seeing if you can meet each of your underlying needs or desires lies at the heart of the collaborative process.

SKILLS NEEDED

The Empathy phase of the B-E-A-R Process requires you to use four skills:

- Understand positive intention
- Understand viewpoint
- Understand importance
- Understand feelings

UNDERSTAND POSITIVE INTENTION

You may recall that one of the skills in the Assert part of the B-E-A-R Process requires the asserter to express his positive intention for the dialogue when getting the other person's agreement to proceed. If that was done, you can fairly easily paraphrase what the person bringing up the issue already expressed as his intention and move on.

For example, Jill could start a dialogue with John by saying she wants to talk about his burning plywood in the fireplace because she knows how important he considers reusing or recycling the wood but she wants to discuss alternative ways to meet those values that will address her concerns as well. More important, she could assure John that she really wants to resolve the issue so she can continue to feel close to him.

If John could enter the dialogue knowing about Jill's underlying intent to feel closer to him, he would more likely listen and communicate in a less defensive way. Someone in Jill's position, however, might not always express her positive intention or even know what it is. In that case, John should search for it, even if Jill isn't saying it or even aware of it. I call this "additive empathy." Additive empathy means going beyond what someone explicitly says to interpret what someone might really mean underneath what they say. Usually, people make negative interpretations of the other's statements or behaviors when there is a disagreement or unresolved issue. For example, John could say, "Jill, why do you always have to have your way. It must be that your parents always treated you like a little princess who could never do anything wrong." Consciously or unconsciously, John intends to make Jill feel guilty for expressing her viewpoint, and he implies selfishness.

Demonstrating understanding of the other person's positive intention, the opposite of this tactic, involves searching for what deeper positive intention the other person might have, even if unexpressed, and then reflecting that back tentatively to see if it is true. For example, John could infer Jill's positive intention as follows: "So are you bringing this up because you don't want to feel this tension between us anymore?" When Jill hears John try to guess her positive intention, it can help her stay focused on her actual positive intention.

Actively looking for each other's positive intention in the process powerfully reframes the dialogue into something more constructive and greatly facilitates collaborative brainstorming of potential solutions later in the process.

UNDERSTAND VIEWPOINT

The first and most basic level of empathy is listening for and accurately paraphrasing the content of another's point of view. "Point of view" includes each person's position on an issue, as well as all the supporting opinions and facts they relate pertaining to that position. When parties fail to demonstrate accurate understanding of each other on the content level, misunderstandings pervade the resolution process. This may seem simple to do, but since conflict usually involves the presence of negative emotions, often with some intensity, many people find it difficult to stay in the cerebral cortex of their brain.

Paraphrasing another person's differing viewpoint also proves difficult because some people do not differentiate between understanding and agreeing. They believe that demonstrating an accurate understanding of another's viewpoint will indicate agreement to the other person, or that their own viewpoint will not be seen as valid, or that they will lose their own viewpoint. Once you understand that you can have differing viewpoints based on your differing life experiences as well as differing cultural and family backgrounds, you can understand and hold two seemingly incompatible views at the same time.

Holding two views at the same time becomes possible once you jettison the "I'm right/You're wrong" way of thinking. This necessary attitude shift for collaborative conflict resolution allows parties to mediate their disputes rather than fight it out with their words, fists, or lawyers. The dialogue necessary for collaborative conflict resolution, whether in an informal setting or a more formal mediation setting, requires a "both/and" type of thinking rather than the "either/or," "right/wrong," "good/bad" of dualistic thinking.

Learning how to demonstrate accurate understanding of another's point of view is an important skill for optimal conflict resolution because it can serve to clarify and rectify basic misunderstandings. If you cannot demonstrate accurate understanding of the content of what someone says, you should ask him to repeat it, or expand on it, so you can understand it. You must have a genuine interest and curiosity in what the other person says and why he considers it important.

Recall the proverbial blind men, each touching the elephant in a different place. Rather than thinking each other wrong, each blind man might better express curiosity about why the others are having such a different experience. Each of them should ask each other about the experience and explore possible reasons for the differences. In this metaphor, the elephant's ear, tail, and leg all represent different histories, experiences, and perceptual fields. Rather than immediately concluding that the other person is wrong, you need to become curious as to why he feels, thinks, and perceives things so differently.

If you can make this transition, you reap significant rewards in expanding your learning, your vision of the world, and, more specifically, your deeper understanding of the person with whom you have conflict. If you don't make this transition, you will stay stuck in seeing an elephant as a rope, pillar, or some other partial reality rather than the whole elephant. In essence, you need to reframe a disagreement as an opportunity to learn a broader reality, a worldview that incorporates a more sophisticated inter-relationship between your perceptions and others' perceptions. When you allow the "you're wrong and I'm right" kind of thinking to yield to "we need to explore each other's perceptions of reality" kind of thinking, you move toward resolution of disagreements and perhaps even toward feeling good about each other again.

In summary, if you can't demonstrate accurate understanding of the content of the other person's viewpoint, you must solicit more about what the other person says until you do understand and can prove it to them by putting their content into your own words until they explicitly acknowledge that you accurately understand their point of view.

UNDERSTAND IMPORTANCE

Though it is often difficult to demonstrate an accurate understanding of the content of someone's viewpoint when emotions run high, it is even more difficult to demonstrate an accurate understanding of the meaning or importance that underlies the other person's viewpoint. For example, beyond John's ability to accurately paraphrase Jill's reluctance to burn the wood scraps from their house remodeling project (the content of Jill's viewpoint), it is even more important that John respond to the underlying meaning or importance of that viewpoint (e.g., she fears the wood might contain toxic chemicals that will release in the air if burned and adversely affect their daughter's asthma). When Jill expressed why she did not want John to burn the wood scraps, and John could empathize with the meaning and importance underlying Jill's viewpoint, he could relinquish his insistence on burning the wood and eventually came to another solution acceptable to both.

This skill lies at the heart of effective conflict resolution. Only when each person understands how or why the content of the other's viewpoint is important, or how the other person has come to her perceptions, conclusions, and behaviors, can they begin to co-create resolutions to their dispute. Our different life experiences, cultural backgrounds, and gender training all contribute to each of us having different assumptions, inferences, and interpretations of our experiences. Hence we each have somewhat different expectations and judgments of how we should do things or how people should behave. These are so ingrained in us that we seldom recognize that we hold these norms.

Only when you understand that each of you touches a different part of the elephant does the disagreement make sense, and only when each party understands how or why the other person arrived at her viewpoint, do you begin to see the other person and her view in a new light. You stop seeing each other as stupid, bad, or naive and settle down to the hard work of finding a solution that both of you can embrace.

Even if a mutual gain solution does not arise, the parties can usually accept a compromise that gets each of them the most feasible outcome under the circumstances. Sometimes the parties can better accept their disagreement once they understand each other's underlying reasons for their respective positions.

This step assumes key importance in the conflict resolution process because once all parties understand more deeply each other's personal stake in the dispute, it becomes possible for each party to begin taking that stake into consideration in brainstorming potential mutual gain solutions later on in the process. Until they mutually understand the deeper personal meanings and importance that underlie each of their positions, this type of collaboration remains unlikely to take place. Rather, each party remains focused on getting as much of what he wants as possible and the more creative mutual gain solutions remain uncovered and unexplored. They polarize rather than collaborate.

The importance that underlies someone's position in a dispute lies at the heart of the issue for each party. Jill did not want the wood burned (point of view) because she was afraid some of the plywood could have glue in it that, when burned, could release toxins into the air. The importance of this for Jill turned out to be her fear that toxic fumes from the glue could seriously harm their daughter's health. Because their daughter already showed signs of asthma, Jill worried that toxic fumes from the glue in the plywood could aggravate her condition.

Although John still did not believe the plywood held toxic glue, and was not worried that burning the wood could harm their daughter, he did finally understand why Jill remained so adamant about his not burning the plywood and could see that she was not acting totally irrationally. He recognized and acknowledged that the plywood could, potentially, contain glue that could release toxic fumes when burned. He also acknowledged that their daughter's health should receive priority. Only when he heard and understood why it was important to Jill that he not burn the plywood was he willing to look for alternative solutions.

Often you need to guess at what is important to the other person in a dispute because he is not aware of it himself. You will remember that this is called "additive empathy." Additive empathy takes you beyond what the other person has explicitly stated. Often, what is most important to a person remains unstated and therefore, the resolution remains illusive.

UNDERSTAND FEELINGS

Feelings result from your interpretation of events and can influence your decisions, opinions, and actions. Sometimes emotions can make you quite irrational. Like it or not, all humans have feelings that can drive the conflict resolution process because conflict typically stimulates intense emotions.

Strong negative emotions, often part of the conflict resolution process, can prevent listening or speaking effectively. Even people well trained in empathy can find themselves unwilling or unable to use these skills when they reach a certain level of anger, frustration, impatience, or fear because the primitive part of their brain has been activated.

Emotions that can normally derail the conflict resolution process can become a useful part of the process if conflicting parties can directly communicate their strong negative emotions respectfully and demonstrate understanding of each other's feelings until each acknowledges being accurately understood. Most people must experience this to believe it. To have your strong emotions explicitly understood, particularly by an adversary, could actually validate and heal, particularly when it combines with an accurate understanding of the meaning and importance of the topic for you. This powerful combination sets the stage for working together on the conflict rather than becoming adversarial.

Empathically responding to another's feelings tangibly helps that person manage the primitive parts of his brain and facilitates the cortex remaining dominant.

Although unusual, it really helps to demonstrate understanding of someone's negative feeling BEFORE speaking from your own frame of reference. Usually, people jump into their own feelings, their own opinions or position, or make inferences about the other's intentions and motivations before responding to the hurt or anger or frustration that the other person feels. I cannot emphasize enough the damage this usually causes in trying to resolve a conflict. One of the main things you can do with or without a mediator's help is FIRST respond empathetically to what the other person feels and says BEFORE you speak from your own frame of reference. In other words, by responding to the other person's feeling first, you quiet down their limbic system enough for their cortex to listen to what you have to say.

In our case example, John empathized with Jill's feelings in various ways. He started out by saying, "You really sounded angry with me for putting that plywood in the fireplace." And later, "I sensed you were afraid of something or felt really urgent about something but I didn't know what." He then finally responded, "I now understand that you were really worried that the glue in the plywood would get into Emily's lungs and make her asthma worse. You were even scared that she might go into anaphylactic shock!" Using feeling words like "angry," "afraid," and "worried" helped Jill to feel that John really understood her and she then could listen more openly to John's experience.

One last point, since people often do not identify how they are feeling or what is most important to them in an interchange, the listener frequently needs to guess the feelings and underlying causes of the feelings. When this is the case, it is usually best to put the empathic response in question form. For example, "Are you feeling afraid that Emily's asthma will get worse if we burn the wood?" rather than putting into a statement like, "You're afraid that Emily's asthma will get worse if we burn the wood." The statement can sometimes come across as too definitive and not tentative enough, particularly when the deeper feeling and meaning are not clear.

SUMMARY

- Identify the other person's positive intention in bringing up the issue.
- Demonstrate understanding of the other person's point of view.
- Empathize with what the other person thinks is important and why.
- Empathize with the other person's feelings about the issue.
- All the above skills demonstrates respect, prevents misunderstandings, reduces emotional temperature, and opens the way for better listening and communicating.

CHAPTER NINE
ACKNOWLEDGE

Demonstrating your understanding of the other person's positive intention for the dialogue, their point of view, what is important to them and how they feel provides a good start, but more can be done to create an optimal atmosphere for collaborative conflict resolution. You might also need to acknowledge some things about the other and yourself to establish an atmosphere that encourages collaboration rather than polarization.

Benefits

The Acknowledge phase of the B-E-A-R Process brings at least four benefits to the parties in a dispute:

1. Clarifies areas of agreement and disagreement.
2. Encourages each person to accept responsibility for his part in the creation or perpetuation of the conflict.
3. Establishes goodwill and a more constructive interpersonal ambiance.
4. Increases each person's receptivity to the other's differing point of view.

SKILLS NEEDED

Often overlooked in conflict resolution dialogues, the following four skills can help move the process forward:

- Acknowledge areas of agreement
- Take responsibility
- Express appreciation
- Accept disagreements

ACKNOWLEDGE AREAS OF AGREEMENT

Typically in a conflict resolution process both parties express their demands autocratically at one another in increasingly volatile or disrespectful ways with little understanding of each other's viewpoint or the underlying meaning or importance. Rather than searching for the other person's positive intentions, we assume negative intentions. Bringing empathy into the process slows down this process somewhat and lowers the emotional temperature. Also, when the participants assert themselves more respectfully, it helps check the dysfunctional emotionality and keeps each party in the cortex area of the brain.

Soon after one person accurately demonstrates understanding of the other's point of view, however, that person tends to move quickly to the part of the conflict over which they have the most vehement disagreement. When that happens, the parties develop a distorted view of each other. Hearing only their disagreements and none of their agreements promotes polarization rather than collaboration. When I experimented with having the parties share any areas of agreement after they empathized with each other, and before they expressed their disagreements, it greatly improved the atmosphere.

Encouraging parties to look for any areas of agreement they can acknowledge, even if it is only 5 percent of what the other person communicated, powerfully contributes to establishing a collaborative interpersonal atmosphere. The parties no longer believe they totally disagree with each other and gain hope for continuing the dialogue. Each experiences the other person as more reasonable and each begins to think less in all-or-nothing terms, feeling the other person both understands them and agrees with aspects of what they say. This softens the entire dialogue process significantly.

In our example of John and Jill's altercation about burning the plywood, they made a significant breakthrough when John acknowledged his agreement with Jill that their daughter Emily's health was more important than burning the plywood to fulfill John's ecological values. John needed prompting to verbalize this agreement, however. He didn't think of saying this to Jill in the heat of the discussion.

It proves useful to clarify ahead of time that agreeing with aspects of the other person's position does not preclude a change of mind later. In other words, no one locks into an agreement until they complete the entire negotiation and accept all the components of the final agreement.

Acknowledging areas of agreement, an integral part of the B-E-A-R Process, usually builds gradually throughout the dialogue. The first few rounds often do not include this stage if the parties are extremely upset or the dispute involves a particularly old or entrenched issue. This step also needs to remain optional, particularly in the early stages of the dialogue, since the parties may truly not see any areas of agreement. Only after each party demonstrates some understanding of the other's viewpoint, feelings, and underlying meaning or importance does this part of the process usually come into play. Once it does, however, it makes an important contribution to the resolution process.

TAKE RESPONSIBILITY

Perhaps the most rare of all the skills in the B-E-A-R Process, taking responsibility, means acknowledging to the other party your own negative contributions to the disagreement or dispute. Many people find it particularly difficult to take appropriate responsibility for their actions, attitudes, and speech that have contributed to the conflict. However, if each person can willingly explore first within himself, and then with the other, how he might have created or perpetuated the situation, a truly collaborative ambiance develops. If both parties can willingly look first at their own responsibility and then the responsibility of the other, without yielding to blame or judgment, they can begin to assess the interactive complexities that characterize most conflicts. They can begin to understand how or why things did not go well or why they have the disagreement.

For example, if George can admit that he often ignores Rose when he watches TV by pretending he doesn't hear her, he has done something significantly beyond empathizing with her hurt and angry feelings. He has taken appropriate responsibility for his part in the dynamic between them. Concurrently, if Rose can admit that she often chooses times to speak to George when he watches TV because she resents how much TV he watches and would like more time together, she has done more than just empathize with his frustration for distracting him from his TV shows. She has taken appropriate responsibility for her part.

Some people take too much responsibility and some too little. Another cornerstone of collaborative conflict resolution, taking appropriate personal responsibility, works best if all parties willingly do it. Even one person's willingness to take responsibility can help the resolution process because it may inspire the other to do the same. Lack of reciprocation can create an imbalance, however, and put the entire process in jeopardy if both parties did indeed contribute to the conflict.

People unwilling to take personal responsibility for their actions tend to externalize responsibility onto others through blame, judgment, accusations, criticism, and defensiveness. Any and all of these methods derail a constructive dialogue and get in the way of solving the problem. Blame and judgment also act as defense mechanisms for avoiding the truly useful strategies of sharing our feelings and what we see as really important regarding the issue. People who tend to externalize responsibility for their part of the problem tend not to engage in a process in which they might feel vulnerable, and they are more likely to hire a lawyer and attempt resolution through a more adversarial route that does not require them to deal directly with the other party and own their contribution to the conflict.

Those who take too much responsibility tend to over-accommodate and then grow resentful later. They also tend to need approval or acceptance, so they have trouble advocating for themselves in a disagreement. They might not even disclose a disagreement, so that the other party remains unaware of a problem. In serious conflicts, such as a child custody dispute in a divorce, these people may need an attorney to represent them because they do not honor themselves enough to represent themselves effectively.

In addition to empathizing with the feeling and meaning of the other party in the dispute, as described in the previous chapter, collaborative conflict resolution requires both parties' willingness to take appropriate responsibility. Those unwilling to take responsibility for their contribution to the conflict or those prone to take too much responsibility often face more difficulty settling disputes in a collaborative way. Parties who take too little or too much responsibility can benefit most from following the B-E-A-R process. This sequence of skills encourages the party who takes too little responsibility to take more and the party who takes too much responsibility to take less. This does not imply that taking responsibility can resolve all conflict or heal all wounded relationships. It does, however, pave the way for a more complete and fair resolution, which we will discuss in a later chapter that covers the importance of apologizing and making reparation.

EXPRESS APPRECIATION

When you explicitly express appreciation for anything the other person does to facilitate resolution, another important part of the Acknowledge phase comes into play. When you can express appreciation for anything about each other, a major barrier to collaboration falls away. The impression that the person with whom you have conflict does not like or accept you creates that barrier. It's that simple. When we have a conflict, we don't like each other, and we find it hard to separate a person's behavior or attitude from the person. When in conflict, most of us project on to the other party that they do not like us. The effect of expressing genuine appreciation in the middle of a dialogue can sometimes feel almost magical.

One small example of this would be if Jill could express appreciation to John for having not continued to put the plywood on the fire in the fireplace when she screamed at him. If Jill could express this to John, he might be more willing to look for alternative ways to use the plywood scraps ecologically.

Victor Borge once said, "Laughter is the shortest distance between two people." Expressing appreciation must be a close second.

ACCEPT DISAGREEMENTS

Not all conflicts reach resolution with all parties getting what they want. Some necessary compromises might give you only part of what you want. Sometimes you reach no agreement at all. However, if you disclose what is truly important to you, demonstrate understanding of what is important to the other, and demonstrate a good-faith effort to reach a collaborative and creative solution, but still fail, you still have a chance to accept your disagreements and move on with your relationship. Although some conflicts reach no resolution, all conflicts need not end the relationship.

An example of this occurred between Tim and Amanda. Amanda, ten years older than Tim and approaching age forty, wanted a child, but Tim did not. He had spent a number of years earlier in life using drugs and had recently embarked on his college education. They truly loved each other, but they were victims of "unmeeting" needs. After empathizing with the content of each other's position as well as the underlying importance–Amanda only having a few child bearing years left and Tim belatedly getting started with his education and career–they deeply understood why they faced a conflict. This couple parted in a loving and accepting way, wishing each other well in their understandable but incompatible life directions.

SUMMARY

- Acknowledge any areas of agreement before or during the discussion of the areas of disagreement.
- Take personal responsibility for your part in the conflict.
- Express genuine appreciation to the other person when warranted.
- Accept any disagreements not crucial to your relationship or to other aspects of the dispute.
- Acknowledging the above components is sometimes delayed until later in the dialogue process.
- The Acknowledging skills promote a more positive atmosphere for what is often a difficult interaction.

CHAPTER TEN
RESPOND

The next phase of the B-E-A-R Process, responding directly and specifically to the other person's I-message, direct request, or proposal, sometimes gets omitted in the conflict resolution process. Surprisingly, people often ignore direct requests or questions from each other as well as sincere proposals and attempts to offer resolutions. Sometimes they ignore each other consciously, but more often they get so involved and attached to their own position or perspective that they do not even hear the other person's proposal or request. Not responding directly and specifically to another's proposal or request usually alienates the other person who perceives it as disrespectful. To maintain rapport you need to at least let the other person know you have heard the request or proposal but choose not to respond right now. It also helps to give a reason why.

BENEFITS

At least four benefits accrue to responding directly and specifically:
1. Clarifies confusion and misunderstandings
2. Demonstrates respect to the other person
3. Encourages collaboration
4. Creates a sense of closure for both parties

SKILLS NEEDED

The Respond phase of the B-E-A-R Process involves four skills:
- Elicit specificity
- Respond directly

- Apologize
- Make amends

ELICIT SPECIFICITY

Although asking the other person to be more specific does not respond directly to the content of her request, I-message, or proposal, it proves invaluable as an interim response when you do not understand what she has said. Often, people unwittingly speak vaguely in a conflict situation because speaking specifically carries more risk. They feel vulnerable and protect themselves behind generalities or vagueness in their communication. When you use vague language, you contribute to misunderstandings that, in turn, exacerbate conflict.

Many people use vague language because they have vague thoughts; others fear specific language because they fear the consequences. Vagueness avoids personal responsibility. People's vagueness is mostly unconscious and unintentional, but they continue it out of habit when they feel afraid, unclear, or need to protect themselves. Because conflict inherently produces anxiety, many people unwittingly hide behind vagueness, abstractions, and omissions in language.

Hence, when in doubt, you should ask for further clarification and specificity and then paraphrase the other person's response to check for the accuracy of your understanding. Asking for specificity usually involves requesting clarity about one or more of the who, what, when, why, and how of the other's message. For example:

- "Who do you mean by 'they'?"
- "What exactly did you say you want?"
- "When would you like me to respond to your proposal?"
- "Why do you need the proposal by Monday?"
- "How would you like to divide our furniture?"

Soliciting specificity helps to reduce misunderstanding. Creating safety in the relationship during disagreements helps people to speak more specifically. Demonstrating understanding of what someone says and acknowledging any areas of agreement helps create this safer environment. In an ambiance of respect and understanding, many parties grow increasingly specific and clear in their language.

RESPOND DIRECTLY

Not responding specifically and directly to someone's request or pro-posal insidiously damages a relationship, often far more than a clear and definite "no" does. People vacillate in their responses to other's requests or proposals for many reasons: fear of hurting the other's feelings, fear of how the other might react, or wanting to avoid the in-teraction. For whatever reason, not responding directly usually harms the relationship and thereby restricts the conflict resolution process.

There are various ways of responding directly and specifically to someone's request, proposal, or I-message:

- Respond positively and clearly: "Yes, no problem."
- Respond conditionally: "Yes, if you _____."
- Respond negatively with rationale: "No, because _____."
- Postpone response: "I need time to ___ and I'll get back to you by ____."

Responding positively and clearly: "Yes, no problem." Let's take an example of Ruth making a direct request such as: "Would you be willing to come home a half hour earlier today and take care of the kids so that I can get to the PTA meeting on time?" If Bill has no prob-lem meeting the request, he should say yes directly and immediately BEFORE discussing any details regarding implementation. For ex-ample: "Sure, no problem. I'll need to catch the train about 4:15 then. I'm okay with that today since I was there until eight last night."

It is best to say yes before you get into the details of implementa-tion because until the other person has heard the affirmative part of the response, she remains in doubt about your response and that does not facilitate discussion of the implementation. Remember, most people feel vulnerable when they make a direct request. If Bill started talk-ing first about needing to meet the 4:15 train, it would have left Ruth wondering if he was saying yes or no. Even Bill saying, "I'm okay with that today since I was there until eight last night" still does not communicate a clear and specific yes.

Responding conditionally: "Yes, if you _____." A conditional response reveals that the recipient wants or needs something in return from the person making the request. For example, Bill could have said: "Yes, I can do that if you're willing to have dinner ready." If the person making the request finds the condition unacceptable, a negotiation may ensue. The next chapter discusses how to negotiate a conditional response. Please note that in Bill's response, he says yes first, and then expresses his condition. This usually works much better than expressing the condition first, as in, "If you're willing to have dinner ready, I can do that." And works significantly better than saying, "No, unless you have dinner ready."

Responding negatively with rationale: "No, because _____."
Giving the rationale for the rejection of a request, an optional but respectful step, may help the person ~~making~~ the request accept a no more easily. For example, Bill might say, "No, I won't be able to come home earlier tonight because I promised George that I would go over his numbers after five so he can turn them in tomorrow morning." This option often precipitates a negotiation if the person making the request does not like or agree with the rationale for the no. The next chapter discusses how to handle this negotiation.

Postponing response: "I need time to _____ and I'll get back to you by _____." This option, although not an explicit response to the content of the request, at least gives a specific response to the person making the request. If Bill needs to think about his response, or needs to get more information before responding, he should explicitly say that to Ruth and not leave her hanging indeterminately. Giving Ruth an estimate as to the time needed before responding and then meeting that commitment always proves helpful. Not giving a time frame for getting back to the person making the request, or not meeting the time commitment, can prove counter-productive and lead to distrust.

For example, Bill could say, " I'll need to talk to George because I promised him that I'd go over some numbers with him after five tonight. I'll see him when I get into work this morning and call you around 9:30. Would that work for you?" It may or may not work for Ruth, but at least Bill attempts to give her as direct a response as possible until he gets the information he needs to make a decision.

By the way, let's say that George doesn't get to the office by 9:30 so Bill doesn't get a chance to talk with him by the arranged time. In this case, it remains extremely important for Bill to call Ruth by 9:30 to keep her informed. This shows respect and maintains Ruth's trust.

APOLOGIZE

As the dialogue progresses and the parties begin to demonstrate that they can assert their points of view subjectively and respectfully and also demonstrate understanding of one another in increasingly meaningful ways, the parties open more to taking responsibility for how they might have contributed to the conflict. Acknowledging your part of the problem and apologizing can help the resolution process immensely. Taking responsibility and explicitly apologizing definitely contributes to an atmosphere of respect and resolution.

Taking responsibility for something differs from apologizing for it. Thus, in the B-E-A-R Process, we list taking responsibility under the Acknowledge phase and apologizing under the Respond phase. Typically, after we have empathically responded to the other person, we then acknowledge our responsibility for something we have done, and then apologize for it. For example, when the husband of a divorcing couple lost money in an investment with community property assets, he could say to his soon to be ex-wife, "I realize how angry and resentful you have been toward me for investing in that REIT without listening to your fears and hesitations. I acknowledge that I discounted your feelings and opinions and went ahead with it without telling you about it. I should not have done that, and I'm sorry."

Apologizing in the Respond phase of the B-E-A-R Process is always optional and does not apply to all conflict dialogues. If it does apply, however, this is an effective time and way to express your apology.

MAKE AMENDS

In some situations, understanding the other person, acknowledging responsibility, and apologizing does not bring resolution. Though making amends does not always apply to a conflict, it often proves useful when the other person experienced some financial or other tangible loss that can be returned, financially compensated for, or mitigated. Rather than continuing to negotiate, you can acknowledge responsibility, apologize, and then offer some kind of restitution or recompense to the other person, thereby possibly eliminating any further need to continue the dialogue regarding all or some part of the dispute. Even if the reparation offered relates only to one aspect of a larger dispute, this kind of gesture paves the way for a more collaborative effort on the remaining aspects of the dispute.

For example, the husband in our example offered to compensate his wife for the total amount lost in the investment as part of the divorce settlement even though not required by law to do so. This gesture proved invaluable because once the husband acknowledged his responsibility, apologized, and expressed willingness compensate his wife for their investment loss in the final settlement, his wife began to cooperate more willingly on the remaining issues involving spousal support and child custody.

Under different circumstances, making amends can take different forms. Let's say the couple in our example did not seek a divorce but wanted to stay married and work on improving the relationship. In this case, one alternative would be for the husband to acknowledge his responsibility and apologize for making a unilateral investment decision on their community property assets (as before) but also make a commitment to not repeat this behavior in the future. If the wife had no experience or knowledge in the investment area, the husband could propose that he do the initial exploration about alternative investment vehicles and then go over the various options with her. He then could outline risk-reward considerations for each investment alternative and include her input in the final decision so that both would feel a part of the decision, however the investment worked out.

We might describe this latter scenario as a "commitment to a change in future behavior," which would then need to lead to the actual behavior change. Only after this new behavior has taken place over time can we expect the wife to feel the conflict has been resolved and trust reestablished. If the husband does not involve his wife in future investment decisions with community property assets, no amount of taking responsibility or apologizing can resolve the conflict. If he cannot change his behavior, he will not resolve the conflict.

SUMMARY

- Responding directly and specifically to the other person's I-message, direct request, or proposal demonstrates respects to the other person.
- Lack of a direct response often proves worse than a negative response because it leaves the other person in a frustrating limbo.
- Eliciting specificity means refusing to fall victim to vagueness, which can leave you powerless in the dialogue.
- Apologizing when appropriate begins a process of reconciliation but often cannot replace acts of reparation or vows to change behavior.
- Following up on vows to change behavior is essential for reestablishing trust and rapport.

CHAPTER ELEVEN

RESOLVE

Once the parties achieve mutual understanding of their areas of agreement and disagreement, the next phase of the B-E-A-R Process, the Resolve part of the model, involves seeking mutual agreement on the issues still in dispute. You observed in Figure 1 how the Assert part of the process initiates the dialogue with one person contracting for the dialogue, clarifying his positive intention for the dialogue, speaking with a respectful tone of voice and facial expression, and giving an I-message, making a direct request, or offering a proposal. The person receiving this message then begins his response by using the B-E-A-R Process (represented by the circle in Figure 1).

The Breathe, Empathize, Acknowledge, and Respond sequence is not cast in stone. The recipient of the asserter's I-message, direct request, or proposal can pick and choose whatever is appropriate to the situation. However, the B-E-A-R sequence often makes both logical and emotional sense for most interchanges. Following the sequence carefully has proven to work most effectively most of the time.

Once the recipient goes through the B-E-A-R Process, which culminates in a direct response to the asserter, that response either serves as his assertion or he adds his own I-message, direct request, or proposal. The asserter then becomes the recipient and goes through the B-E-A-R sequence in turn (see Figure 2). This back and forth continues until both parties to the dispute understands their own and the other person's positions, proposals, feelings, and what is most important to each of them about the issue at hand. With this mutual understanding, they become much more likely to work together collaboratively on searching for a mutual agreement.

Once this mutual understanding has been achieved, the parties can then leave the sequence of the B-E-A-R Process and proceed to the Resolve step in order to reach a mutual agreement. The mutual agreement phase differs from the mutual understanding phase in that both parties now understand what they still disagree about and what underlying needs and interests are important for each of them to have satisfied. With this mutual understanding, they can then commit to working together to find solutions that will meet as many of those underlying interests as possible for both of them.

The dialogue in the Resolve part takes on a different flavor in that the parties work together to explore and discover mutually acceptable solutions. If disagreements arise during the resolution process, however, the parties may need to return to the earlier stages of the B-E-A-R Process to make sure they once again have mutual understanding.

BENEFITS

The Resolve part of the B-E-A-R Process offers the following benefits:

1. Facilitates creative problem solving
2. Improves the quality of the resolution by providing a broader array of potential solutions than either party could provide alone
3. Provides clarity and specificity once an agreement is reached
4. Improves cooperative implementation of the agreement

SKILLS NEEDED

The Resolve part of the model requires four steps performed sequentially:

1. Brainstorm options
2. Evaluate options
3. Delineate agreement
4. Implement agreement

Once the parties have come to a clear understanding of each other's differing viewpoints or positions as well as the underlying meaning and importance of those positions for each, they should then agree ahead of time to go through the four steps in order.

BRAINSTORM OPTIONS

Brainstorming is when everyone involved in the dispute tries to come up with creative ideas of how to meet everyone's important needs and interests in the resolution of the dispute. Once the parties agree to leave the mutual understanding sequence of the B-E-A-R Process and engage in the resolution phase, they need to agree that they will not criticize or evaluate each other's ideas during the brainstorming process. Criticism or evaluation during the brainstorming phase can inhibit the creativity of the parties.

Once the parties begin to brainstorm potential options for solving the unresolved issues remaining between them, they should use their knowledge of the underlying meaning and importance for each of them as important criteria for brainstorming potential solutions. Each party should think not only of his own underlying interests, but also of what the other considers important. Each party uses his creativity to suggest solutions that meet as many of both parties' underlying desires and interests as possible.

For example, when John and Jill started brainstorming about what they could do with the plywood other than burn it in their fireplace, Jill thought of using the plywood for another building project. When John laughed and started to deride her idea as totally unrealistic because the plywood was in very small pieces, I interrupted him and reminded him of the brainstorming ground rule of not criticizing others' ideas and instead using it to come up with another idea of his own. He stopped and thought awhile and then said, "I know, I could bring it down to the recycling center where they ship wood off to a place that grinds it into even smaller pieces and they press it into larger sheets that can be used for construction." This ultimately became part of their resolution and it pleased John that he had come up with his own solution that met his ecological values.

EVALUATE OPTIONS

Next, the parties review each option, keeping in mind what was important to each of them, to see which option (or combination of options) might best meet both of their needs. Although this process can prove difficult in complex conflicts, if the parties keep focused on each other's most important underlying interests and needs, they have the best chance of finding the best "mutual gain" solution. This might require compromise solutions (i.e., each party might not get everything he or she wants). I have experienced some amazing results, however, with both parties feeling that they got everything they wanted from a truly creative solution.

In the case of John and Jill, Jill got what was important to her by protecting their daughter from aggravation of her asthma. John got what was important to him by finding an ecological solution to getting rid of the plywood.

This phase usually involves reviewing the list of potential solutions created in the brainstorming phase in order to see which one might work the best for both parties. Often the parties find a way to combine their various ideas in a solution neither of them had thought of on their own.

Often the parties shift their chairs around so they sit side-by-side, looking at the brainstormed ideas on the flip chart in my office. This symbolic shift from facing each other directly in order to reach mutual understanding, to sitting side-by-side to reach mutual agreement marks a turning point in the collaboration process. The parties now work together collaboratively to meet their own and the other's needs.

DELINEATE AGREEMENT

Once parties achieve an agreement, they should either write it out so that each person can review it and reflect upon it, or summarize it verbally in terms as clear and specific as possible. You might not need to put less formal negotiations in writing. The more specifically you mutually delineate the agreement, however, the less likely it will unravel over time.

A good test for specificity is whether each party knows who should do what by when and how it should be done. If the parties need a legal document, each party's consulting attorney may need to review it.

IMPLEMENT AGREEMENT

Implementing the agreement characterizes the mutual action phase of the B-E-A-R Process. An agreement proves only as good as its implementation. The more the parties have come to a mutual understanding of what was important to each of them in the conflict, and the more collaborative the mutual agreement phase has been, the more likely each party will implement the agreement in a cooperative and responsible manner.

Complex agreements can require more specific delineation of the action steps necessary to implement the agreement. Clarifying in a final written document who does what by when can prevent conflicts during the mutual action phase. Parties should explore any possible blocks to implementation as well as ways they can facilitate each other's implementation once the agreement is reached. Parties may also wish to set a time in the future to evaluate the effectiveness of the agreement and whether the agreement needs revision to meet changing circumstances.

SUMMARY

- The Resolve (mutual agreement) part of the B-E-A-R Process should come only after the parties have come to a mutual understanding of the underlying issues and what is most important to each party in resolving the dispute.
- The parties can begin the brainstorming process when an atmosphere of mutual understanding, trust, and respect prevails.
- Using their awareness of what is most important to each of them as their criteria for brainstorming ideas of how to resolve the issues, they can then move to evaluating those ideas based on the same criteria.
- The parties can prevent misunderstandings when implementing the agreement by delineating the agreement verbally or in writing and summarizing "who does what by when."

PART FOUR
THE B-E-A-R PROCESS IN ACTION

Chapter Twelve includes an edited transcript of an actual counseling session with a married couple demonstrating how the B-E-A-R Process can be used to teach couples who want to stay together how to communicate more effectively. Chapter Thirteen illustrates how the B-E-A-R Process works in a series of three mediation sessions with a couple that has decided to end their marriage. The names and identifying information have been changed to protect the privacy of each couple.

Therapists can use the B-E-A-R Process whenever a potentially adversarial or conflictual issue arises between couples as well as to help couples communicate more effectively when making difficult joint decisions.

Mediators can use the B-E-A-R Process to assist two or more people to reach a settlement agreement that maximizes cooperative implementation. It is particularly useful when couples reach an impasse due to emotionally volatile issues or misunderstandings.

Anyone interested in learning how to resolve conflicts more effectively can benefit from reading one or both of these transcripts because they illustrate how real people are struggling to resolve their issues using the B-E-A-R Process. The model can be used in a variety of contexts in addition to the marriage counseling and divorce mediation settings.

CHAPTER TWELVE

THE B-E-A-R PROCESS IN A COUPLES COUNSELING SESSION

After nine years of marriage, Cliff and Leah have been feeling more distant from one another recently. Leah, in particular, has felt distant from Cliff. They have been coming for counseling for about four months and have agreed to learn the B-E-A-R Process for resolving their conflicts and to discuss difficult issues. Comments about how the counselor attempts to facilitate the B-E-A-R Process along with how the couple's communication does, or does not, illustrate the B-E-A-R Process have been italicized.

Cliff walks into the office and immediately begins a cough that is about 4.2 on the Richter scale. I notice that his nose is very red as he says hello with a Johnny Cash-sounding voice. Leah looks healthy but weary.

THERAPIST: How is each of you tonight?

CLIFF: I feel miserable, but I wanted to come anyway.

LEAH: I'm okay, just a little tired.

THERAPIST: Since you've got a cold *(looks at Cliff)* and you're kind of tired *(looks at Leah),* we might want to go slowly tonight. If there's an issue that you both would like to discuss, I can continue to coach you through the B-E-A-R process like we've done before. My hope is that if we go through this process enough times in our sessions, you will be able to use it at home more effectively. Is that okay with each of you?

The therapist attempts to contract with Cliff and Leah to use the B-E-A-R Process during the session. You may wish to refer to Figure

1 throughout this transcript so you can gain a better perspective on how the whole process fits together, the main goal of presenting this transcript. The therapist also structures how he would like to proceed in the session by describing his role as a communication skills coach using the B-E-A-R Process as the guide.

LEAH: Yeah.

CLIFF: Sure.

THERAPIST: So, how have things been going between the two of you?

LEAH: Not as wonderfully as I would like. There's not been anything in particular, but I've felt a general less than wonderfulness *(she laughs and looks at Cliff)*. I feel like you've been kind of short with me lately, and again I don't know if it's a general irritation you're feeling toward me or if it's just general stress. But nothing really... *(Pause)*

THERAPIST: Major?

LEAH: No.

THERAPIST: But you want things to be better, you want things to be more ... what?

This comment attempts to empathize with Leah and to encourage her to express herself more specifically to Cliff. While I list the skill "use specificity" under the Respond phase of the model, it helps when the person asserting is specific as well because it prevents confusion on the part of the listener.

LEAH: Positive, good!

THERAPIST: Where are you Cliff?

CLIFF: I can remember maybe a couple of times. I don't remember how we resolved them, or what I said even, but I do think there have been some moments this week where both of us were kind of short with each other...and then we let it drop. But it may have been just me.

THERAPIST: You've noticed some impatience between the two of you but you're not sure if it was just you or not?

The therapist continues to model empathy by demonstrating understanding of the content of what Cliff says.

CLIFF: Yeah, definitely. It may have been only me in that I was, you know, stressed with something else.

LEAH: Yeah, I've also been aware that you're sick. I tend to sort of let a lot slide, give you the benefit of the doubt, try not to take it as personal, and assume that there's other stuff going on. But it's been wearing on me a little bit, because I don't know if that's what's going on, because the way it comes across is that you're irritated with me, and not anything in particular, just a general tone. But I don't know, maybe you are?

THERAPIST: Would you like to check that out with Cliff? You could ask if he's aware of anything about you specifically that he's been irritated with.

The therapist coaches Leah to make a direct request, one of the skills in the Assert part of the model.

LEAH: Is there anything that has been going on lately that you've been finding irritating or are you not even aware that that's going on?

CLIFF: *(long pause)* I don't think so. I think that my sense of the times when that's happened is that they're very moment-specific, and maybe I'm just not seeing underneath it but I don't...

THERAPIST: When what's happened?

Cliff has had a tendency to use vague language with Leah in previous sessions, so the therapist encourages him to be more specific about what he means by "the times when that's happened."

CLIFF: If I've been short with you, my memory of those times, and I'm having trouble getting really specific actually. My responses concretely had to do with whatever was happening at the time, and not a general feeling about you...or a deeper feeling about you. Which doesn't mean that it isn't amenable to working on. Obviously, there are things that could change with those interactions. And I hope, genuinely, that we can have a way of talking about it at that time too. As you said, check out whether there's something bigger underneath it, and obviously that's the time when we have a better chance of getting our finger on the pulse of it.

LEAH: I can't even think of anything in particular, it's just this general feeling I've had and I don't know that it's worth every single time that you're short with me that we have to talk about it. Because a lot of time I could just write it off as Cliff is preoccupied, or Cliff is busy with something, or he's not feeling well. I don't feel like I have to pick at you every time with "That's a really irritating response" or "You were really short with me just then." I don't feel like that's going to contribute to anything. I don't think I should expect you to be perfect, or that you should expect that of me every single moment. And so that's why I don't know if how much of it has to do with the fact that you're sick and trying to pull all this stuff together and, even though you're having really positive experiences at work that there's a certain level of stress of being in a new environment and dealing with that. So to a large extent I've just ignored it pretty much. But it has bothered me.

THERAPIST: *(To Leah)* It's really okay to make an explicit request for clarification. Like "Are those times when you're short with me indicative of something deeper about me, or not?" It's a "me/not me" differentiation you want, I think. That's a valid inquiry.

This is the therapist's attempt to validate Leah's desire to know more specifically how Cliff feels about her and to go ahead and ask him whenever she wants clarification. This illustrates the "make direct requests" skill under the Assert part of the model. It also illustrates the therapist's attempt to coach Cliff to be direct and specific to Leah's request, the skills needed in the Respond phase of the model. Intimacy withers without specificity as vagueness usually increases the other person's frustration and the potential for misunderstanding.

THERAPIST: *(To Cliff)* I sensed you really did go inside yourself to think about whether there really was something about Leah that was bugging you and you essentially got the answer no, there wasn't anything about her that your "short comments" were the tips of the iceberg for. Is that accurate?

Here the therapist empathizes with Cliff to make sure he understands Cliff accurately and models for Leah that empathy here might work well after she has gotten a direct response from her direct request.

CLIFF: Yeah, you got it.

THERAPIST: *(To Leah)* And is that what you wanted to know?

LEAH: Right. But I don't think that it's productive to do it every single time.

THERAPIST: I agree. It's useful, however, when there's been a pattern going on for some time.

LEAH: We do that with each other once in a while. One us will say, "Hey, what's going on?" And we'll be able to say, "I'm sorry, it's not you," and the other person will say, "Well, don't take it out on me."

CLIFF: Or the kids!

LEAH: Or the kids, whatever…to be able to just absorb the stress.

Something just lit up in Cliff about this topic of not knowing if the other person or something else causes someone's negative mood. This changes the focus of the session for a while on how they relate to each regarding their two children.

CLIFF: Yeah, it's true and actually that helps me a lot in thinking about how to deal with you when you're stressed out with the kids and you're taking it out on me. What I've been striving for in that situation is how to draw the line without getting you angry. I understand that the kids frustrate you, but I don't like it when you take it out on me; that hurts. Please just tell me what you want me to do in a non-confrontational way. I also think it would be good for me to be willing to let a little bit of that roll off my back. Maybe gently nudging you and reminding you that it's not productive to take that out on me now.

Cliff makes an effort to speak respectfully and subjectively here by giving an I-message to Leah so as not to alienate her. The I-message is integral to the Assert part of the model and departs from previous sessions when Cliff was full of You-messages like "Get off my back!" or, "You're always harping on me!"

LEAH: Well, I do do that. *(To therapist)* We've got this five-year-old who's going through another really defiant stage and it's hard to walk out of being really frustrated with her and into being calm with Cliff. And so what I do is I come in and say, "Cliff I can't stand it anymore! Go deal with her!" And he's like, "Why are you yelling at me?" *(To Cliff)* I don't mean to be yelling at you. I mean to be just expressing my frustration, but it feels like I'm yelling at you and blaming you. And yeah, I don't want to do that, but I think to a certain extent I'd like it if you could just absorb it, see it for what it is, and deflect it or whatever.

Here Leah is in the Acknowledge phase of the B-E-A-R Process. She "owns" that she does yell at Cliff about the kids in a way that makes him feel blamed. Cliff's new ability to speak more subjectively by giving an I-message rather than a You-message is actually working. In previous sessions, they would have been fighting tooth and nail as to who was at fault, rather than looking at what each is doing to contribute to the other's reactions. Leah then moves to a direct request for Cliff to understand sometimes that she is just frustrated with the kids and not angry with him.

CLIFF: You mean just interpret it differently. Like if you're yelling downstairs, "Cliff, get over here, now!" Instead of my normal interpretation of it, which is *(Cliff tries to model Leah's demanding tone of voice)* "Cliff, how come you didn't come here five minutes ago? I needed you and you didn't come."

Cliff is learning. He starts out with empathy: "You mean just interpret it differently." This lets Leah know he is hearing her request to not take her yelling from frustration with the kids so personally. He then takes ownership for how he does often misinterpret her as judging him for not helping her in a more timely way.

LEAH: Right.

CLIFF: That is how I hear it. And often enough in the past, I've reacted to that message and to that message alone and I just stoked your fire at the moment when you were already going strong, by throwing it back at you immediately.

Cliff both acknowledges his role in this pattern and empathizes with Leah both in his words and tone of voice. Again, this contrasts to his defensiveness in the past. For the first time in our work together, he seems to be truly trying to understand how Leah might feel in the situation and reflects that understanding back to her explicitly.

LEAH: I wouldn't mind if you hear me sounding like that *(the demanding tone of voice Cliff just modeled)* if instead of saying "Don't take it out on me!" you could say "Okay, take a deep breath," to let me know that I'm stressed out. Or "Okay, take a deep breath, I'll go deal with it."

Leah is in the Assert part of the model, making a direct request for how Cliff can better respond to her when the kids are stressing her out. In previous sessions, when either of them got so upset that they could not hear the other or when they started yelling derogatory things at each other, I would have them take a time-out to close their eyes and do some deep breathing to calm them down until their heart rate was more normal, and then phase them back into the B-E-A-R process again. Leah has found this technique very useful in the sessions because she becomes "flooded" very quickly. Hopefully this method of cooling down will generalize to times when she gets flooded at home.

CLIFF: Sure.

LEAH: That's not an accusing message, that's kind of a helpful message.

CLIFF: Right.

LEAH: Let me know that I'm taking it out on you, that you're not misinterpreting it, but that I should calm down.

As Cliff uses his empathy and acknowledging skills more effectively, Leah's tone of voice softens and she opens to making a direct request for how she would like Cliff to be with her when she reaches the end of her rope with the kids. This is a significant change for Leah because she historically has gone into a judgmental and demanding place with Cliff very quickly, which then triggers his defensiveness, which triggers even more frustration and demands from Leah. By using the skills in the B-E-A-R Process, they are learning how to break a pattern in their relationship that has built for years and has grown quite frustrating for both of them. This also illustrates how quickly Leah and Cliff can get triggered into the primitive parts of their brain and how that escalates things between them. Breaking these difficult patterns takes time and effort, but experiencing the difference in the sessions motivates couples to use the skills outside the sessions.

THERAPIST: You're each trying to break an old pattern here, both within yourselves and between you. Identifying a pattern is difficult because a pattern by its very nature is unconscious. But with each other's help, you can identify it now. If you can't identify it on your own, you have each other to remind you. For you, Leah, your pattern is getting very frustrated and then unconsciously moving into your demanding and judgmental place. If you can catch yourself, you can try transforming your demanding tone into a respectful request, like asking for help rather than ordering Cliff to help. For you, Cliff, your pattern is to get defensive; you read criticism into what she says or get immediately defensive when she does criticize or judge you. Working on paying attention to what is going on under her demands by being more empathic can help you with this, like realizing that she's really frustrated with your daughter and not you.

If couples can't identify when they get caught in a pattern, or if they don't have enough rapport with each other to help each other become more aware of when the other person gets caught in a pattern, the B-E-A-R Process may prove too difficult to learn at that point. Before continuing to work as a couple, they may need some individual therapy to clear the negative experiences and traumas that underlie their conditioned responses.

CLIFF: Yeah, what you just said was what I was beginning to see for myself. I want to be able to be the kind of person who, when she's angry or hurting, can see that more in the moment and be aware enough to be able to respond with more understanding to her being upset, or ask her if I can help. I suddenly held up that model *(Cliff points to the B-E-A-R Process chart on an easel in the office)* to what I've always done, and found myself wanting, and I suddenly realized it's the B-E-A-R Process I want to use. I want to be like the person who responds to that stressful situation in a way that empathizes with you *(Cliff looks sincerely at Leah and his tone of voice is new and heartfelt)* and not always read your tension as something that's directed at me. More important, even if something is directed at me, I want to be able to respond in a way that tries to understand that the tension you're giving out is an effort to communicate how frustrated you really are in that moment with whomever, so I can maybe help you in some way rather than defend myself. And I can see how being able to respond that way would be greatly helped by practicing and thinking about the various parts of the model.

This was one of those rare moments when a client has a "Eureka!" experience. Cliff really understood the importance of getting inside of Leah's frame of reference, particularly when she is upset. Cliff finally understood why we practice the B-E-A-R Process in the session: so he could use it when he really needed it at home. The B-E-A-R Process, when followed, helps each of them move out of the primitive parts of their brains during emotional upset and into their cortexes where they can have a broader perspective and think more clearly.

Cliff is not just learning the model from his head, but his heart now follows. If he has any chance to get out of his old conditioned defensive responses that he learned as a child trying to protect himself from an overly intrusive mother, it's now. He has married someone who triggers that history, but he now has the opportunity to break a cycle that could break the marriage.

THERAPIST: It can be just one sentence and you're doing both the Empathy part and the Respond part.

The therapist points first to the Empathy phase of the Model and then to the Respond phase on the chart. It often helps to have a visual display of the B-E-A-R Model available to clients so they see where they are in the process.

CLIFF: Yeah, and I can also see that if at the same time Leah can see her part in it...

THERAPIST: That's right. *(Therapist turns to Leah)* What I suggest here is coming from more of a request mode like "I'd like some help" or "Can you help?" rather than "Cliff, get your ass in here!" Then you're allowing him to play the knight in shining armor coming to assist you.

The therapist points to the "Make direct requests" component of the Assert part of the model to help Leah see her work in this particular interchange. Giving examples of both the demand mode and request mode enables the client to experience the comparison directly.

LEAH: Right, right.

THERAPIST: And he can feel good about himself helping you rather than feeling judged and demanded upon.

LEAH: So instead of coming out and saying, "I can't deal with Emily, you go do it," I could come out and say, "I'm really frustrated and I can't deal with Emily, can you come and help me?"

THERAPIST: You got it.

LEAH: I can see how just changing that could help. Like I just say to her, "You go brush your teeth!" you know, which is what I normally do. Then I give up and say *(to Cliff)*, "You go deal with it!"

THERAPIST: Both of which are demands.

LEAH: Yes, they are demands!

THERAPIST: It's not very inviting.

LEAH: No, it's not, I can see that. *(Pause)* At the time when it's happening, it seems perfectly reasonable to me, but I can see now it's a demand and it comes across as blaming–"Why aren't you already here!"

Leah also now sees her part in the interaction pattern. She takes responsibility for her part. This is in the ACKNOWLEDGE phase of the model.

LEAH: Although I think that you *(Cliff)* often just step in and say, "Okay, I'll go in and do it."

This is crucial! Leah acknowledges to Cliff that he does sometimes just come and help without getting defensive, and her tone of voice carries a genuine appreciation in it. When acknowledging one's non-facilitative part in an interaction combines with acknowledging what the other does in a facilitative way, along with some appreciation, the emotional ambiance of the dialogue changes significantly for the better. You have two people much more willing to work together on resolving their issues.

CLIFF: A lot depends on the context of how we feel about each other.

LEAH: That's right! *(Laughing)*

THERAPIST: Yes, the two of you could begin identifying things you can do for each other and with each other that will build a better ratio of positive to negative experiences with each other. The little positive, helpful things you could do for each other to build that more positive context you were talking about, Cliff. *(Therapist turns to Leah)* This also gets to what I interpreted you to be saying earlier tonight to Cliff. Even though things have been going pretty well, your vision for this relationship is that it could be even better. There's more potential here for intimacy and making each other feel good and supported.

LEAH: I'm feeling that very strongly.

THERAPIST: Searching for ways to be attentive to one another and doing nice little caring things doesn't have to be nights on the town wining and dining. It can be small things. Could you each begin to think about trying that with each other?

LEAH: Yeah.

THERAPIST: I'm talking about over the next few months, building this into your relationship.

LEAH: I would like to do that. I would like to make a commitment to that. Really making that a priority. Because I know that it would make me a lot happier, and I believe it would make you *(to Cliff)* a lot happier too.

CLIFF: I very much want to commit to that. I'm trying to leave behind any feelings I have about what I have or haven't done. I'm trying to feel about it as a step out into a new day kind of approach to that kind of commitment. Because I think my own pattern is to get obsessed about what I don't do and continue to not do it.

LEAH: I have to say that I'm a little concerned about you in this regard in terms of your tendency when there's something like this, an expectation that you set for yourself, that it becomes a performance that creates a kind of pressure on you.

CLIFF: I know. I'll figure out some way to avoid it.

LEAH: Well, no, it's not that. I think that you set yourself up. Like it has to be the most brilliant thing ever or you shouldn't do it because it's going to fall flat.

CLIFF: Right, the most perfect expression of that is not being able to write my dad for months and months when all I need to do is send a note.

LEAH: Yeah, it's like you have to write the opus of the century instead of just a card saying "Hi Dad, great to get your letters, like to talk to you some time," or whatever. *(Leah turns to the therapist)* Cliff feels like he has to type a ten-page letter that captures everything he hasn't said in all these years. And so nothing gets produced. *(To Cliff)* I just want to make sure you don't set yourself up and feel like, "Oh, God, it's been three days and I haven't done anything," you know what I mean?

CLIFF: Right...right. *(Pause)*

THERAPIST: I think she's asking you to demonstrate that you understand what she's trying to say to you.

The therapist senses that Leah wants Cliff to understand what she is saying here so he coaches Cliff to demonstrate his understanding by paraphrasing in his own words what Leah has been saying, which illustrates the Empathy phase of the model.

CLIFF: I hear you say that you're concerned both that I may fall into that kind of pattern with this new commitment and...

THERAPIST: What pattern?

The therapist again asks Cliff to be more specific in his language.

CLIFF: That I might fall into the pattern of becoming depressed and self-criticizing about what I haven't done and that somehow causes me to continue to fail to do it. I think I also heard you say that you don't necessarily want to be instrumental in sending me off on that path by saying I really want us to make this commitment and making it into a heavy thing. You're just trying to say, look, I'd much rather just invite you into this without any judgments. I want to go in this direction with you and it would be good for both of us, and you'd much rather have it be that kind of a positive role for you and me.

LEAH: Right. And I want to clarify that further. One of the concerns that I have is that if you are busy doing other things and then suddenly after two weeks you think, "Oh my God, it's been two weeks, I haven't done anything, now I have to do two weeks worth all at once." That's what I'm specifically afraid of. I'd rather that after two weeks and you realize it, then you could just...

CLIFF: Get you a flower.

LEAH: Or write a note that I'll see on the mirror. You know what I mean? It doesn't have to be that you're building up an account that you then have to meet at a certain rate. That's what I'm concerned is going to happen!

CLIFF: Like it will be a burden...

LEAH: Yeah, like a burden. If it's a burden, it defeats the purpose!

CLIFF: Right.

LEAH: It should be a joy.

THERAPIST: Keep at it, Cliff. Make sure she knows you've heard her and then we'll get to any part of it that you can acknowledge or agree with.

The therapist observes Leah becoming adamant here and that this is really important to her, so he coaches Cliff to continue to empathize so Leah feels heard. He also lets Cliff know that when he has demonstrated his understanding enough to Leah, he can then look for any areas of agreement he has with her before sharing his perspective, which illustrates the basic Empathy, Acknowledge, and Respond phases of the B-E-A-R Process.

CLIFF: You further clarified that a part of what you've seen me do in the past is that, as the time gets on, I tend to look at that whole span of time as increasing what I should be doing, and you want to make it clear that those are not your expectations, and that you are not wanting to put that kind of a "should" on me about any kind of gap in my doing it or not, that even something small is fantastic no matter when it comes.

LEAH: Yeah, that's exactly right and I want to be able to do the same for you.

Leah's voice grows soft and gentle here, unlike the earlier part of the session. Cliff's empathy seems to have a very soothing impact on her.

THERAPIST: You also were saying, I think, that you didn't want Cliff to feel as though he had to do major things. You want to relieve him of the obligation to do big or impressive things for you. Is that part of it?

LEAH: Right. Absolutely.

THERAPIST: It could be just really little things that let you know that he cares about you and is thinking of you.

LEAH: Right.

The therapist here models for Cliff even more specific empathy for Leah. The more deeply and accurately Leah feels understood, the more likely she will open up to Cliff's perspective later on. The therapist has the choice of demonstrating it for Cliff or coaching him into putting Leah's communication into his own words, or both. The therapist senses that Cliff has reached his limit and decides just to model it and let Cliff come from his perspective next, first by acknowledging or agreeing with any part of what Leah has said, and then to come from his perspective in the Respond phase of the model.

THERAPIST: How about you, Cliff, anything that you are willing to go along with or agree with?

CLIFF: Yeah. I agree with it and I also really appreciate that she's that sensitive to my difficulties.

THERAPIST: Your pattern of feeling obligated to do bigger and bigger things as time goes on?

The therapist both empathizes with Cliff and encourages him to use more specific language.

CLIFF: Yeah. In this Acknowledge phase, I'm taking responsibility for the patterns that she and I are describing, but I don't really feel blamed about it. So it's not like I have to apologize or accept the burden of something. I don't feel that you're blaming me for it. I feel you're inviting me to come out of it.

LEAH: I don't want to add to your anxiety.

A nice long comfortable pause settles in here with them looking fondly at each other.

THERAPIST: Very nicely done, Cliff. Do you have any response from your frame of reference?

Now that Cliff has done a good job of both empathizing with Leah and acknowledging his part in the dynamic between them as well as expressing his appreciation for how she is communicating with him, the therapist prompts him to move on to the Respond phase of the B-E-A-R Process.

CLIFF: *(Long pause)* Yeah, I genuinely want to be giving you those expressions and I want you to feel appreciated by me. *(Pause)* I also want that from you again. Because I know there have been times when I got that much more from you and I want that again. It meant a lot to me.

Cliff's tone of voice makes it clear that this is a heartfelt request, unlike earlier sessions when he came almost totally from his head.

LEAH: Can you tell me specifically what kinds of things you would appreciate from me?

Leah demonstrates that she is learning the B-E-AR Process here by asking Cliff to be more specific. In earlier sessions, it was often hard to understand Cliff because he spoke so generally and abstractly. The therapist intervened a number of times with Cliff to speak more specifically in his communications and coached Leah to ask for that specificity when she needed it.

CLIFF: I just always liked the little things you used to buy me. I didn't necessarily know how to handle it then. I'm telling you now that they were very important for me at really crucial times, and I want that feeling again...from you.

LEAH: I have to say I have a little anxiety about it because I have found in the past that...I mean a large part of why I stopped those gestures was that I didn't ever feel like they were appreciated or acknowledged to the extent that I would have liked, and so it felt like they were pointless gestures to a large extent.

Leah's reaction here is quite justified. Cliff didn't acknowledge her attempts to show caring through her gifts, and she feels somewhat hesitant to do it again. The therapist is monitoring the B-E-A-R Process, however, and Leah has jumped to her point of view before empathizing with Cliff. She has skipped both the Empathize and Acknowledge phases of the model. The therapist needs to intervene here or things can get off track pretty quickly. Cliff has made a very heartfelt request and owns that he could not respond very well to Leah's gestures in the past, and if she does not empathize and acknowledge quickly, he will quickly regress and start defending himself.

THERAPIST: I'd like you to hold off with your response to Cliff for just a moment and ask if you'd be willing to let him know what you're hearing from him now about back then.

LEAH: Yeah, I think what you're saying is that although you appreciated the gestures that I made in the past to demonstrate my affection, you didn't at the time necessarily know how to respond to them. But you realize now that they were important and valuable for you, and you would like it if I resumed making those kinds of gestures because you do realize that they're valuable.

CLIFF: Yes!

LEAH: And you believe that you would be able to respond in a way now that would let me know that. So you're demonstrating an awareness of the anxiety I've had about that.

CLIFF: Right.

LEAH: You look tentative; like there's something I'm not saying.

CLIFF: No, it's just that there's something in addition to it. Everything you said is right, but there's kind of like this larger feeling that I *really* want it now.

LEAH: But you didn't want it before?

CLIFF: No, I'm saying–

LEAH: You *do* want it now.

CLIFF: I'm telling you I <u>really</u> want it.

LEAH: Yeah.

CLIFF: I mean all the stuff that you said is true. I did say that and those are all parts of my statement, but the basic communication I'm trying to make is that I feel really warm about what you were capable of doing in those times. I feel like, in some way, wherever that came from in you, you were doing a lot to bring us through some, what in retrospect were pretty hard times. You know what I mean? It's like you showed some kind of strength to do something that turns out was actually very important! And that's also my way of saying I want that again. I want that feeling from you again. Regardless of whether I'm giving you that feeling, I'm saying I want it from you. *(Both laugh)*

THERAPIST: Are you also saying that you're willing to respond more appreciatively now?

CLIFF: Yes, in the past I feel I didn't necessarily have a good way of responding to you or didn't know how. I want to be able to respond to that better in the future.

LEAH: So you're saying that now you want to let me know affirmatively that you would like that positive pattern to resume, and that you're ready for it. You feel like you will be able to respond to it in a way that'll let me know that you value it. And you're letting me know now that it is valuable to you.

CLIFF: Right.

THERAPIST: There's one other piece that might be important here. *(To Cliff)* That you're also acknowledging to Leah now, after the fact, that when she did give you those little gifts, that there is now a very deep, heartfelt, and profound sense that that was really very significant in helping you get through some things that you were not as conscious of back then, or at least you didn't know how to respond to, but you're trying to say now how deeply meaningful and significant those little gifts actually were for you.

The therapist tries to model for Leah how to empathize on a deeper level of feeling by her tone of voice, which is impossible to convey in writing. The therapist also models more specificity.

CLIFF: Yeah... *(Pause)* Yeah, I mean it's hard for me to imagine what it would have been like if she never did it.

THERAPIST: *(Again, to Cliff)* So even though Leah didn't know how deeply you did appreciate it, because you weren't very good at expressing and acknowledging your appreciation at that time, that's why she got the feeling that it wasn't all that important to you. But what you're saying now is it was just your inability to know how to respond. Upon reflection, it really was extremely important to you. Is that accurate?

CLIFF: Yeah.

THERAPIST: *(To Leah)* Want to try it? I think it's important that Cliff hears it from you.

LEAH: Yeah. *(Leah pauses and speaks with a much deeper, more heartfelt voice from within herself.)* You're saying that you realize now that the gestures I made were really important, even though at the time you weren't able to express that or acknowledge it. Or maybe weren't even aware within yourself of their significance back then. But you realize it now and you want to have that feeling back. Is there something more?

CLIFF: No, that's right.

THERAPIST: The only thing I would add is you *really* want it back. It's a really deep desire and longing.

CLIFF: Yeah!

LEAH: The longing that *I've* been feeling all along.

THERAPIST: *(To Leah)* Yes! That's right!

LEAH: *(To Cliff)* Do you feel it? Do you really feel like you know that feeling?

CLIFF: Yeah.

LEAH: In a way that you understand or identify with my feeling about it?

CLIFF: Yeah, I think so...

LEAH: The longing?

Leah really wants to know if Cliff experiences the same kind of longing for her love and attention that she has longed for from Cliff. This remains extremely important for Leah because this is what she has missed for a long time from Cliff. She realizes that if Cliff experiences the absence of her love and attention, partly because she no longer gives him little gifts and tokens of her affection, then he might understand why she might not feel loved and cared for when Cliff does not give her small gifts and tokens of his love and affection, or respond to her little gifts.

CLIFF: I have a longing, the significance of which is that I want those behaviors from you that tell me how you're feeling about me. I long for that.

LEAH: I feel like having my voice reflected at me.

CLIFF: I'm suddenly realizing that I am identifying with you.

Cliff laughs with the sudden realization that the longing he feels in the moment is the same longing that Leah has expressed to him for a long time, that he now experiences the loss of appreciation and attention from her that she has experienced from him for some time.

LEAH: That's great! I love to hear that! I've never had that feeling that you've identified with that or even understood my feelings about it.

CLIFF: I never did either. In fact, as I said it tonight and am saying it now, it didn't occur to me that I'm identifying or modeling how you have been feeling. I just thought about what it made me feel like and what it feels like now to look back on the feelings of when I did get it.

Cliff continues to have difficulty being clear and specific about what he is saying. The "it" here refers to Cliff's feelings of love, affection, and appreciation from Leah when she would give him small gifts now and then. He is gradually getting out of his head where he has been most of his life and beginning to become aware of his feelings as well as Leah's feelings.

CLIFF: And I just realize, wow, does it mean that if we start doing this process that I'm going to get that again? *(Cliff is now raising his voice in excitement.)* Yeah! I want that again! You know what I mean? That all went through my head. I didn't really think about identifying with your longing. But I can see it's a parallel.

THERAPIST: Good. Would you be willing to demonstrate again to Leah now that you understood what she just said?

Cliff continues to return to his frame of reference here, which is fine, because it's important he continue to feel his longing for Leah to resume her gestures of little gifts that communicate attentiveness and affection toward him. It is also crucial, however, that he let Leah know, specifically, that his longing for feeling her love resembles her longing to feel his love.

CLIFF: You said that you feel like your longing is being reflected in...

THERAPIST: Longing for what?

The therapist coaches Cliff to be more specific again. Leah can begin to trust the shift Cliff makes here only if he puts his empathic response into language so concrete, and in a tone of voice so heart-felt, that she feels beyond a shadow of a doubt that he accurately and deeply understands her.

CLIFF: That your longing for that connection, you want that expression of connection from me.

LEAH: Yeah. I'm hearing a reflection of what I've been saying and it makes me hopeful, but it also makes me kind of wary. It makes me really hopeful because I finally feel like at last Cliff gets it. *(Leah turns to the therapist.)* At last Cliff understands what it is I'm looking for because until you said that tonight right now *(Leah turns back to*

Cliff), you haven't really understood what it is I want. And what the feeling that I'm looking for is. Which comes about from the demonstrations that I'm asking for. And I feel like maybe now it's clicking with you because you're feeling it yourself. And so maybe you're getting clearer that that's what I'm looking for too! I'm hoping that that's registering with you. Like you're not only saying, "Oh, this is what I want," but also "Oh! That's what Leah wants too!" *(Now Leah's voice is raised in excitement.)* "That's what she's been talking about all this time!"

CLIFF: Yeah, I see.

LEAH: What I'm hoping for is that you now know what it is that I'm looking for, and I'm a little concerned that's not happening, that you're not seeing it from my point of view. That you're still seeing just the first part, the "Oh, I *(Cliff)* remember what it was like when Leah gave me little gifts," but you're not doing the second part of "Oh, that's what Leah wants too!"

CLIFF: Okay, so there's a few levels there of what you're trying to communicate. You're saying that you see the reflection and you hope that in bringing up the fact that you see the reflection, that I'm going to notice that I may have discovered an insight or a feeling which I can then apply to understanding your longing.

THERAPIST: For?

CLIFF: For that clear expression from me.

THERAPIST: For those behavioral things that would be comparable to her giving you little gifts, but something from you that demonstrates your caring and appreciation for her.

CLIFF: Right. And you're concerned that I may not make that leap to the next level of understanding that the feeling I had is a window for me to understand your feelings.

THERAPIST: Good job, Cliff. So what's happened here is that you more deeply understood one another in terms of how important the demonstration of the care, thoughtfulness, and love you have for each other is on an ongoing basis. It doesn't have to be every minute or every hour or even every day, but whenever there's an opportunity to do that demonstrating, which can take a lot of courage because it can be a vulnerable thing to do since the other person may not notice or care every time. What you're hearing is you both now want those demonstrations of caring. Over time, though, a pattern inhibiting those acts of caring has built up. There's a history here that you need to overcome. Reparation needs to take place. My recommendation, as a way to end our session tonight, is that you each begin to express your caring for the other in those small gestures. Without any feelings of obligation, which is what you *(Leah)* were trying to say to Cliff: "Don't make this into an obligation or duty!" You *(Leah)* only want it when it's genuine.

LEAH: Yes.

THERAPIST: And for you *(Cliff)* to only do it when it's genuine. But now you have the consciousness of how deeply significant it is for Leah because you became aware tonight of how deeply significant it was and is for you.

CLIFF: Yeah.

THERAPIST: That's a very new and precious place now. But you both might be a bit rusty, so have a lot of latitude on it. No Pulitzer Prize expectations here. Whenever you sense the other person is attempting to demonstrate caring, let the other person know you're appreciative. That's the way to begin to build the caring and love back up again.

CLIFF: Get in there and make a lot of mistakes.

THERAPIST: Yes, it's the intention here that's important and not the perfect execution. Good work! Both of you! And *(to Cliff, referring to his cold and cough)* under significant diminished capacity!

LEAH: *(to Cliff)* Yes. Thanks.

Cliff smiles broadly and then erupts into another horrendous coughing spell as the session ends.

This session illustrates how the B-E-A-R Process reduces defensiveness and facilitates partners to hear and understand each other on the deeper level of what is important and how they are feeling. The Acknowledge phase of the model, optional in the early stages of the dialogue, becomes increasingly important because parties in conflict need to experience the other person acknowledging his part of the problem and accept responsibility for it as well as do something more constructive.

Specific language helps to minimize misunderstandings, and takes eternal vigilance on the part of each person. Asking for specificity from the other is as important as speaking with specificity to the other.

Finally, note that the therapist both models these skills in his interactions as well as coaches each party in the skills as they interact with each other. Couples like Cliff and Leah need to practice the B-E-A-R Process with each other outside the session when they have the time and energy to do so. Generalizing these skills from the therapy office to the home setting does not happen automatically. Setting time aside weekly to consciously practice this process helps couples use these skills more spontaneously when they need them.

CHAPTER THIRTEEN
THE B-E-A-R PROCESS IN MEDIATION

Mediation, a method of resolving disputes by having two or more parties engage in a dialogue without fighting or litigating, usually consumes less time and money than hiring attorneys to represent each party. A collaborative process rather than an adversarial one, mediation requires people to represent themselves in the dialogue and to negotiate directly with each other rather than through someone else.

Mediation may not suit all circumstances. For example, when one of the parties does not have enough internal strength for self-representation, or when one of the parties to the dispute easily intimidates the other, mediation alone may not serve effectively. However, if each party can understand the other person's perspective and still hold his own perspective, mediation often provides a viable alternative to litigation.

The B-E-A-R Process facilitates the balancing out of power between the parties if the imbalance is not too great. If one party tends to dominate, the B-E-A-R Process requires that person to not interrupt the other person, to listen carefully, to empathetically respond, and to acknowledge any contribution to the problems between them *before* responding to the other. A person who tends to dominate in a conflict resolution process often omits each of these things.

On the other hand, the B-E-A-R Process requires the less dominant party to assert his point of view or position in a clear and specific way, which often he has not had the personal power to do. This process provides the time, the space, and the safety to do that without interruption and to get an empathic response from the dominating party, often unprecedented in the relationship.

The B-E-A-R Process gives the mediator the structure and the sanction to guide the parties through a mutually respectful process.

I have personally experienced couples that had already decided to get a divorce change their minds and hearts after experiencing this process. The process gave them a way to talk about and negotiate with each other around conflictual issues that they never knew existed. Once they learned how to do it, they decided to stay together. Although not common, it does happen. More frequently, couples that have to continue working together because of co-parenting responsibilities have found a way to do that with reduced animosity. They learned how to communicate in a more respectful way with each other so they could make better collaborative decisions about their children after the divorce.

Other couples have found that once they engage in the structure of the B-E-A-R Process, they can resolve what they previously considered immovable impasses. Once they learned how to get at the personalized meaning and importance of the issue for themselves and for each other, a resolution emerged that had not occurred to either of them before. For example, this often occurs when someone finally admits he did something wrong or unfair and apologizes for it. Sometimes that party needs to make reparation in a financial or other way in the negotiation; other times, the other party needs only to hear that apology before agreeing to a settlement. Explicitly taking responsibility for any wrongdoing, lie, omission, or unfair act can provide a powerful healing experience for both parties.

Just being understood by the other party can help healing. I recall one experience in which the wife broke down into tears of gratitude after I coached her husband to respond empathically to her. He did what I believed was an extremely poor job of it. He was off on the feelings, vague, and somewhat inaccurate on the content and meaning of what his wife had said, but he accepted my coaching in making his responses more accurate. In spite of how poorly he did, his wife broke down into tears because, for the first time in their relationship of thirty-two years, he tried to understand what she said before he either criticized her or just ignored what she said and went on with his point of view.

He seemed totally unaware of how he had been relating to her all those years, and amazed at how deeply his attempts to understand his wife impacted her. This couple came to realize that they each had parents who related to each other in the same way they had been relating to each other. They each had lived out what they had experienced in their families of origin. They literally did not know they could relate otherwise until they entered into the B-E-A-R Process.

Even the B-E-A-R Process does not always work out successfully, however. The process promises clarity of communication and of the issues; it does not promise resolution. At times, one or the other of the disputing parties can not abide by the ground rules of the B-E-A-R Process, and some people simply can not or will not demonstrate understanding to the person with whom they disagree. They either cannot differentiate understanding from agreement, or they flood so badly that they cannot engage in the process. Other times, the disagreements have festered so long that one or both parties have grown extremely inflexible. This process also breaks down if one or both parties withhold information (e.g., hiding assets), lie, or try to cheat the other person. The process most commonly breaks down when one party, used to intimidating and dominating the other party, refuses to continue with the process because he feels a loss of control over the other person and the situation. This most severely tests the personal strength and skill of the mediator. If the mediator fails to hold to the structure of the process, negotiation can disintegrate quickly.

Finally, when couples are attempting to decide whether to divorce, the B-E-A-R Process often helps each party determine whether the other party is willing to learn a way of communicating that could help them resolve their disputes on their own. When both parties learn to use this method to resolve their disputes, the couple often stays together. If one party (e.g., the wife) is unable or refuses to learn the B-E-A-R Process, the relationship usually ends because the other party (the husband) sees that the failure to learn the process signals that he needs to leave for his own health and welfare.

Also, when one person in a relationship has suffered intimidation for years by the other, she often does not have the internal strength or perspective to leave. Once it becomes clear that the dominating person will not learn a process that would treat the other more respectfully, she often has the cognitive and experiential clarity to leave.

In one example of this, the wife of a recently separated couple, no longer willing to accept her husband's treatment, went to live with a friend for a few weeks. Having endured his control and domination for more than two decades, she finally could take it no more, but she also felt guilty for leaving. By playing on that guilt, he had almost persuaded her to move back in. On the recommendation of her friend, however, she made her husband come in for a mediation session as a requirement before she moved back in. He very much wanted her to move back, so he reluctantly agreed.

As I structured the ground rules for the B-E-A-R Process and got to the part where each person would need to demonstrate that they accurately understood what the other had said before they responded from their own perspective, he interrupted me. He said that he was unwilling to do that with someone who was always "wrong." I then tried to clarify that demonstrating understanding was not necessarily agreeing with the other person. He could still disagree with her or think her "wrong." He said he refused to do that. I'm not sure he understood the difference, although I gave him a couple of examples to make sure.

I then reiterated that to help them with their issues I would need each of them to abide by that ground rule because I had observed that if someone would not willingly demonstrate understanding of the other person in a relationship, even while not agreeing, it left no basis for a healthy or mutually respectful relationship. Without looking at either of them, I said that if someone is not willing to listen and hear me out, I have no standing in the relationship. If I have no say or sovereignty in the relationship, I ultimately become a "non-person". It would prove unhealthy for me to stay in that relationship because I would eventually deteriorate emotionally and psychologically.

The wife appeared quite surprised and said she had felt like that for twenty years. I told her that she could choose to move back in under the same conditions that had pertained for twenty years. I, however, would not work with them, even if she were willing to proceed, without her husband abiding by that ground rule in our sessions.

In short, I tried to role model how to honor one's self. She sat for a long time, and her face kept changing, as if she were growing up before our eyes. She finally stood up and said in a rather surprised but pleased and strong voice: "I don't feel guilty anymore." She then calmly walked out.

INTRODUCTION TO THE THREE MEDIATION SESSIONS

A group of eight attorney mediators met with me once a month for approximately six years to learn how to facilitate a more collaborative communication process in the context of mediating divorce settlements and commercial disputes. I learned during those years that working toward mutual understanding between conflicting parties helped significantly in getting to a mutual agreement and that an agreement arrived at in that way held up better over time. Unless each party understands why the other person remains upset or adamant about the issue at hand, as well as the personal importance or significance the issue has for the other, they will not work well together toward resolving the dispute. True collaborative resolution of a conflict usually requires deep, personal, and mutual understanding *before* parties attempt to come to an agreement or settlement. Until each party understands the deeper significance of the conflict for the other, true mutual understanding remains unlikely. Without this deeper mutual understanding, a true collaborative process eludes them and chances for an optimal resolution of the conflict decline.

Alternatively, deep mutual understanding does not guarantee mutual agreement. It might only lead to increased clarity that they can never reach a mutual agreement. This might lead to a compromise, which does not fully satisfy either party but does the best they can do under the circumstances. Other alternatives obtain as well. The parties might enter into a collaborative law process in which their attorneys attempt to resolve their differences collaboratively. Some attorneys now experiment with adding coaches for each of the disputing parties. The more traditional paradigm of coming to a settlement involves the parties hiring attorneys to negotiate a settlement in a more adversarial manner. If this does not work, the case goes to court and a judge makes the final decision.

I have found that deep mutual understanding of what each party holds important provides the key to making the collaborative process work. An agreement implemented from a deep level of mutual understanding more likely holds up over time and functions more effectively. This proves very desirable when circumstances force the parties to have continuing contact or requires them to coordinate their behavior as, for example, in a divorce where the former husband and wife have joint custody of their children and need to continue co-parenting.

The following annotated transcripts of three audio taped mediation sessions an attorney mediator conducted with a couple going through a divorce demonstrate how the B-E-A-R Process can help people in conflict work through difficult issues in a mediation session. It particularly illustrates how it can break through an impasse in a conflict with intense and entrenched emotions.

I have refrained from extensive editing to make the sessions more readable and less time-consuming in favor of keeping the true length so the reader can get a realistic picture of an actual mediation session. I have changed the names and identifying information to protect the privacy of the couple.

Brad and Sue, married for twenty-one years, have no children, and decided to try mediation to reach a divorce settlement. After attending four mediation sessions, they stalled in the process of achieving a settlement agreement because of Sue's unresolved feelings of betrayal. In the preceding session to the first session included here, the mediator had suggested trying the B-E-A-R- Process to break through the impasse. The couple agreed to try it in the next session and to have the session taped.

Although the mediator contracted to use the B-E-A-R Process in the preceding session, she had not gone into detail about what the process would require of each of them. The session begins with the mediator describing the B-E-A-R Process, structuring how they will go about using it, and getting a more explicit agreement from each party to voluntarily follow the mediator's guidance through it. This preliminary structuring and contracting proves essential for success. Without advance commitment, the structure of the process might not hold. People strongly resist changing communication styles, and the new skills in the B-E-A-R Process often prove difficult to learn, particularly when emotions and stakes run high and the primitive parts of the brain take over during the kind of stress that conflict often precipitates. If the mediator gets an agreement from both parties up front, she can then use that agreement to enforce the structure of the B-E-A-R Process without making the parties feel picked on against their will. It frees the mediator to stop the process and coach each party to use the skills and steps with less resistance.

We learned that without the mediator taking an active role in structuring the process, getting a contract from each party to use the process, and assertively requiring the parties to abide by the sequence of steps in the process, the parties' old and defeating communication patterns would quickly reestablish themselves.

Comments about the mediator's interventions, along with comments on how the couple's communication does or does not illustrate the B-E-A-R Process, appear in italics.

THE FIRST MEDIATION SESSION TRANSCRIPT

MEDIATOR: So this process is called the B-E-A-R Process and it takes a little while to explain each step to you, but I think if you understand what the steps are and the rationale for each step, you'll understand how it might help us break through the impasse we all felt at the end of our last session.

The mediator has a chart of the B-E-A-R Process on an easel in her office and refers to it from time to time. We have found that having this visual aid helps people orient themselves to the steps in the process during the early stages of using it. The reader may wish to refer to Figure 1 throughout this transcript to help in learning it.

MEDIATOR: One of you begins by Asserting. The underpinning in this whole process is speaking to each other respectfully. What we're trying to do is avoid you triggering each other's intense negative emotions during your discussions so you can each remain as calm and rational as possible, so you can listen to each other accurately.

So one of you starts by asserting your point of view, or an issue, or a request, and to do so in as respectful a way as possible. By doing that, you are more likely to be heard in a less defensive way. When you're asserting, we ask you to talk about you and your experience rather than talking about the other person, characterizing them, or making interpretations, etc. It's really like making I-statements if you've heard that terminology before. Speaking from your own experience rather than speculating about what the other person's experience has been or should be, and to talk about what is important to you, why it's important to you, and how you feel.

While one of you is asserting, the other person is on what we call the Breathe stage (the mediator points to the Breathe step in the model on the chart). The Breathe stage means taking responsibility for your own emotional responses and realizing you do have control over how you are going to respond. One of the things that help you control your emotional temperature is breathing deeply. Often when we hear something that's difficult to hear, we either stop breathing or we start breathing very shallowly. Another reason why this step is here is that there has been some research by John Gottman, who wrote a book called *Why Marriages Succeed or Fail.* He has measured the heart rate of couples when they are in conflict. What he has found is that people in conflict, when they get to the stage of "flooding," they no longer can process well, think well, speak well, hear well. They are in a place where they are really not functioning well and it's useless to continue to have a conversation at that point. In fact, he says it usually takes about twenty minutes to recover, providing there's no more stimulation, to a normal state. So that is part of what this process is about. It's to help both of you not get to that flooding stage. All it takes is about a 10 percent increase in heart rate and you're beginning to flood.

So while you are at the Breathe stage, you are listening to and observing the other person who is asserting and you're monitoring your own emotions, you're reminding yourself to breathe, and if you're getting upset, let me know so we can either call time-out or work with it so you don't get to that "flooded" stage.

Once the person has finished asserting, and I'll ask you to keep it fairly short at first because this is a new process that you're trying out, we ask the person in the Breathe stage to move into the Empathy stage of the model. In this stage, you express in your own words what you heard the other person saying. Because you have to do that, you have to listen really carefully. It helps for you to really listen for understanding and then put it into your own words to demonstrate that you've heard the other person accurately. One of the rationales for this is that much conflict is based on misunderstanding, and if you take the time to listen carefully and restate what you heard the other person say and check out "Is that accurate?" that clarifies things and sometimes the conflict goes away. Even if it doesn't go away, at least it has narrowed it down so you know what the real issue is and then you can focus on that. So what we ask is that you summarize the content of what the other person has said and also what it means to them, so they really feel understood.

Empathy doesn't mean agreeing with the other person. You can demonstrate that you understand somebody and still disagree with him or her. What I'm going to do in these first few rounds is model empathy for you. I will demonstrate understanding by empathizing first and then ask the person who is at the Breathe (listening) stage to do it. So the asserter will hear it twice, first from me and then from the other person.

Now the next stage after you've empathized is Acknowledge. The tendency is that when it's your turn to respond, we tend to immediately go to what we disagree with. So before you jump to responding,

I'm going to ask you if there's anything the other person has said that you can agree with, that you can express appreciation for, that you can accept even if you disagree, or anything that you can take responsibility for.

This, I think, is the most powerful part of the process. Any acknowledgment you make, however, must be genuine. If you can make a genuine acknowledgment, this is the grease that begins to smooth the friction of conflict. Feeling respected and understood changes the dynamic between people, as does having the other person not disagree with everything you have just said. So even if it's only five percent of what somebody has said, if you can acknowledge that you agree with something in a truthful way, the other person will be more open to continue negotiating. They won't be left with the distortion that you disagree with everything they have just said. This is what often happens if you jump right to the part you disagree with, and it usually makes coming to a resolution much harder.

Respect is not just about what words you use, but also your tone of voice, your body language, your attentiveness–that's all a part of the gestalt of respect. Then once you've done all of that–listening, empathizing, and acknowledging–you have earned the right to respond. And again we ask you to do that respectfully and specifically to what was raised. Then it's also a time to apologize or make reparation, but that's usually down the line a bit in the process.

The Respond stage is responding to what has been specifically raised by the other person and the Assert part is bringing in new material from your own perspective. So this is basically the mutual understanding process.

As you see on the chart, there is a final stage called Resolve. So you will take turns asserting your issues and points of view and going around the circle in response until you have mutual understanding of the unresolved issues between you. Once you have mutual understanding, you will go the Resolve stage to get mutual agreement. The steps there are brainstorming options, evaluating them, and then delineating an agreement.

SUE: Which is where most people want to go right away. They hear what the problem is and then they want to problem solve.

MEDIATOR: Right, and this might seem like a slow process. Spending time on getting mutual understanding might seem like a waste of time to some people, but I find it's much more efficient if you do it this way.

BRAD: It makes perfect sense.

MEDIATOR: So are you each willing to give this process a try?

The mediator first looks at Sue and then Brad. Without this crucial contracting part of the mediation, the parties could become quite offended when the mediator interrupts the dialogue to coach them. This focus on the B-E-A-R Process keeps the parties in the cortex part of their brain so they don't as easily emotionally "flood," triggering the primitive parts of their brains.

SUE: Yes.

BRAD: Certainly.

MEDIATOR: Now, Sue, Brad raised an issue last session that he wanted to talk about, about how the two of you have been negotiating. Is that topic okay for you to talk about?

SUE: Sure.

MEDIATOR: And you *(Sue)* can later bring in your own new material. You said something had made you angry and that's also something you may want to bring in at some point, okay? *(Pause)* Why don't we start then with Brad? And Sue, I'm going to take notes and you may or may not want to take notes, depending on how good a memory you have. You might just write down memory tips so you can summarize accurately what Brad says. We're not going for perfection here, especially as we begin.

So, Brad, to the extent that you can face and speak directly to Sue, please do. It's a dialogue between the two of you. Sue, if you could show respect by listening carefully and having eye contact with Brad that would be good. But if that's too hard, it's okay not to.

So, Brad, why don't you start? I might stop you if it goes on too long, but I want you to get enough out so we can get started.

The Mediator makes sure each party knows what to do during this first interchange. After describing the whole B-E-A-R Process, the mediator goes back over the first step again. If the parties can stay focused on the process in the beginning and remain open to coaching, the entire mediation will go smoother.

BRAD: As we've gone through this mediation process together, I think the thing I feel most upset about is that when we entered into a relationship I understood that we had a verbal agreement about how our property was split. I remember talking about having a prenuptial agreement even before we moved in together. It was a topic you had reminded me of several times when we got married, and we've always handled our relationship from a point of view of dividing our resources based on what we contributed. That's certainly the way we've run our household budget during the entire time we've been living together.

I don't feel upset that we're dividing our property in half, but I do feel upset that the whole negotiation process has taken us to a place where you're going to end up with more than half of our property and that you will have spousal support. My fear is that the safety of the resources that I've built up over the years, that I've mostly but not entirely been responsible for building up, is going to evaporate and I won't have the safety of having some financial resources to fall back on. *(Pause)*

MEDIATOR: Sue, what I'm going to do is empathize first in my words and then you do it in your words. Okay, Brad, what's upset you the most as the two of you have been negotiating in this mediation process is that the way the negotiation has been going seems contrary to you in terms of what the former understanding has always been between you and Sue, particularly around property. It sounds like from your perspective, that was based on a percentage allocation of what each of you contributed, that you contributed in proportion to what your respective earnings were. It sounds like the two of you discussed having a prenuptial agreement, but I'm deducing that you decided not to do that and you just worked from a verbal agreement. Is that accurate?

BRAD: Yes.

MEDIATOR: And you thought you'd be dividing resources based on the respective contributions you each made. And at this point in time, you're not so much upset about actually dividing the property in half, even though you contributed more than 50 percent to the accumulation of that property. The part that sticks in your craw is that Sue, in addition to that, is asking for spousal support, and that means she is going to get more than half, and that creates some insecurity for you in looking at the nest egg you've built up disappearing.

BRAD: Yes, that's correct. It's actually fear.

MEDIATOR: Okay, so you're really feeling financial fear looking toward the future.

BRAD: Right.

MEDIATOR: And where you thought you had some resources to fall back on, it looks like you're not going to have that.

BRAD: That's what I'm afraid of.

MEDIATOR: You're afraid you're going to go through those resources, or you're not going to have a cushion that you were hoping to have.

BRAD: That's right.

MEDIATOR: So did I basically get it accurate?

BRAD: Yes, that was a good reflection.

MEDIATOR: Anything that I missed or got wrong?

BRAD: No, those are the key things. That's my upset and that's my fear.

Notice how carefully and specifically the mediator goes through each of the points Brad brought up and responds to the feelings as well. She even stops to check with Brad whether she got the most important points before she goes on. Notice how Brad gets to a clearer understanding of his feelings (fear) upon hearing the mediator's empathic response to his upset. All of this very importantly demonstrates empathy, not only for Sue who watches in anticipation of having to do it next, but also Brad, who gets to experience what it feels like to be listened to and accurately understood.

MEDIATOR: So those are the two important things to get. *(Pause)* Now, Sue, I just want to acknowledge that it might be very hard to reflect this back.

SUE: Okay.

MEDIATOR: Are you ready?

SUE: Yes...So, Brad, what I hear you saying is that you felt we had a verbal agreement regarding property and that we had spoken about a prenuptial agreement but we never created one, and that you've provided more financial support over the years. You're not upset that we're doing what the state law requires is a fifty-fifty split, but you're upset because you believe that I'm going to receive more than half of the property in spousal support. You're watching your safety, that is, your resources, evaporate leaving no support for you financially and you're scared. Did I miss anything or did I rephrase anything incorrectly?

Note that the part about what the state law requires was not part of Brad's communication. Note also how this could be felt as a subtle way for Sue to be already defending her position under the guise of empathically responding.

BRAD: I'm not exactly scared as I watch resources evaporate. It's more that I'm afraid that the way we negotiate, that when it's all said and done, I'm not going to have very much to fall back on.

SUE: What I just heard you say is that you're afraid you're not going to have much to fall back on.

BRAD: That's right.

MEDIATOR: Very good! Sue, before you respond, is there anything here that you can acknowledge, anything you can agree to, appreciate, accept, or take responsibility for?

The mediator points to the Acknowledge phase of the model on the chart. Sometimes this stage serves as an optional part of the process early on because the parties don't trust each other or the process yet. Nevertheless, since we have found it really does facilitate things in a very positive way, it is best to get parties to do it as early as they can.

SUE: I agree that we talked about a prenuptial agreement a long time ago and we were kidding back and forth because I was naive that we would be together for a long time. *(Some negative emotion is creeping into Sue's tone of voice at this point.)*

MEDIATOR: So that's what you can acknowledge. You acknowledge the prenuptial and...

SUE: I can also acknowledge that you've put in financially a lot more than I have. And I acknowledge that I've put in support other than financial–

MEDIATOR: Okay, that would be part of the response.

This very critical feedback to Sue at this stage in the mediation says to Sue she can't get into her responses by calling it an acknowledgment. To have let this go unnoticed might begin alienating Brad and convey to Sue that she can circumvent the process. You will observe as we move forward the importance of keeping each party to the structure of the process; otherwise, things will unravel very quickly.

SUE: That's going into the response, okay, so I agree that you put in more financially than me.

MEDIATOR: Okay. So now Sue gets to respond and this is the part for you *(Brad)* to listen, observe, and breathe, and if you want to keep notes, please do. I will also model the empathy.

Here, the mediator has again structured Brad's role as he prepares to listen and empathically respond.

SUE: So I acknowledge that you have put in more financial support. I feel that I have put in more household support, giving time to take care of the house and other things. I've probably done the majority of the yard work and cleaning the house. You have helped when I've asked, but you went out and made the money and we did the traditional split where the man makes the money and the woman supports the household. One of the reasons I wanted you to seek legal counsel is because I had, and I knew what was coming, and I was hoping you did too when you made your final decision. I'm sorry that you're finding this out so late and that you now feel that you're not going to have anything to fall back on...I have a lot less too; I thought I would be with you. *(Sue starts to cry and her voice gets almost inaudible.)* And you rejected me, and you led me on.

MEDIATOR: Okay, I'm going to ask you to speak from your experience, how you feel.

Sue slips into You-messages here, accusing Brad of rejecting her and leading her on. This very common kind of communication proves extremely provocative and dysfunctional for the conflict resolution process and this example beautifully illustrates why the B-E-A-R Process works well in the mediation of conflict. Allowing these kinds of You-messages severely sabotages the mediation process. The mediator appropriately intervenes here by asking Sue to stay with her own experience rather than accusing Brad of what she believes he has done to her. At this point, the mediator might choose to explain the three components of an I-message (Sue's feelings, a non inflammatory

behavioral description of Brad's behavior, and the tangible conse-
quences for Sue) and then coach her to use this structure to give the
I-message in lieu of the You-message. For example, as an I-message
in this context, Sue might say something like, "I have a lot less too
because I really wanted our relationship to continue and I felt devas-
tated when you told me you wanted a divorce."

If the mediator had stopped Sue here to get a contract with
her regarding her willingness to learn how to give an I-message
rather than a You-message, many of the problems later in the me-
diation might have been avoided or at least reduced. Sometimes
someone in Sue's position is not willing to learn a new and dif-
ferent way of communicating and then the mediator has to de-
cide whether to proceed or not. From my perspective, one of the
reasons Brad and Sue are getting a divorce is because Sue gives
You-messages (makes accusations and interpretations) and has not
known how to give I-messages.

What follows is an example of what can happen when one party
to a dispute vents her hurt and anger through various forms of You-
messages and how that plays out without her being taught and guided
to give I-messages.

SUE: My experience is that you started an affair with someone
else, and when we talked about changing the ground rules, you didn't
tell me you had started an affair already. When I made the agreement
that I made, and you also agreed, you said that we would still be the
primary couple. I feel you broke every ground rule we had in place
and that's why I feel so betrayed.

This You-message in I-message clothing often occurs. The phrase
"You started an affair" is actually an accusatory interpretation of what
happened, is quite inflammatory even though she prefaces it with "My
experience is that." It constitutes an interpretation, not a behavioral
description. Sue's interpretation, accurate or not, does not reflect an
I-message and can derail the process. The mediator could coach her
into an I-message here, reminding Sue that when she initiates from
her own perspective, she needs to avoid making any interpretations
or accusations, even if she thinks them accurate. Sue needs help in
translating her feelings into I-messages. For example, she might say,
"When I found that you had put a note in your calendar about you and
Amy around three weeks before you and I had agreed to change our

ground rules, I was deeply hurt because it looked to me like you were already in an intimate relationship with her."

The mediator might not have interrupted here because sometimes the person needs to get out their accusations and interpretation and their resulting feelings before they can accept coaching. It is often difficult to know when to stop the process and coach the client into a more constructive communication or when to let it go. Since this happened early in the process, I believe much of what transpires later, similar to the above, might have been prevented. But intervening early also runs the risk of alienating Sue from continuing the process.

SUE: I apologize if you don't see it that way, but that is the way I see it. I found an anniversary in the calendar that you put in for Amy and you. It was three or four weeks before you and I had changed our ground rules. That hurt me so deeply I can't tell you. So I'm sorry, again, that you feel that I'm going to get more than my fair share, but I put twenty-one years into this relationship and I feel that you just threw me out with the trash, because you were afraid to talk to me and tell me how you were really feeling. I would hear things like "Well, school is ending and I'm not sure what my next path will be." At no time did you say you were unhappy with our relationship and that's what I'm upset about too. I feel betrayed by that.

Sue starts out with a better I-message here, but then a phrase like "I feel you just threw me out with the trash" exemplifies an accusatory and inflammatory You-message. If Sue were open to learning how to communicate this in a more effective way, the mediator could have helped her formulate some of the valid points she tries to make into I-messages: "Brad, I often did not know how you were feeling and that was not only confusing, but it didn't give me a chance to rectify what wasn't going well between us. I felt powerless when that was going on."

The mediator chooses not to surface these You-message attacks; instead, she asks Brad to be empathic to Sue. Someone as angry and hurt as Sue may need some empathy before being open to communicating with an I-message.

MEDIATOR: Okay, are you complete enough for the moment?

SUE: Uh-huh.

MEDIATOR: *(To Brad)* So I'll empathize with Sue first and then ask you to. *(To Sue)* So you see that you're relationship was set up in a kind of a traditional way. Brad brought in more money than you did and you tended more to maintaining the household and the yards. You had consulted with legal counsel and you were aware that there were things that Brad might not be aware of around the divorce and that's why you really wanted him to see an attorney as well to get educated. You also acknowledge Brad's fear that he's going to have less than he thought he was going to have, but you also have less because you thought you were going to be with him and then you would have all the resources as well. You get that Brad talked about the initial financial understanding and he feels that that's not being honored here, but you feel that there were a lot of other ground rules that the two of you had and that he broke those ground rules. And that's why you feel so betrayed. And I didn't hear everything about the anniversary, but it was something you saw on the calendar and it was very painful. And you're sorry that Brad sees this as you're getting more than your fair share, but you feel you've invested twenty-one years in this relationship and you feel you have been discarded. And something that's painful for you is that you didn't realize, because from your perspective Brad didn't communicate to you, how unhappy he was in the relationship or what was not working for him in the relationship. And so that feels like a betrayal that this information was withheld from you so you couldn't do anything about it. Is there anything that I missed? Or is that basically accurate?

SUE: Yes, that's accurate.

Note how clearly and specifically the mediator delineates all the major content and feelings that Sue expressed to Brad. This empathic response not only demonstrates for Brad what to do next, but it also gives Sue the direct experience of feeling accurately and fully understood. The mediator's doing this in the initial stages of mediation serves many purposes. It helps the parties to feel that the mediator can understand them, which paves the way for each of them to emotionally hire the mediator. It begins, slowly at first, to give the parties a feeling of safety. They not only know the mediator can understand them accurately, but that she will also coach the other party to understand accurately. This feeling of safety can only come slowly because most people in a divorce have not felt this for a long time (if ever). People will not self-disclose much unless they feel safe. They will also refuse to lower their defenses unless they feel safe. Collaborative

*conflict resolution builds on people feeling safe enough to expose vul-
nerabilities and get through the accusations and misinterpretations
that conflict often stimulates so they can share what they really feel
and what they really think important. Empathy provides the major
tool to begin this trust-building process, and the mediator here demonstrates how that process can begin.*

MEDIATOR: So Brad, can you do that in your words?

BRAD: Sue, I heard you say that you feel like you contributed
more to our house. That you did most of the gardening, most of the
housework, and I also heard you say you wanted me to get legal counsel when we entered into this process because you didn't think I understood the consequences of getting divorced. And I heard you say
how betrayed you feel, and that you feel especially betrayed because
you found something in a calendar in your Macintosh, or probably in
your address book, that suggested that Amy and I had some kind of
relationship before you and I ever talked about our relationship. And
you also feel betrayed because you believe I had feelings about our
relationship long before I ever opened the topic of talking about our
relationship, the discussion we had like in early or mid March?

SUE: I think it was earlier.

BRAD: Does that pretty much cover what you said?

SUE: Are you empathizing or acknowledging?

MEDIATOR: He's just asking if he was accurate.

SUE: What you said is true. *(Her tone of voice is quiet and
resentful.)*

BRAD: I certainly acknowledge you contributed more to the garden than I have. You've worked in the garden much more than I have.
I acknowledge that I didn't go and talk to someone legally before we
entered into the mediation process. And I acknowledge that there is a
date in the address book entry for Amy on March 4, which was a week
to a week and a half before I asked for a conversation, and when you
and I sat down and talked about how I was feeling in our relationship.
I actually really appreciate how betrayed you might feel seeing that
date. I don't know if I can fully appreciate it, but I acknowledge it.

Sue begins to cry here and there is a long pause.

MEDIATOR: *(To Sue)* Keep breathing.

SUE: I can hear… *(Pause)* Please stop looking at me. I'll respond. *(Angry tone of voice toward the mediator)*

MEDIATOR: So it's okay to go on?

SUE: Yes.

MEDIATOR: *(To Brad)* So, anything else to acknowledge?

BRAD: Those are the things I can acknowledge.

MEDIATOR: Okay, thank you. I think it's important for Sue to hear some of the things you said.

BRAD: I do have some specific responses.

MEDIATOR: And it's your turn now to do that.

BRAD: I always felt like I held up my side of the housework. I've done most of the cooking and a lot of the grocery shopping and plenty of housecleaning over the years. So I don't feel that is way out of balance, and to me that's kind of a "nit" at this point.

Here Brad gets into subtle pejorative comment about Sue nitpicking, which the mediator could pick up. The mediator needs to decide when to intervene and when to let things go. The better the trust base and rapport the mediator has with each party, the better she can give feedback or interrupt to make a communication more optimal. If anything, this seemingly small word "nit" can carry a connotation that can set Sue off. The earlier the mediator catches this and helps the person translate it into less inflammatory communication the better. For example, she might help Brad say the last sentence in a more respectful way, such as "So I don't believe the division of labor we had around the house was imbalanced in any significant way."

BRAD: The March 4 date that is in Sue's address book entry is the date that Amy came over to do computer work at our house, and she had dinner with us, and you *(Sue)* went to bed early and she *(Amy)* and I had a really intense discussion after you went to sleep that night. She and I kissed each other goodnight. It felt like a significant moment to me, but it wasn't a moment where we were physically intimate in any way. It just felt like...the reason why I put that entry for her in the address book is because it felt like the moment that our relationship in some way became a possibility. And it's also the moment I realized, and this is moving over into an assertion, it was actually the next day or two after March 4 when I realized I felt really incomplete in our relationship. That I felt parts of me had died in our relationship, and when I sat down and talked with you about our relationship, my intention was absolutely to try and make it work. I didn't sit down and talk with you to try and find an escape hatch from our marriage. So I did not have an affair before you and I talked about it and before you suggested that that was an option. *(Sue makes a facial gesture of disbelief.)* It's true!

Brad responds to a nonverbal communication of disbelief by Sue. At this time, the mediator could remind Sue that certain facial gestures are a form of response that, when engaged in at this point, do not follow the B-E-A-R Process to which she has agreed and can actually be detrimental to getting resolution.

BRAD: And it was actually my intention through those months when we tried to make all of that work that you and I were going to work. *(Sue makes a snorting sound.)* It really was; you can snort, but it really was true that I wanted our relationship to work, and during that period when, you know, the three of us...we all knew about each other when we were sort of in that triad relationship, that was a horrific time for me. But even then I did not expect our relationship was dissolving. *(Long pause)* I feel really sorry that this has unfolded the way it has.

The mediator must monitor nonverbal communication that expresses the listener's point of view, disbelief, or disagreement because such expression violates the B-E-A-R sequence by responding, usually disrespectfully, before the listener has empathetically responded and acknowledged any areas of agreement. This can inflame the speaker and derail the process. In this case, Brad continues and the mediator chooses not to intervene and remind Sue of the agreement that she will stay with the process and show respect even if she feels anger or disbelief. Sue may need coaching to close her eyes, breathe for a while, and recommit herself to the B-E-A-R Process.

MEDIATOR: Okay, I'm going to summarize first and then ask you to, Sue. So Brad, first of all, as far as the housework goes, you feel you did most of the cooking and most of the grocery shopping and some of the house cleaning, so you feel you held up your end there, that there wasn't a real disparity in how that was handled. You really understand how painful it must have been for Sue to discover in the calendar the March date with Amy's name and yet you want Sue to understand that that was the day she came over to spend time with the both of you and it was when Sue went to bed that you and Amy had a very intense discussion and there was a kiss good-night, but it wasn't being physically intimate. But it was the first time you really sensed how much you had been giving up of yourself in your current relationship and it was shortly thereafter that you raised these issues with Sue. So you want to be clear you had not had a prior affair at the time you raised these issues. You were really honestly approaching Sue with the intention of asking what can we do to make the relationship better. You had not done anything prior and it wasn't an escape hatch or a way out. You were really serious about seeing what could make this relationship work. And I gather that even after the two of you talked about changing some of the ground rules in your relationship and the possibility of having relationships with other people, you want Sue to know you did not already start having a relationship before you had that discussion. And it sounds like there was a period of time when there was kind of a triad relationship and that was very hard on you, and even during that time you still expected you and Sue would stay together. And you're really sorry at this point how things have unfolded.

BRAD: That's a good reflection.

MEDIATOR: Okay, Sue, it's your turn.

SUE: You say that you feel you held up your side of the household. I have no idea what a "nit" means, but you said it. Something about a nit?

Although perhaps not an optimal time, the mediator could have intervened here to help Brad use more specific language as well as choose a less inflammatory phrase. She might have Brad describe more clearly and respectfully what he meant by a "nit." If Brad could not do that, she could have role-modeled a communication such as "I truly don't think there was a significant discrepancy in the amount of time and effort you (Sue) spent on household chores and the amount of time and effort I spent on different but comparable household chores and activities. In other words, the time and effort I spent shopping and cooking and sometimes helping clean the house was relatively equal to the time you (Sue) spent on the garden and cleaning the house more frequently than I. I think the difference was relatively minor." After the mediator role models this, she then would have Brad say it from his perspective but with the same non-inflammatory and respectful tone. I cannot overemphasize the importance of catching inflammatory language, gestures, or facial expressions to minimize flooding so that the primitive parts of the brain do not take over.

SUE: You stated that you've done most of the cooking; you've done some of the helping. You're trying to imagine how painful it could have been my discovering the anniversary date in the computer. You mentioned that it was just a goodnight kiss, you had not begun a new relationship, but it did begin the possibility and you started thinking that you were feeling incomplete and part of you had died and started thinking about that for a few days. You state that you weren't trying to find an escape hatch from our marriage but for some period you felt incomplete. You didn't see our marriage dissolving and you feel sorry how this has gone. Am I basically accurate?

BRAD: Yes, that's accurate.

MEDIATOR: Anything she missed that's important to you?

BRAD: No.

MEDIATOR: That was good work, Sue. Is there anything you can acknowledge?

SUE: I acknowledge you did most of the cooking. You'd rather cook than clean. And you're a fantastic cook; I acknowledge that with fifteen more pounds on my frame.

Again, the mediator could have Sue recommit to in a clean, direct, and respectful manner despite her hurt, anger, and resentment.

SUE: I acknowledge that you did do some housework. I heard you say you felt my pain when you made the comment about my discovery. I agree that we both thought something was missing in the relationship. I felt you were distancing from me. I acknowledge that. I acknowledge how difficult everything was. I watched our marriage dissolve. And I'm also sorry. *(Sue starts crying again at this point.)* So now I'm going to respond.

Notice Sue's growing awareness of slipping into her own frame of reference in the acknowledgment phase of the model. The mediator at some point could acknowledge Sue's increase in awareness, often more effective than just pointing out when she does not follow the model. It reinforces not only the increased awareness but also the mediator's "base" with Sue, which could help later should the mediator need to interrupt Sue and have her speak more respectfully from her perspective.

SUE: When you kissed someone that you're attracted to, you broke a boundary, you broke a ground rule, you betrayed my trust, you betrayed our agreements, and you broke our marriage vows.

The mediator has the option to let these accusatory You-messages go for now and allow Sue to express her anger via accusations, or to stop her and coach her into translating these You-messages into I-messages. To the degree that Sue can and will give I-messages, and to the degree that Sue has emotionally hired the mediator, I recommend the mediator stop Sue in this case, empathize with her feelings, interpretations, and accusations, but then remind her of the agreement to use I- messages and recontract with her to learn how to do this in the mediation.

This can help keep both Brad's and Sue's emotional temperatures down. Although Brad probably did not disclose his feelings and often withdrew emotionally, Sue's propensity to make interpretations without checking them and to get angry and accusatory based on her own interpretations, likely provided one of the reasons he disclosed little to her. That dynamic in their marriage reenacts in the mediation. To the degree both parties wish to learn from their mediation experience, I recommend interrupting and translating the You-messages into I-messages. For example, Sue could rephrase her statement more respectfully with an I-message and still not dilute the intensity as follows: "I felt incredibly angry and hurt when I learned you had kissed Amy good-night that evening after you told me you wanted to end our marriage and have a relationship with her. It made me wonder whether you knew much earlier that you were going to leave me but didn't tell me."

Perhaps the mediator assessed that Sue needed to express all these things and that she might not willingly take coaching at this time until she got all of this out in an accusatory way. If the other party can handle it emotionally, which Brad seems to do here, it may help to let Sue vent awhile and then, after receiving some empathy, perhaps she can rephrase things in a more constructive, I-message way.

As Sue continues in this manner, we will use it as an opportunity to identify the various kinds of You-messages such as accusations, interpretations, and war words.

SUE: You had the beginnings of a new possibility of a new life with someone else *(interpreting Brad's thoughts)* and when we changed our ground rules, you said nothing. You didn't say you were already attracted to someone *(interpretation of Brad)* and I find that out of integrity. You stated that you weren't trying to find an escape hatch from our marriage, but yet I feel you weren't actually willing to have the two of us explore what was wrong with the marriage before you brought in a third party *(not a feeling but another interpretation of Brad)*.

Sue communicates her interpretations as facts and indicates no openness to having the accuracy of her perceptions or interpretations confirmed or disconfirmed.

SUE: That option was never suggested. We should have gone to marriage counseling and neither of us suggested it. And I didn't know you already had someone lined up and ready to go *(inflammatory wording and interpretation)* because you never brought that forth the whole time! The three-way was horrific! I watched our marriage dissolve. I told you I was watching our marriage dissolve. *(These move closer to an I-message)* I was watching you build a new life with someone else because you were so enamored with her it didn't matter what I said *(interpretation of Brad)*. You forgot my birthday *(interpretation)*. You told me you'd purchase something for me when you went to Spain and you didn't. *(This is a better behavioral description.)* You were so out of relationship with me *(interpretation)*. She absorbed your total world *(interpretation of Brad)*. That's my experience. *(It is actually her interpretations and judgments.)* And I still have to ask you, are you having an affair with this woman? *(This is a good example of a direct request.)* You never even told me because you understood that we had an agreement to wait three months (*Interpretation. Note how she makes an inference about what Brad thought without checking it. Rather she treats her inferences as facts and then makes decisions on those inferences as facts.)* And I acknowledge that. We've talked about this before. For me it was just another pattern of withholding and deceit *(Notice how she prefaces this with the words "for me" but then proceeds to make an accusation about Brad.)*, which a lot of our relationship was. And I'm sad that our relationship has ended this way because I would really like to be able to find in myself to be your friend again. *(This gets closer to an I-message.)* But every time you state that you've been in integrity, I tend to disagree because already in your heart you started distancing from me.

This interpretation assumes she knows what went on inside of Brad's heart at the time. It should be emphasized that Sue's interpretations may be accurate. They are, nevertheless, interpretations and spoken as facts. Interpretations, accurate or not, spoken as facts, serve to disrupt the mediation process. I-messages are a much better way of communicating because they only express a behavior description of what happened and the feelings of the person communicating the I-message. At minimum, the mediator should keep asking Sue to check her interpretations with Brad. In addition, she should encourage Brad to self-disclose in a clearer and more specific way, leaving less room for Sue's interpretations.

SUE: And whenever I tried to see if you could slow down, like giving you the letter and asking you to step outside the relationship, I was attacked. *(It would help here to get the behavioral description of what Brad actually did or said rather than use the word "attacked.")* Anytime I made a comment about Amy you defended her and attacked me. It was really hard to experience your rejection month after month, week after week. *(This reflects more of an I-message)* And I don't expect you to ever understand how you shattered me.

The word "ever" here acts as an all-or-nothing "war" word, which usually alienates the other person. Also, the phrase "You shattered me" is an excellent example of an accusatory You-message. An example of an I-message here would be "When you defended Amy I felt shattered."

SUE: I will never trust another human, another man, the way I trusted you. My innocence is gone. *(The tone of voice here is blaming and accusatory.)*

MEDIATOR: And one of the problems with this process is that at some point we have to end and someone always gets left hanging. So I don't think we have the time for you (Brad) to empathize, but I think a lot got said that needed to get said.

This is a very unfortunate time for the session to end. Sue really needs to hear an empathic response from both the mediator and Brad in order to get through her feelings of hurt and anger as well as her blaming and accusatory tone. Sue should not leave feeling she has said her piece cleanly and respectfully. Likewise, Brad should not leave feeling misinterpreted, sad, guilty, or hopeless about ever getting a resolution.

MEDIATOR: Think about whether you want to pick up from here next time. We'll talk about it. I've taken notes and I can empathize with what Sue said and have you do that, or we could start fresh with a new assertion, or we can go and talk about substantive things. Let's just kind of let this settle and let you reflect on it and lets talk about it next time. How it was for you, what you got from it, whether you want to do more of it or not. Is there anything either one of you needs to say right now before we wrap up?

An alternative statement here could be something like: "I'm very sorry we have to end here because of the time. I think it is very important that both Brad and I demonstrate our understanding of how angry and hurt you feel, Sue, and for you, Brad, to have a chance to respond. We will need to begin with this next time and I realize you both may feel left hanging at this point."

BRAD: *(To Sue)* I think I heard everything you said. *(To the mediator)* I guess my concern about this process is that what we're doing right now, actually we're sort of at a stuck place, or I feel stuck because there's nothing I can do or say that's going to make Sue feel better. So I feel stuck.

Whether or not Sue's interpretations and accusations are true, Brad feels stuck because Sue has told him that he will never understand how what he has done has shattered her, one reason why they may not reach a mediated settlement. This crucial moment in the mediation reveals that Sue's belief that Brad lied to, betrayed, and rejected her blocks them from coming to a resolution. Without a resolution of these beliefs and her accompanying feelings, they may not resolve the more tangible issues of the divorce.

MEDIATOR: Well, I heard you *(Brad)* say what you believed to be your truth, and what you would really like right now is for Sue to accept that and believe that and therefore release her pain. And that would make you feel better. Sue is not at that place.

BRAD: Right.

MEDIATOR: Right now my sense is it's too early for you *(Sue)* to get any perspective about this situation and at this point you feel totally betrayed and very much a victim, right?

SUE: I feel betrayed yes. I don't feel a victim. I had a part in this too. I acknowledge that, I've acknowledged that from day one. The part that hurts is the withholding of information and that's been a part of a pattern for our relationship–control issues. He who holds the deck of cards has control. You withhold the knowledge; you know it and I didn't. So Amy and Brad were privy to what was going on in their relationship. They didn't tell me!

MEDIATOR: Sometimes something has to happen before there's something to tell.

Now that the mediator has essentially ended the session, it leaves room for Sue to stray outside the structure of the B-E-A-R Process even more.

SUE: A lot was happening, and I felt that I took accountability throughout this entire process and I actually don't think the two of you *(Brad and Amy)* have.

MEDIATOR: So is that something that you want?

SUE: I don't actually expect Brad and I to see eye to eye on this situation. We both remember it differently and we *always* will. *(Again, the all-or-nothing language comes in here unchallenged.)* I don't *ever* expect him to really understand my feelings and I can't accept...I don't understand his.

The verbal slip "and I can't accept" pinpoints the issue here. She understands that Brad feels alienated and withdrawn from her to the point that he has chosen to end their marriage. Sue has not accepted or resolved this yet and it blocks the mediation process in terms of getting to a financial settlement.

MEDIATOR: Okay, we'll have to stop here.

The mediator could have coached Sue on communicating more respectfully with I-messages in this session. If Sue could not do that, the mediator could remind Sue of the B-E-A-R Process ground rules and then role model for awhile how to turn her You-messages into I-messages so Sue could learn how to do it.

The session ended at an extremely awkward time. It would have helped if the mediator could have empathetically responded to Sue, followed by Brad's empathic response. For both to hear her fully might be healing for Sue and open her receptivity to coaching to hear

Brad's responses. It would not resolve everything, of course, but it could initiate a more constructive and respectful attitude during the mediation process. With time as an issue, the mediator could ask Brad to think about the truth of Sue's accusations and interpretations so he could clarify things at the beginning of the next session. This might partially ameliorate Brad's likely feeling of being left hanging at this point. Ending intense mediation sessions can prove difficult.

On the other hand, the session accomplished a great deal. Brad expressed how he feels it unfair for Sue to get more than 50 percent of their joint resources, given their verbal agreement that they would contribute in proportion to their income and that he contributed more and felt he had done roughly his share of the household chores. He also expressed his fear that he might not have enough financial resources on which to fall back.

Sue got to express her anger, resentment, and hurt regarding her perceptions of Brad's withholding information about his feelings about their relationship and getting involved before he had been honest with her. A major issue, Sue's belief that Brad betrayed her, arose. She also believes she did more of the household chores and therefore deserves more of the resources even though she acknowledges contributing less financially to the relationship.

Brad and Sue are beginning to learn the B-E-A-R Process, which takes time and effort to learn. It often helps for the mediator to remind them of this learning curve and to give positive feedback on their progress at the end of the session.

THE SECOND MEDIATION SESSION TRANSCRIPT

Brad and Sue, reluctant to proceed with the B-E-A-R Process after the last session, felt unable to get through to each other. The mediator reminded them that the last session had ended due to unfortunate time limitations and encouraged them to try one more time to see if they could break through the impasse. They reluctantly agreed in order to avoid entering into the more costly and potentially more emotionally adversarial alternative. The mediator asked if Brad remembered what Sue had said at the end of the last session and asked to start there.

MEDIATOR: *(To Brad)* Do you want me to empathize with Sue first?

BRAD: No, I actually think I can pick it up. So what I heard you say, is that...

MEDIATOR: I want you to be careful. When you said, "So what I heard you say," it was a little dismissive in your tone of voice. To the extent that you can, really convey what you think her experience is so she feels that you get it.

This intervention on the part of the mediator, particularly at the beginning of this session, could help coach Brad into speaking more from his heart when he empathically responds to Sue and also when he communicates his perspective and feelings. If so, the mediator can then go a long way in facilitating the process in a way that will bring emotional closure for Sue. Unless Sue can "feel" that Brad understands how hurt she feels because he left her for another woman, and that he accepts at least some part of his contribution to the relationship ending, the mediation will not succeed.

BRAD: Okay. I understand that when I kissed someone else in our house at the beginning of March, you believe that I started a relationship. Or that that opened up the possibility of a relationship with someone else, and that I actually had the intention of pursuing that in early March. And because of that you believe when we talked about our relationship in mid March, which is probably about a week and a half after I kissed this woman, that I was withholding information, that I wasn't telling you how I actually felt about her and I didn't have the intention of keeping you as my primary relationship and that I wasn't being true to our marriage.

MEDIATOR: Do you get that that's how she really feels?

Brad empathically responds accurately to Sue's beliefs, inferences, interpretations, and accusations, but not to her feelings. He does not explicitly respond to her feelings of anger and resentment, partially as a result of her inferences. Feelings of hurt, anger, and resentment are very much a normal part of someone's response when a partner leaves. However, Sue's interpretations that Brad purposely withheld information from her and betrayed their agreements exacerbate these feelings. We don't yet know the accuracy of Sue's interpretations and accusations of betrayal.

BRAD: Yes! I understand that.

MEDIATOR: *(To Sue)* Do you think he understands that?

SUE: *(To Brad)* I think you understand my feelings and what I anticipate you saying is "That's not true." And my response to "That's not true" is "You said it last week."

MEDIATOR: I don't want you to go there yet.

This very important intervention by the mediator, this early in the session, communicates to Sue that she cannot circumvent the B-E-A-R Process and get into her response out of the sequence, and the mediator retains control of the process. Sue again not only anticipates Brad's response, but also makes an accusation based on a response that Brad hasn't given. This provides an optimal time for some restructuring and recontracting with Sue. Just as the mediator coaches Brad toward a more feeling response, the mediator could coach Sue toward less accusatory and interpretive communications and more empathy.

MEDIATOR: In some way, you're expressing this, Brad, as though it's incredible to you. And I believe that it is incredible to you, that you don't understand why she doesn't believe that you understand her, how she's not getting empathy from you.

BRAD: Okay, I hear you.

SUE: It's like telling me I'm wrong. That's how I feel...

MEDIATOR: Yes, and at this stage in the process, you're trying to say it in a way that you are fully accepting that for her this is the way it is and it's true for her.

I believe a number of things happening here complicate the process. First, Brad cannot empathetically respond to Sue in a way that Sue "feels" understood. The mediator rightfully tries to coach Brad to take this step because it is crucial if this couple is going to come to a mediated settlement. If Sue does not feel that Brad understands her devastation at being rejected for another woman, she probably will not negotiate a settlement on the financial side of things.

Second, Sue wants Brad to confirm her view of what happened as the truth and not call her "wrong." Perhaps Brad cannot because they have yet to differentiate between perceptions, interpretations, inferences, and actual fact. If, in fact, Sue's accusations are all true, Brad not only needs to more empathetically respond to Sue in a more

heartfelt manner, but also acknowledge (i.e., agree with and take re-
sponsibility for these actions) and then respond by apologizing and
offering some form of reparation. If Brad believes that some or all of
Sue's inferences and accusations are inaccurate, however, he needs an
opportunity to express that and to get an empathic response from Sue,
whether she believes him or not.

Third, and particularly troublesome at this point, Sue does not
seem aware of her inferences as inferences. She sees them as facts
(truth), so anytime Brad's frame of reference does not agree with her,
she sees him as telling her she's "wrong." Brad's history of not shar-
ing things from his perspective honestly and explicitly has likely set
up this pattern. This has added to Sue's propensity to make interpre-
tations because she misses some of the data, and then gets angry and
accusatory, causing Brad to withdraw and withhold all the more. This
pattern does not have to change totally in mediation, as it would if the
couple planned to stay together and were in marriage counseling. The
pattern needs to alter just enough for Brad to see that his not speaking
explicitly, even if it angers Sue, hinders a mediated settlement, and for
Sue to see that treating interpretations as facts, and then making ac-
cusations based on those interpretations, will not lead to the truth she
wants so badly from Brad.

BRAD: It's really hard for me to...like...disconnect from myself enough to do that. I mean from a really impersonal place I can do that. But I don't know if that would actually serve.

MEDIATOR: No, I don't think that's going to quite do it.

SUE: That's why I don't think I can ever see Brad where he lives, and he can't see me where I live. That's why it's such a hard place to be bridged.

MEDIATOR: But what I'm getting is that this has been a pattern throughout the whole relationship.

SUE: I didn't know it existed because he was helpless...

MEDIATOR: Do you think you in any way colluded with that?

The mediator checks to see if Sue can take responsibility for her part in the relationship not working.

SUE: Oh, sure. My accountability? Denial is great! When things started coming to light, I remember Brad saying eight years ago when we began EST that there was something wrong with the marriage. He didn't say, "I'm not happy." There was something wrong with the marriage. Okay, so then we both got into EST and started working the process and went through our various pieces, as you said a little while ago, you thought we'd resolved the issue. The issue was just covered over with EST.

BRAD: I agree with you.

SUE: So it got put on hold and it still wasn't addressed.

MEDIATOR: I guess I'm getting that Sue's not really heard by you *(to Brad)*, and yet you seem to be a very conscious and sensitive person. So I believe you can demonstrate a deeper understanding of her, and that's why I want to keep working with you so you can get there. I think it could just open something up and release some pressure. My sense is that there is this terrible container of pressure between the two of you, and if we could open up just a pinhole, it could begin to release. So that's what I'm looking for.

BRAD: Okay.

MEDIATOR: I know it's hard.

BRAD: Well, I guess where I'm sort of stuck is you know... I love you, and I've always loved you. I still know the place inside me that loves you. So...to connect to that and be... *(Sue starts to cry here.)* Yeah, and just the... *(Brad starts to cry as well.)* So it's really hard for me to connect to that in the face of all the distrust and sense of betrayal that you're expressing toward me.

I see this as the turning point in the mediation. When Brad says he still loves Sue, and comes to tears saying it, it provides one of the things Sue needed to experience. Sue needed to feel Brad's love for her or to feel his sadness about the loss of their relationship, or both. This provides a crucial part of what she needed to move on in the mediation as well as in her life.

MEDIATOR: When we as human beings are in pain and conflict, we tend to shut down, and we think that will protect us and we feel safer that way.

BRAD: I understand, but there's a difference between saying, "I feel betrayed" and "I feel like you betrayed me."

MEDIATOR: Even to say "I feel betrayed" is something being done to you. So "hurt" might be the actual feeling...

BRAD: So the hard thing is to always peel it away and say how I feel, and not imply something about the other person and just have my feeling.

MEDIATOR: Yes. It takes a willingness to be vulnerable, and you have to feel like you're not handing ammunition to the other person.

BRAD: At the moment, I feel like I'm handing ammunition to the other person, because every time I bring truth and honesty into this space, it gets turned around as a weapon to prove that I'm not trustworthy. So the more I talk about what actually happened for me over the last year, I don't feel received in any way, I just feel like I'm handing ammunition over to Sue.

MEDIATOR: So the more honest you are, the more evidence there might be for Sue to attack you?

Brad expresses what it feels like when Sue cannot demonstrate her understanding (i.e., be empathic). Unless Sue attempts to understand Brad's perspective, even if she doesn't believe him, he will continue to find it difficult to feel safe enough to speak honestly. This does not mean that Sue could not also express her frame of reference, but Sue has mostly failed to empathize with Brad's point of view. Some people hesitate to demonstrate their understanding to something they don't believe or accept because they don't differentiate between empathy and agreement. Whether this is true for Sue or not, I believe Sue's lack of empathy has contributed to problems in the relationship all along. Brad's lack of honesty and Sue's lack of empathy produce a pattern that makes Brad even less open and honest and Sue even more interpretive and accusatory. Surfacing this cycle may or may not help in the mediation context, but it would prove central in a counseling setting. For mediation, the parties only need coaching into doing this by keeping them in the B-E-A-R structure, so they can develop just enough of a mutual understanding to negotiate a settlement.

BRAD: That's actually my experience in our mediation. For instance, Sue and I fully shared calendar and address data and I obviously didn't put anything in there that I felt was sensitive or secret. It got picked up and used as a piece of ammunition to prove that I violated ground rules in our relationship. When I've talked to Sue about what actually happened and how I felt it gets reflected back to me as proof that I was out of integrity, when, in fact, I'm actually just trying to describe how I felt about her and our relationship through this crucial period that we're talking about. This was a period when I never imagined that I was going to be in relationship with another woman. But Sue is firmly convinced that I was imagining that I was going to be in a relationship with another woman.

MEDIATOR: So that's very painful for you, that you are coming from your honest part and declaring that you had no intention, not even thought of being in relationship with another woman, and Sue...

BRAD: Oh, it crossed my mind. Let's be honest, it crossed my mind! But it wasn't my intention. Over the last several decades, I've run into a number of women that I've thought, "God, I wonder what it would be like to be in a relationship with her?" but that doesn't mean that I've gone and done it. And that wasn't my intention last March.

MEDIATOR: So you're acknowledging that you have found other women attractive and that that's not abnormal, and the main thing is what you choose to do with those feelings.

BRAD: Right.

MEDIATOR: And that you felt that you acted in integrity and in accordance with the rules of your marriage, the understanding between the two of you that you would not act on those feelings.

BRAD: That's correct. I made that choice over and over. And I made that choice last March. I chose to initiate a conversation with Sue about our relationship because I realized there was a place in me that I felt really off in our relationship and it was sort of reflected back by this experience with this woman. But it wasn't about creating a relationship with that woman; it was like "Oh, if this can happen, what's going on in our marriage?" And then I started to actually realize that we had a problem. So I initiated a conversation that was actually very difficult for me to initiate and it was a very scary experience because of our past experience of talking about our feelings and having these conversations. It's been very hard in the past, and then, you know, events unfolded. It was like...this year unfolded the way it did, but my intention was never to rip apart our marriage. And it never even occurred to me that that would even happen. In June, when Sue asked me to move out, I was shocked because... *(Sue nonverbally expresses disagreement.)* I was! I mean it just didn't occur to me that that was where we were at.

MEDIATOR: So when you initiated the conversation, which was very difficult for you to do, that felt being in integrity with yourself and you needed to do that.

BRAD: Yes.

MEDIATOR: And that was March, and even through June...

BRAD: Well, then I engaged in this relationship in April. So then it unfolded in April and May, and Sue knew about it, and I was gone for a period of three weeks in there.

We are now getting into Brad's perceptions and experiences in March when Sue interpreted that he was out of integrity and accusing him of already having an intimate relationship before they had the talk. If we believe Brad, it appears that at least some, though not necessarily all, of Sue's accusations are inaccurate. For example, we gradually learn that Brad has had a hard time bringing things up to Sue and that he has a hard time being open and honest about things he anticipates will upset her.

MEDIATOR: And did you feel having the affair was in or out of integrity at that point.

BRAD: It was in integrity. Sue suggested that I do it, not specifically with this person...

SUE: I didn't know you already had a person picked out.

Not only out of the sequence of the B-E-A-R Process, this interruption again forms another inference communicated as fact, the kind of thing the mediator needs to point out so as not to let Sue continue to communicate her perspective out of sequence. This kind of comment by Sue causes Brad to feel attacked and unsafe.

For the mediation to work better, the mediator would need to re-contract with Sue not to express her frame of reference (either verbally or with facial gestures) until after she has demonstrated accurate empathy to Brad. It often helps if the mediator can give a good rationale for this by explaining again how staying within the process serves Sue's interests. For example, after reminding Sue of her agreement to follow the ground rules of the B-E-A-R Process and how this can ultimately facilitate them to come to a better resolution, the mediator can also express to Sue that if she demonstrates understanding to Brad before she comes from her frame of reference, it might help him to feel more safe and therefore express more openly and honestly to her about what really goes on inside of him. She will more likely get the full truth this way, rather than making him more defensive and guarded. It does not mean that she can't later express her own point of view if she disagrees with him or does not believe him. She also does not have to hold back her emotions as long as she does not blame Brad for those emotions. She needs empathy about the difficulty of doing this when she feels so strongly and has felt frustrated for such a long time. Nevertheless, if she wants clarity and resolution, the B-E-A-R Process could benefit her if she can stay within the structure.

BRAD: I didn't have a person picked out! *(Some anger now in Brad's tone of voice.)*

MEDIATOR: Can you understand how it looks that way to her?

BRAD: Yeah, I totally do.

SUE: I'd like to ask a question. We had an anniversary coming up on Monday. What does that anniversary mean to you?

BRAD: That was our first date; it was the beginning of our relationship.

SUE: But yet that's not the anniversary that's in the calendar for us. The anniversary for us in the calendar is...

BRAD: Our wedding anniversary.

SUE: So knowing what I know about us and seeing the date in the computer on March 3 or 4 or whenever it was, can you see how I would...where I was coming from and how that would happen?

BRAD: Yeah. I totally get that.

SUE: Can you see my point of view? You'd been attracted to this woman for many, many years.

BRAD: We've been friends for many years.

SUE: You said there was an electricity when you went on a motorcycle ride together.

BRAD: We also held a really good boundary about it. We always held really good boundaries.

SUE: And then you broke a ground rule in our house and you didn't tell me. *(Her voice is getting increasingly angry and accusatory here.)*

MEDIATOR: Which ground rule?

SUE: Kissing someone in our home!

BRAD: I'm not aware that was a ground rule.

SUE: We had a ground rule long ago, not in this house, no touching, and that happened from EST when it happened.

BRAD: Oh, right. Well, but we kiss people. I kiss people goodbye...

SUE: You kiss people, but do you put an anniversary date about it in a computer? *(Very accusatory tone of voice again and all three people start talking at once in an escalating manner. No one hears anyone else.)*

This sequence exemplifies what can quickly and predictably happen once the mediator allows the parties to get away from the structure and sequence of the B-E-A-R Process. Many people consider this an inevitable part of the conflict resolution process, but I disagree. Once the parties agree to hold to the process, the mediator can prevent these kinds of interactions, which add nothing to the process and takes the parties further from a resolution. In the resulting confusion, they learn nothing. As primitive parts of their brains take over, they feel less and less safe, so they accuse, defend, argue, and lose ground. Sometimes in the very early stages of a mediation, the mediator might want to allow this to occur, not only to diagnose the communication patterns in the relationship, but also to let the parties experience how quickly things deteriorate when they leave the B-E-A-R Process, a very familiar pattern to each of them. I rarely find this useful. More frequently, the parties in the mediation, all too familiar with this pattern, don't need the demonstration again in the mediation. Whenever it occurs, however, the mediator can usefully call time out and recontract for the parties to go back to the B-E-A-R Process.

BRAD: So here's where we're stuck...

SUE: I state my feeling of how I feel, you make me wrong, then I make you wrong, and we keep going back and forth.

BRAD: That's what we do, right.

Sue does not see that what she regards as stating her feeling is actually a You-message in the form of an accusation or interpretation and not a feeling. Since she views her interpretations as facts, when Brad does not agree with her interpretation, she feels he makes her

wrong. This complicated pattern drives their communication prob-
lem. If this couple wanted to stay married, they would need to address
this issue. In mediation, it needs identification and management just
long enough to get a settlement.

For example, Brad needs to respond as deeply as he can to Sue's
feelings of hurt and devastation in reaction to his choosing to leave the
marriage for another woman. He needs to respond to how Sue feels
rejected, hurt, and betrayed. He could respond to how difficult it must
have been to know he was attracted to this other woman before he
became intimately involved with her, even if it happened after he had
the conversation with Sue in which they changed their ground rules.
He then needs to acknowledge the accurate parts of her accusations,
however small. Only in this way can she begin to see his honesty and
openness. He can even empathize with how easily she might infer that
he had intentions of getting into a relationship with this other woman
before he felt he actually did, given the circumstances. Empathizing
with and acknowledging all that could, potentially, break through to
Sue. Even more important, it remains crucial for Brad to clearly ad-
mit his difficulty in being fully open and honest with Sue about difficult
things, without making her totally responsible for that.

MEDIATOR: So can you *(Sue)* see how he feels that when he's
honest with you, he feels like he's supplying you with ammunition?

SUE: So, I would ask a question.

Note how any time the mediator asks Sue to own her part in some-
thing, she changes the subject.

MEDIATOR: Well, can you see or understand that?

SUE: I can see that. Why would you put an anniversary date in
for a friend that you kissed? You didn't do it for anyone else!

Sue's sentence "I can see that" fails to express empathy. The me-
diator needs to coach Sue to put into her own words what she under-
stands Brad to have said and how he feels about it, even if she doesn't
believe him and even if all her accusations are true. If she misses this
step, Brad will not feel safe enough to speak honestly with her. The
mediator might assure Sue that if she demonstrates understanding to
Brad, it does not mean she has to believe or agree with him. She will
get a chance to express her own frame of reference. She only needs
to empathize first and then say what she has to say. When Sue tacitly

says, "I can see that," she does not demonstrate in her words that she actually does understand how Brad might feel hesitant. Optimally, the mediator needs to recontract with Sue regarding her willingness to abide by the B-E-A-R Process. Without Sue's explicit willingness to let the mediator guide the mediation process, the mediation will remain cumbersome, inefficient, and possibly ineffective.

BRAD: That's a fine question!

MEDIATOR: Let's rephrase that. What caused you to put that date in the computer?

The mediator attempts to demonstrate the difference between an accusatory question and a sincere open-ended question showing genuine curiosity.

BRAD: Stated that way that's a perfectly reasonable question. I put dates in the computer that I have a hard time remembering or that I want to remember. I've never had a problem remembering February 1 for us. *(Sue starts to interrupt.)* Let me finish, please! So I put our wedding anniversary in the computer because that one is not as significant to me and that's the one I have to pay attention to. You don't even normally remember our anniversary date. *(Brad now gets his jabs in as well.)*

SUE: I've forgotten it once, just like you did.

BRAD: So it was May when I put that date in the computer and by May I was in relationship with Amy.

SUE: What does that March date mean to you? *(Spoken like a prosecuting attorney.)*

To lower the emotional intensity and to make sure Sue hears Brad accurately even if she does not believe him, the mediator should require Sue to respond here empathically before allowing her to ask more questions. The mediator should not only make sure Sue heard this information, but also explore the implication of this new data in regard to her inferences.

BRAD: It was when she and I first had a conversation when we connected in a way that felt profound to me.

SUE: And let me reflect back to you what you said two weeks ago about that. When we had this conversation two weeks ago, you said, "It was a possibility of beginning a new relationship."

This interaction, again out of the B-E-A-R Process, suggests the mediator needs to coach Sue in "sandwiching" empathy in between her questions, so Brad can feel accurately heard and that Sue does not misunderstand or misinterpret his answers. Since inferences and interpretations abound for Sue, having her pause and respond empathically to Brad's answers, while difficult, is crucial for the mediator to break the pattern that has not only contributed to the demise of the relationship, but could also abort the mediation process. If someone gets to ask repeated questions, particularly with an accusatory tone of voice, it can feel like an interrogation, which leads to withdrawal or defensiveness and does not facilitate further dialogue.

The next few minutes involve similar accusatory questions and defensive answers uninterrupted by the mediator. We pick up where Brad is trying to answer Sue's question about when he thought the relationship was over.

BRAD: My life felt like a disaster in May and June. So that was an incredibly difficult period in my life and I don't know...I was intensely unhappy, I wasn't happy anywhere I was. It was difficult for me spending time with you, it was difficult spending time with her, and it was difficult spending time by myself. It was awful. Somewhere we were damaged at that point.

SUE: You betcha.

BRAD: I would say so too. But I can't actually put my finger on a place where, you know, I actually couldn't say...

SUE: So let me tell you from my experience where our relationship was damaged.

BRAD: Okay.

Brad heaves an audible sigh of frustration here. I believe it would have been important for the mediator to ask if Sue would be willing to empathize with what Brad has said here before expressing her frame of reference again. Many people would have already shut down by this point and Brad is getting close.

SUE: When you told me you were in love with another woman.

BRAD: Okay.

SUE: Because in my eyes you violated every rule we had in place. And to follow it up you said, "And I'm not willing to let her go."

(Sue's voice is very angry.) "I want to explore this other relationship and see where it leads me." You never said, "I need to let her go and see if we can make it and go into marriage counseling." You were so focused on her and not me. *(Sue starts crying and is obviously in great pain and anguish.)* It's why I feel so betrayed after twenty years.

MEDIATOR: You feel that Brad did not give your relationship a full last try by him being willing to set aside another relationship, which he was in with your permission, although you didn't have all the details...

SUE: I didn't have all the details and I didn't agree to what happened. And a part of me took the accountability and said I changed the ground rules. I allowed this to happen. Maybe this is what's supposed to happen. Not knowing, I didn't find out about the kiss until August.

BRAD: Amy and I didn't have a relationship and didn't even talk about a relationship until April.

SUE: *(In a very angry and intense voice)* DON'T MAKE ME WRONG!

BRAD: Okay. So, okay...

SUE: DON'T MAKE ME WRONG!

This excellent example of a You-message reveals Sue accepting her own inferences or interpretations as truth and if Brad doesn't agree with her, he makes her "wrong." If Sue had held to the structure of the B-E-A-R Process, she would first demonstrate that she understood Brad and then express her frame of reference. Again, I believe this impasse comes from Brad's resistance to disclosure and Sue's propensity not to differentiate between her inferences (in the vacuum of Brad not being fully honest) and facts. This distortion continues to obstruct the mediation process.

BRAD: I don't intend to make you wrong. I want to tell you I agree with you. I agree with you that when I told you I'm in love with another woman–that was a huge turning point for us.

SUE: Yeah!

BRAD: And at that point I had at least as much attention and energy going in her direction as I did in your direction, and I did not make some final attempt to make our relationship work. We didn't even talk about that.

MEDIATOR: So you're really acknowledging all that.

BRAD: Yeah.

MEDIATOR: You're acknowledging that that was the turning point in your marriage when you openly acknowledged you were in love with another woman.

BRAD: I can feel like what it would be like to receive that. I mean I can't fully... I'm not you, but if you turned around and said something like that to me in the middle of our marriage, I would have felt devastated!

SUE: Yeah!

BRAD: So I really get that!

SUE: Do you mean to hold the accountability for your part in all of it?

BRAD: It makes it even worse.

SUE: It makes it even worse? *(Sue continues to cry with deep anguish.)*

BRAD: Right.

This would provide a good place for the mediator to coach Brad in specificity, a very important skill in the Respond phase of the model. The mediator could step in here briefly and either ask Brad what he means by "It makes it even worse," or the mediator could make a tentatively stated interpretive lead by saying something like: "Do you mean by "it makes it worse" that when you take responsibility for your part in the relationship ending, it makes it even harder emotionally for you to deal with the end of the marriage?" She could follow up by, "What specifically do you take responsibility for in regard to the relationship not working?" This could provide part of what Sue needs to hear to feel some resolution.

SUE: And then when I asked you to go to marriage counseling you said no. I asked you in July and you said it wasn't an option. I asked you again in September and you confirmed that it wasn't an option. So our marriage was gone!

BRAD: So...I hear that that was really the devastating moment for you.

It would help here for the mediator to assist Brad in putting into words the details about the "devastating moment" and how it made Sue feel. Soliciting Brad to speak specifically provides another crucial part of the mediation process. The questions in parentheses in the following exchange are suggestions for how the mediator could coach Brad to speak more specifically.

BRAD: I actually sat with the feeling of *that (What do you mean by "that"?)* you know I meditated on it *(What do you mean by "it"?)*. I sat in therapy and talked about it *(What do you mean by "it"?)*. I've turned this *(What do you mean by "this"?)* inside out just to feel our relationship on both sides, so...

MEDIATOR: You've really tried to sit in her shoes...

BRAD: Yeah.

MEDIATOR: And tried to really feel like what it felt like to her.

BRAD: Yeah, it doesn't take a rocket scientist to recognize that when your partner says I'm in love with someone else...

SUE: *(Laughs in a very strange way and shouts)* YOU'RE FUCKED!

BRAD: That's right!

SUE: I mean, c'mon!

BRAD: So, I'm...

SUE: And what do you do?

Brad tries to communicate his understanding of how hurt and devastated Sue felt here, but Sue doesn't let him. She interrupts him two times in a row when he attempts to empathize with how it felt to her. Optimally, the mediator would slow the process down here and ask Sue not to interrupt Brad and just to listen to him try to demonstrate to her his understanding of how it felt to her when he told her he was in love with Amy. She doesn't need to empathically respond to him here, but she does need to give him a chance to empathize with her and to hear it and let it soak in as much as she can. Sue's willingness and ability to let Brad try to demonstrate his understanding of how devastating it was for her to hear him say that he was in love with another woman lies at the heart of the issue and could prove pivotal to getting a mediated settlement. As mentioned earlier, Sue needs to hear two things from Brad: that he understands deeply how it devastated her when he rejected her for another woman, and that he accepts responsibility for some part of what went wrong between them.

BRAD: Right, it's even worse! So all I wanted to say was the big turning point in our relationship for me was when you asked me to move out. So at that point I went "Oh, my God!" and I had to flip over to a completely different side of myself to prepare to live alone, to separate, to let go of the cats, to do all of this you know...I had to handle my life, I had to find a place to rent, I had to think about moving, the reality of our relationship ending came in when you asked me to move out. And that was the moment for me that was devastating. So when we had a conversation in July, I was already halfway out the door, I'm energetically pulling out, I'm making logistic preparations to be elsewhere, I was unwilling to enter into couple's therapy in July.

SUE: And you kept saying, "I haven't–

MEDIATOR: Before you jump in, can you let him know you understood him?

This was a very important intervention by the mediator and it begins to reestablish the B-E-A-R sequence to get things back on track.

SUE: I understand that, and we talked about this before, that you said that was the devastating point for you when I asked you to move out and take some time for yourself and figure out what you wanted to do.

BRAD: Can you imagine what it would have been like, to reverse roles?

Brad finally asks Sue to empathize with him. He is becoming aware that all along Sue has not demonstrated understanding of his frame of reference. He now asks for her to do that because he has not only struggled to empathize with Sue, but has also received empathy from the mediator, so he knows its importance.

SUE: Yes, when I'm in your position and if I didn't want to go, I would have said, "What can we do to see if we can save this? I don't want to leave."

MEDIATOR: But that's you putting you into it. Can you...

SUE: So I understand from your point, just as May devastated me, my asking you to leave devastated you. *(Bravo! Both for Sue and the mediator for not letting her go on before empathizing.)*

BRAD: It was the ultimatum you gave me; you didn't just ask me to move out. What you said was–

SUE: I want a monogamous relationship.

BRAD: That's right. If you can't let go of this other relationship and recommit to a monogamous relationship the way we held it before, we started unzipping this whole mess–

SUE: Well, it was–

MEDIATOR: Wait. Let him finish.

BRAD: If you can't recommit to a monogamous relationship, I need you to move out! That's actually what you said.

MEDIATOR: And so, what did that mean to you? *(Soliciting specificity)*

BRAD: That meant I had a choice. The only way I could stay in the house was to release my relationship with the woman I had fallen in love with...I wasn't willing to do that.

MEDIATOR: So you were on another track.

BRAD: I was sort of in this inner place where I was split.

SUE: And that's the whole thing that I kept feeling. Underneath all of this were the unspoken words "I'm not willing to give her up to save our marriage." *(Very bitter, angry tone of voice here.)*

BRAD: That's right.

MEDIATOR: And that's–

SUE: And that was never spoken. Instead what I kept hearing was "I haven't made that decision yet...I haven't made that decision yet."

MEDIATOR: So you were projecting that Brad knew where he was in his feelings but didn't convey them to you.

The mediator attempts to get Sue to see that she is projecting something on to Brad here, but it does not get through.

SUE: Actually, what I said was "If you want me to sit here while you build another life with another woman and be okay with it"...and you denied it and you said, "No that's not true." And I said, "Yes it is!" You and she keep asking more and more from me and I'm the bad guy, I'm the outsider...but I'm YOUR WIFE! *(Both anger and tears here)* By you just saying "I'm not willing to give her up because I'm in love with her" doomed our marriage. And that's what I kept feeling as an undercurrent, that was the elephant at the time. And even when I asked you when you were moving out if there was still the possibility, you kept telling me you might return. But when I watched the process of you moving out, there was no way you were going to return. You were setting up your life to go off and do your own thing. Yet I felt led on for two and a half months.

MEDIATOR: That's the key for you? You felt led on.

SUE: Yes.

MEDIATOR: Okay, let me check something out. *(To Brad)* Do you feel in your heart that in any way you led Sue on? *(To Sue)* And I don't want to create any ammunition here.

BRAD: No.

MEDIATOR: But I think this is a critical piece for you *(to Sue)*. And what is true for you? *(to Brad)*

BRAD: It's certainly important to me...At the time that Sue asked me...sort of gave me that ultimatum...I knew that I loved this other woman and I knew that I loved Sue and I felt really torn and I didn't know what I wanted. I was unwilling, actually, to make the choice.

SUE: Right.

BRAD: I was really unwilling to choose and I guess what I did is, I just put myself in this situation that was going...it was a tense difficult place, something was going to shift. The other woman was going to drop out and say, "I can't do this." Sue was going to drop out and say, "I can't do this." I was going to drop out and say, "I can't do this." One of us was going to do that and I couldn't choose. I wasn't willing to let go of Sue, I wasn't willing to let go of the other woman, and I never intentionally led Sue on. What I didn't do was tell her fully about how I was feeling because...it just...we didn't handle it well together. When we had conversations like that, Sue's response was to get very, very upset, which

I can certainly understand. She'd get really upset and really BIG and all of this response would just be coming at me and it was more than I could handle. So I never intentionally led you on...

Sue needs to hear this extremely important admission on Brad's part. Even though Brad honestly expresses his ambivalence, with which Sue may or may not empathize, he acknowledges that he "didn't tell her fully about how he was feeling." Sue needs to hear and understand this admission because it validates, in part at least, that he kept her in the dark, which not only agitated her, but also drove her to make inferences. In the absence of the full truth, people often try to fill the void with their own inferences, accurate or not.

Optimally, the mediator would empathize with Brad's admission that he didn't tell her all of his feelings and then have Sue put into her words that she heard Brad taking responsibility for his part in the process.

BRAD: From my perspective, I wasn't lying to you. I didn't have the imagination that the other woman and I could create a life together. I didn't have that imagination. I don't know what else I can say about that.

The mediator could coach Brad into speaking even more specifically about his contribution to what happened. To illustrate what taking responsibility in the Acknowledge stage of the model might sound like, Brad could say something like: "I really understand how you could interpret my deep ambivalence and indecisiveness, along with my unwillingness to choose and declare myself unambiguously for you and our relationship, and my inability at the time to tell you fully all that I was feeling that I was consciously leading you on. The fact is I was so confused I was possibly hedging my bets so if things didn't work out with Amy and me, I could come back. My inability to make a clear decision, and leading you to believe something might work out for us provided a safety net for me. I didn't realize at the time how crazy making and cruel that was to you. I see it now and I'm profoundly sorry."

BRAD: But once you asked me that question *(again, he needs to speak more specificity as to what question)*, I on some level did choose.

MEDIATOR: Not choosing is choosing.

BRAD: Yeah.

Sue weeps in the background.

MEDIATOR: And that's what I'm getting that will help Sue see this, is that you did make a choice by not choosing to let go of the relationship with the other woman and work on the relationship with Sue. From your perspective at the time, you felt you couldn't choose. So you were kind of waiting for somebody else to choose. And you kind of went, well...Sue had asked you to move out, you started in that mode, and something needed to give somewhere so that's the direction you went.

The mediator could add: "And so you acknowledge now that you actually did make a choice by not choosing."

BRAD: That's accurate. So by August I moved out. I lived alone in August. I saw the other woman several times during the first part of August; fortunately, she was gone for most of August. So then I just got to sit in my own place and I was living alone for the first time in over twenty years, which was a shocking and difficult transition for me. I mean really horrific, actually. And fortunately, I had most of that month to sit and chew on what do I want to do now. And by the end of August, living alone was okay. I started enjoying having my own space and then Sue and I were talking in mid September, when she was pushing up the schedule and asking me to make a decision and not sit in this limbo place. She wanted to know by November 1 and my response was "I'm not moving back toward you, I'm actually...the whole pattern of what had happened for us for months is moving...separating...is moving further and further apart."

MEDIATOR: So you found it hard to reverse the momentum.

BRAD: That's right. That's one way of looking at it. I hadn't really thought about it as momentum.

SUE: You split off all contact with me and kept seeing her. So of course the momentum is going to be in that direction. It doesn't take a rocket scientist–

MEDIATOR: Can you let Brad know you heard him by putting it into your words? I know it's hard.

SUE: What I heard you say is that you spent most of August by yourself and that you contacted her only a few times. And you said that I kept pushing up the timetable and you felt yourself withdrawing.

MEDIATOR: *(To Brad)* Is there anything else you feel she needed to hear. You said a lot of other things. Is there anything else you need to hear from her?

BRAD: I don't know how important or significant it is. In this conversation, we sort of walked ourselves through this entire torturous period of time...*(pause)*

SUE: When you moved out, you told me that you hadn't made a decision yet.

BRAD: Yeah, that's true.

MEDIATOR*: (To Sue)* You don't look like you think that's true.

SUE: I don't think that's true because of your actions; your behaviors didn't match what you were saying. So when you moved out, you brought a brand new piece of furniture. Within a few days to a week, you bought a washer and dryer and ordered a brand-new bed. You were setting up a household.

BRAD: I knew I was going to be living on my own for at least a couple months. *(Sue laughs derogatorily.)* I was sleeping on the couch; I had stuff in boxes –

SUE: Let me finish! So for most people who think they might return, they're not going to spend lots of money. They'll borrow things from other people; they'll move into an apartment, they'll lease things because they might return. That's why I felt led on. You're telling me one thing and then I find out you bought a washer and dryer, you got new furniture, and then I come to your home and her things are decorating the house everywhere. And yet you told me there was a possibility of us getting back together. *(Sue starts to cry here.)* The direction was away from me and yet you kept telling me you hadn't made a decision yet.

BRAD: Uh-huh.

SUE: Can you understand the depth of pain caused by her presence in the house and mine wasn't there?

BRAD: Yes, I understand that.

Again, Brad does not speak specifically enough, and the mediator needs to help him, either by asking him to put into his own words how painful it was for Sue to see anything of Amy's in his apartment or to model the empathic response first and then have him repeat it in his own words.

SUE: Yeah, I kept being told, "I haven't made that decision yet."

MEDIATOR: And that hurt.

BRAD: I Imagine that it did feel awful, and I can certainly understand that. There were two of the three pieces of furniture that came from our house. I'm sure it felt strange to be sitting on things that came from our house in an alien environment with other people's stuff around. A lot of the things in the house were borrowed, and mostly when Amy and I talked during August and September, we talked about how we were not going to be seeing each other and how much time we needed to be alone. We weren't talking about how we were going to create a new relationship together. When she came back after her trip and we saw each other in early September, we were happy to see each other, but we were not making plans for how we were going to create a relationship. We were actually talking about how much or how little we could see each other and still give me the space to be by myself. That's actually what we were talking about. In fact, it's still what we talk about.

MEDIATOR: So are you saying that did not mislead Sue? She was sensing that you were clearly pulling away. Was there any sense that you could go either way at that point from your perspective?

BRAD: *(Sigh)* I guess on some level I was trying to create the space for it to go either way. So I felt really wounded by having to leave my house, my cats, our marriage, and I felt really adrift. Living alone was a really new experience, so I was just sort of in this place where I wasn't one thing or another. I was just actually trying to create my own space. I didn't even know what it would feel like to create my own space. I'm swimming in a bunch of stuff that's borrowed and I don't know how I want to decorate it. I don't know what I want to hang on the walls. So most of my attention was going mostly on that. And I was getting help from other people, Emily, Judy, Jim about how to create my home. And I was sleeping on the couch.

MEDIATOR: You're attention wasn't going toward relationship in either direction; it was kind of relationship with yourself. How were you going to create a home for yourself that would feel like home. And what I get was the most devastating for you in that time period was being asked to leave and leaving everything that was comfortable and familiar.

BRAD: Yeah. So that was where most of my attention was going. There was also a big part of my attention…my attention to myself was going there, like how do I nurture myself? Why do I feel so needy, to feel pulled to be with other people? It was almost intolerable for me to just sit home alone. And I'm not talking about Amy; I'm talking about I want to be out with Emily or Jim or in a bar or listening to music or a movie or something. It was just hard to be in the house. So that's what August was like, and so most of my attention was going toward creating a home for myself. Not a home for Amy and me, a home for myself. And when Amy came back, then there were two conversations starting to happen. So what am I doing with my marriage? How do I feel about you? *(Sue)* Can I actually come back in and create a life with you? Coming from this place that I'm starting to feel in myself? How do I feel about Amy? Is there actually a possibility that we could create a life together, because there's nothing idyllic about that either? So that's pretty much what was happening in September when we sat down. And when you asked me the question…when you kept asking me to make up my mind or give you an indication–

SUE: When we met a week later–

MEDIATOR: *(The mediator indicates non verbally that Sue should first respond.)*

SUE: You just said that it was really difficult for you being alone in that month of August because you were learning to be alone and you wanted to do anything other than being alone. And boy, do I know that feeling!

BRAD: Uh-huh.

SUE: And you were trying to figure out what is my marriage, what's going on with my relationship with Amy, and feeling really lost and adrift and then you had all this stuff around you that wasn't your stuff and it was borrowed stuff and you were trying to figure out how to work with it. And then you started conversations with Amy. I don't know how to acknowledge anything about those conversations you had.

Sue shows improvement at empathy when reminded by the mediator but misses the part about the content of Brad's conversations with Amy regarding how much or little time to spend together so he can have more alone time.

MEDIATOR: You did acknowledge and understand the feeling of being alone...

SUE: I understand how you felt alone, I understand the feeling of having all kind of weird stuff in your house that is not really yours, wow, how do I make it mine but it's not mine because it's borrowed...

BRAD: Right, I don't even know how long I'm going to be here.

SUE: And I can understand the lost feeling, and that you didn't know how long you were even going to be there. And then when I asked you what am I supposed to do with your things, all you said was that I don't need to suit you. And when I asked if there was any reason I should sit around, you said no. But you were never clear. What changed in a week? How did you make the decision?

Sue makes progress here in her attempt to be empathic and then asks a direct question.

BRAD: I understand your question. And there isn't anything that changed in the week. But what happened for me was I remembered the feeling of just sitting with you and talking with you and the whole pattern of what had been happening for us is that we had been moving further and further apart whether it was through your actions or my actions or our actions.

SUE: I-statements please!

BRAD: Okay, so I was just feeling the whole momentum of what had unfolded for months and I heard you asking me to make a decision, that we originally talked about the end of the year and you didn't want to wait that long, so you wanted a decision by November 1. So I was sitting and thinking, okay, that's only six weeks away, what is going to change in the next six weeks? What is happening for me? And then, actually, all I did was kind of drop into my body and said "Guts, what's the truth? What's the truth?" And my gut feeling was that we're not going to make this work. We're not really back together.

SUE: So question–

MEDIATOR: First, can you respond to...

Without reminding Sue early on in the mediation that she has agreed to respond empathically to Brad until he feels understood before she comes from her frame of reference, the mediator needs to keep reminding Sue of this step now. I don't believe Sue ever understood that she agreed to do this or its importance in the conflict resolution process. This may need reiteration many times to one or both parties. For example, if Sue could see how she creates stories and misinterpretations in the vacuum of Brad's lack of clarity, perhaps she could also then see that, by responding empathically and asking for more specificity, she would have a better way to get more specificity from Brad.

SUE: So you acknowledged what I said about the sequence of events and I asked you the question of what changed? What happened? And you said that you actually checked in with your guts and said that's true.

BRAD: I also said that nothing changed.

MEDIATOR: It was kind of in response to what you felt was pressure.

Rather than coach Sue toward more empathy, the mediator tries to model it for Sue and to help Brad feel more understood. This may be sufficient to get a resolution.

BRAD: Right.

MEDIATOR: And the time frame didn't seem that far away, so you felt you then chose to check in with your gut at that point, rather than wait for six weeks and your gut said...

BRAD: It's pretty clear I actually had a clear gut level feeling–

SUE: Can you tell me from your gut, if you can remember, why couldn't the marriage work, why had you released it, why was no effort made? Because personally, for me, I didn't want you to go. And I kept telling you that. And I kept feeling you move farther and farther away. So when you make a "we" statement, it's true for you, but it's not true for me. I told you that in Hawaii too. I don't think you heard me. My feeling is that you haven't wanted to hear me all along because it made it harder for you to make your choice. And I kept trying to tell you "being in love" doesn't last. Love does! And that's what I offered you again. And you said no.

Sue asks a direct question about why Brad decided to let the marriage go and then honestly acknowledges she didn't want to end the marriage.

BRAD: I can't answer your question about why. Not from a gut place. It's just a gut feeling. I mean I have all my thoughts and under-standings and my awareness through therapy, feedback from friends, and all sorts of other data, I guess, or other people's commentary, but that's not a response to your question. From a gut place, I don't have an answer.

MEDIATOR: What else did you hear her say?

BRAD: I heard you say that love lasts, and being in love doesn't, and that even when we met in September that you had the hope and the intention that we would get back together. *(Long pause and Brad starts to cry.)* That brings us to the point where we contacted you *(to the mediator)*.

When Brad puts into his own words that Sue wanted the marriage to continue he uncovers his own emotion of pain and sadness. I be-lieve Sue needed to witness that before she could begin to shift from her emotional stasis.

MEDIATOR: You've traveled a long way and now you've come to this point.

(To Sue) So that was another devastating thing for you in September, when it became clear that your hope that the two of you could work on the marriage and you could get back together was destroyed.

SUE: Yes, I made that offer and I was turned down. *(To Brad)* So you asked me to trust you, every time I offered you my hand it was slapped away, every time I tried to reconcile I was turned away.

MEDIATOR: Sue, do you think he should have gone against his gut? By going with his gut is that slapping you away?

SUE: I would have liked to have seen a greater period of time with no contact with either of us and then make a gut decision. Personally, I don't think you gave yourself enough time.

MEDIATOR: So that's your...

SUE: So that's my interpretation. So in my view, I don't think at that time you should have followed your gut. I wished you the best, but it made it kind of clear in some respects that you actually left in July...with no intention of returning. And you couldn't admit it to yourself, so how could you admit it to me?

MEDIATION: And that's your interpretation of it.

SUE: That's my interpretation...I'm the one who actually had to ask you to leave and make a choice. I mean I was losing my mind a couple of times at home. I lost it. Brad witnessed it. I said I can't do this any more; you're making me crazy.

MEDIATOR: So you were feeling great internal pressure, and that was causing you to create a time line.

SUE: *(Defensive tone of voice)* I had no one to talk to for many months. I was doing it all on my own. They had each other to talk to. Brad and I couldn't talk about the situation anymore because my energy would get too big, so he would shut down. I didn't know who to talk to, and when I tried, I got slapped down.

BRAD: I hear you saying "slapped down" and I hear you talking about how, from your point of view, I had no intention of coming back to live with you again, and I can understand how it might look that way. But I can tell you from the inside, that wasn't my experience. I spent the first couple months in that house doing temporary things. I bought the cheapest stuff I could. You know I got a washer and dryer because I just refuse to go to the laundromat twice a week. I spent $200 on a junky used pair of machines. I didn't make big investments. I didn't make investments in the house. I didn't talk to Amy about long-term relationship stuff, and in fact I didn't talk to her about you and me. I've always held a pretty solid boundary around our relationship, and I haven't discussed our relationship or our mediation process with her. I don't know what else to say about that period. I'm sorry you felt slapped down. You've used that phrase several times today and–

MEDIATOR: It's one way of saying rejected?

SUE: Yeah, rejected, and I'm not as important as she is. We're in love, so everything she says, she walks on water. I'm just in the way!

MEDIATOR: So again, that's your story.

SUE: That's the way it felt!

MEDIATOR: And of course there's probably no way you would not feel rejected.

SUE: No!

MEDIATOR: Perfectly normal. Of course you would feel rejected.

SUE: How could I not?

MEDIATOR: But could you reflect back what Brad has just said...like he didn't make big investments...

SUE: You didn't make big investments, you actually didn't spend a lot of money, that you were not talking to her about our relationship, you weren't even talking that much about your relationship to her, and that you understand how I might have felt slapped down.

BRAD: I also did feel a lot of pressure throughout that period to make a decision.

SUE: The pressure was yours! When we originally went into our triage, you were supposed to make a decision by December 1, but you said November 1. I actually moved it up one month, but you moved it up two. My experience is the pressure was coming from within you.

Without continuing to remind Sue that the B-E-A-R Process requires her to empathize first and only then come from her perspective with I-messages, and then coaching her to do it, this pattern will just keep repeating.

MEDIATOR: So you're saying both of you were creating that pressure to make a decision.

SUE: I don't like living in limbo; no one does *(defensive tone of voice)*. But I thought going to the end of December...I didn't want to go through the holidays that way so I had to move it up to December 1. And then when I made that suggestion, Brad said no, let's move it up to November 1. And then when we got together in September and I asked what was the purpose of this meeting, he said, "Well, just to check in with each other." And after we did logistics, it was "My feeling is I don't want to be married to you." And so I asked, "Is this a decision?" And he said, "No, its a choice, these are my feelings." I asked, "Are you going to change your mind in six months or a year?" And he said, "No, I don't think I'm going to change my mind." I said, "What's the difference between making a choice and making a decision?" I didn't really understand what you had said at that point, and then I said, "Actually, it sounds like you can't love me the way I need to be loved."

BRAD: Right.

SUE: And you said, "That's absolutely true."

BRAD: That was actually a very profound thing to say.

SUE: After he gave me the explanation, which I didn't understand, I felt into myself, what it sounds like, feels like, is that you can't love me the way I need to be loved. And you said that was absolutely true. *(Sue is crying here)*

BRAD: And that was actually the statement that brought clarity, certainly for me. And it was a–

SUE: And that's when I said, so it sounds like you need to seek your own…

Sue interrupts Brad again at what might have been an important communication. It takes a lot of assertiveness on the mediator's part to monitor and enforce the B-E-A-R structure at times like this, but it brings many rewards. This is one of those times that interruption must not be allowed. Brad was potentially about to say something that he had clarity on, the lack of which has driven Sue crazy for years, and then she cuts him off from saying it, a loss for both of them.

SUE: So, again, I'm the one who had to act. I'm the one who had to leave. I'm the one who had to put it in words.

BRAD: Uh-huh.

MEDIATOR: So you're the person who provides clarity in this relationship.

SUE: Well, I used to be the rock too. I was always there.

BRAD: I would say ultimately that I think that you have been the person who has provided clarity in our relationship.

SUE: I never wanted the relationship to end.

BRAD: I understand.

SUE: I believe that a big part of the relationship ending is you not being able to tell me how you feel. For whatever reasons, you haven't been able to tell me how you really feel, or maybe you didn't really know how you really felt.

BRAD: That's certainly been true lots of the time.

Brad acknowledges his inability to disclose his feeling to Sue. It would be good for the mediator to coach him into putting this into his own words so Sue could hear him saying it. (This is the Acknowledge phase of the model).

SUE: So that's a really big piece of it. That's one of the reasons we're not in relationship anymore, and that's why...and my hurt is... because I didn't know how you were feeling, there was nothing I could do to help make the relationship work one way or another because you were holding all the cards. By me not knowing that there's a problem, there's nothing I can do to try and work with you to solve the problem. Because I don't know it exists.

Sue finally feels exonerated after she explains her view that the re-lationship didn't work because Brad couldn't tell her his feelings that rendered her powerless. Having Brad acknowledge this part of his re-sponsibility is a major piece in getting emotional resolution for Sue.

MEDIATOR: *(To Sue)* So you're very good at analyzing what's wrong with Brad or what Brad contributed. Before this last period from March on, going back the other twenty years, what part can you own?

The mediator takes a risk here by asking if Sue can take some responsibility for what went wrong in the marriage, a skill in the Acknowledge Phase of the Model. Without this step of getting the par-ties to take responsibility for at least some part of the problem, they can remain fixated on the other person's fault, which does not bode well for a mediated resolution. The person who feels done unto of-ten resists taking any responsibility for any part in what happened. The B-E-A-R Process purposely puts this into the dialogue because we have found it a powerful way to facilitate a more collaborative atmosphere.

SUE: I was living in denial. But when we chose the ground rules in our relationship, one of the ground rules of our relationship was we're going to speak the truth to each other and not make it safe. We're going to be willing to say what we need to say and I honored that. When I was upset, I told you. I put ground rules in place for myself. When I was upset with you, I would tell you within thirty-six hours. That was to make sure I told you my truth. And what I hear you saying through all of this is that you didn't honor that ground rule when we put it into place eight or nine years ago. And what really hurt was when you didn't tell me the truth about everything. We had that ground rule in place and that was supposed to be happening. And I've been telling you the truth. Well, I'm sorry, you haven't been telling me the truth.

Note how quickly Sue gets away from taking any responsibility for her part. In response to the mediator's question "What part can you own?" she states, "I was living in denial," but immediately begins to focus on what Brad didn't do.

MEDIATOR: You feel that you abided by the ground rule and Brad didn't.

Here the mediator empathically responds to the content about Brad but not to the part for which the mediator actually asked. In a sense, Sue manipulates the content of the dialogue. Ideally, the mediator could say: " So you feel that you abided by the ground rule and Brad didn't. And did I also hear you say that your part in what happened between you was that you were living in denial? Could you say more about how your denial contributed to things not working?"

BRAD: The ground rule was not about always telling the truth; the ground rule was about if you have something to say, if there's something you're upset about, then you need to talk about it within three days after the time it happens, seventy-two hours. That was the ground rule.

SUE: That was my personal ground rule.

BRAD: That was one of the three ground rules we set up for us.

SUE: I remember a ground rule saying that we're choosing truth over safety.

BRAD: I remember we talked about that. We had three ground rules: the ground rule of monogamy, the seventy-two-hour rule, and... what was the third ground rule?

SUE: That divorce was not an option.

BRAD: That was the third one.

SUE: We're going to do whatever it takes to make this relationship work.

BRAD: So those three ground rules were set up.

SUE: I'm sorry. I disagree. The ground rule for me was to make sure I told you within–

Here Brad interrupts Sue. The same standard of no interruptions needs to apply to each party.

BRAD: Well, we set the intention to tell the truth, and to be honest, and this is where I've been out of integrity. *(Long pause)* I haven't been willing to say how I've been feeling. And it is true that Amy and I have set a ground rule of being completely honest with each other at all times and that is mostly to force me to be in integrity with myself. There are times when painful things would come up or when I would have a feeling or a doubt, I wouldn't express them to you because that's when we would have blow-ups. That's when, in my experience, over and over again, it wasn't safe for me to talk about my feelings, and I really want to own my side of that...that I was unwilling to take the risk! This isn't about Sue making it unsafe, this is actually about me being unwilling to take the risk of saying what was actually true for me and spending the time to connect to it and say it regardless of what kind of blow-up I was going to have to face. And that's where I've been off. I mean that's actually been shocking for me to actually spend a lot of time connecting to what I'm actually feeling because I've mostly suppressed that and that's sucked the juice out of our relationship.

SUE: That's what I've been waiting for you to say!

BRAD: Oh boy!

This provides an excellent example of someone taking responsibility for his or her contribution to the problem. Brad could have blamed Sue for not making it safe for him to express his feelings by blowing up or by just not being empathic, but he doesn't do that. He explicitly states that it isn't about Sue not making it safe but about his unwillingness to take the risk of speaking honestly about his feelings. He says what Sue has not only been waiting for him to admit, but also provides a turning point in reaching a settlement agreement. This demonstrates the power of the acknowledging skill of taking responsibility in the B-E-A-R Process.

Optimally, both parties can do this, but sometimes only one of the parties needs to do it in a mediation setting. In this case, Brad may or may not need Sue to own her part. He may want her to, but since he was the one who decided to leave, he is less likely to need her to.

It would probably be enough for him to just resolve the divorce with a reasonably fair settlement. Sue, on the other hand, needed to hear Brad take responsibility for his part before she would willingly come to a settlement agreement. If Brad could not take responsibility for his part, Sue might continue to punish him in the financial part of the settlement.

SUE: Instead of blaming me for being an emotional being, which I've been for the last twenty years, to actually own that you were unwilling to be mature enough to say what needed to be said.

Ideally, the mediator could coach Sue to demonstrate that she actually heard Brad's taking responsibility for his part of their relationship problems and expressing her appreciation rather than letting her slip in another dig about his lack of maturity.

Both parties have missed that Sue's contributions to the problems in the relationship have been her propensity not only to blow up, but also to make accusations, to treat her interpretations as facts, to interrupt, and to avoid empathy when they had a difference of opinion. In a couple's counseling session, these issues would need attention. In this mediation session, the major obstacle to a settlement agreement has surfaced by Brad owning up to his fear of telling Sue his honest feelings without turning it around to make it her fault. Brad's taking responsibility produces the key in this mediation for them to reach a financial settlement.

BRAD: It's not about being mature. It's about the fact that I am a fear-based type; I am always paralyzed by fear. It's just where I'm really conflicted.

MEDIATOR: This is a part of your makeup and just making a rule isn't going to change it.

BRAD: That's right.

MEDIATOR: It's much deeper and it requires a lot of work and time to be able to do it.

BRAD: That's part of what's been really difficult about my therapy this year. That's actually what I've had to drop into. And so I'm well aware of the fact that my willingness to get into conflict would have been really good for us.

SUE: Which you wouldn't have with me.

BRAD: That's right. I was afraid to initiate it.

SUE: And then I was always the bad mommy.

While it helps for Brad to continue to take responsibility for his part in what went wrong in the relationship, and for Sue to feel exonerated, it would also help here for the mediator to have Sue empathically respond to Brad's confessions of responsibility to make sure she hears them and for Brad to feel understood. Somehow when a person finally hears the other admit responsibility, it ironically proves very hard to hear and believe, but putting what the other person owns into one's own words facilitates this process. Evidently, the scar tissue from such a wound shields hearing and requires many repetitions before the message penetrates enough for the listener to absorb and believe it.

BRAD: I'm practicing taking the risk of telling the truth. If there's a sacred teaching from our marriage for me, it is that the worst thing I can do is not be completely honest and not tell the truth no matter what the consequences.

MEDIATOR: *(To Brad)* Makes it a lot harder later on, don't you find that?

BRAD: Yeah, I mean its pay me now or pay me later.

Brad has gone through most of the stages of making reparation: empathy, acknowledgment of his part of what went wrong, apologizing for it, and finally as the Resolve stage will illustrate, his willingness to make reparation. It might help for the reader to review how these skills are listed under the Empathize, Acknowledge, and Respond phases of the B-E-A-R Process by reviewing Figure 1.

BRAD: We've gotten to an amazing place, and it's at the end of our time. I'd just like to bring up two questions: a sort of metaphysical one and a practical one. My metaphysical question is that...I feel like I am being really accountable here and I'm really sorry that I didn't take more risks, that is where I failed you, and failed us. I have no idea how you would answer that question for yourself. I really don't, but I would be curious to know. In other words, what could you have brought to our relationship that would have changed it? I'm just curious.

Now that Brad has owned up to his part, he asks if Sue will do that. If Sue could reciprocate, it could help them to come to a settlement agreement more easily and collaboratively. On the other hand, even if

Sue is not willing to reciprocate, they have still moved closer to a settlement. Sue may still want him to pay for abandoning and betraying her, but since he has admitted his part, she is less likely to make unreasonable demands that would require them to go the more adversarial route. The role of empathy in this model plays a particularly crucial role because it makes taking responsibility somewhat safer. Brad has had just enough empathy, particularly from the mediator, that he can acknowledge his part. Without this, I believe the likelihood of a mediated agreement would decline significantly.

Additionally, Sue needed an arena in which to express her feelings of anger and hurt to an empathizing ear. The mediator has done this well and has coached Brad to empathize as best he could. Sue needed someone to hear how Brad betrayed her by not meeting his commitments, so she could feel exonerated of blame and humiliation. Once she has expressed her feelings and opinions and hears empathy for them, she can more likely move on to a settlement. Optimally, Sue could have learned more about how to empathize, give I-messages, and take responsibility for her part in the problems, but, as noted previously, this is not necessary to get a settlement.

MEDIATOR: We could take this up next time.

BRAD: Yeah, it's just something to think about. And the other question is...I've made an offer about resolving our finances, dividing our finances. I've offered you more than 57 percent of everything we own. I've offered you 35 percent more than I would get, okay, and I would like you to consider what you actually want and need as we divide our resources. It's just a question for the next couple weeks because I've made an offer and so on some level–

SUE: Well, I'm thinking about it.

MEDIATOR: *(To Sue)* It might be good for you to come in with something like a proposal or–

BRAD: Yeah, a proposal, make a counterproposal.

MEDIATOR: Fine. *(To Sue)* So those are two questions. Are you willing to entertain those?

SUE: Yeah. I have to write them down.

The second mediation session ends much better than the previous session. Since we don't know how much of Brad's acknowledgments

Sue actually heard we can't really know with any certainty what will happen in the next session. If Sue has heard Brad, they will more likely be able to address the financial part of the settlement agreement in a fruitful way. This session illustrates how the B-E-A-R Process, however imperfectly implemented, can create a structure by which parties can express their perspectives fully and have them heard, without interruption, and then have them understood (empathy). If this can create enough of a safe environment for the parties to share more honestly and fully what they really want in the settlement and why, it will significantly facilitate the process.

Each party empathizing with the other can also create enough safety for one or both parties to begin acknowledging areas of agreement and taking responsibility for their part in what happened. This taking personal responsibility creates an interpersonal ambiance more conducive to an agreement that each party considers fair. They can tailor the agreement to fit their unique needs and priorities.

THE THIRD MEDIATION SESSION TRANSCRIPT

MEDIATOR: We ended our last session with you, Brad, asking Sue two questions. Something about her part in what happened in your relationship overall, and then you wanted her to consider your proposal.

SUE: What I've discovered through therapy about my part in all of this is that I let the pattern continue that should have ended twenty years ago. Basically, when we met after the birth of Dottie and we went to your apartment and you told me point-blank, "I cannot be in a relationship with you and be monogamous with you," at that time I gave up my personal value of monogamy to stay in relationship with you. I betrayed myself to stay in relationship with you. I did that for twenty years! I thought when we got married that you had agreed to monogamy. I continued that pattern, thinking, and by you not saying anything, that you had agreed to that rule and that you were in agreement with how I was feeling. I didn't discover that pattern until we were sitting in this office. By you not saying anything, you weren't actually agreeing with me, you were just not saying anything. So I took your silence as agreement and that's how we operated for twenty years.

BRAD: We talked about it a year or two ago.

The mediator should have here asked Brad to respond empathically to Sue, both to make sure Brad heard Sue answer his question, and for Sue to feel heard. This major acknowledgment on Sue's part could shift the tone of the entire mediation. When something good like this occurs, the mediator can reinforce it by empathizing with it. The mediator might coach Brad to do the empathizing, but the mediator can do the empathizing as well, as long as this important statement of acknowledging her part does not pass without response. It also would encourage Sue to stay with her part of things rather than deflecting the focus to Brad.

SUE: Then about six years ago, you betrayed yourself and gave up your values to stay in relationship with me, whatever those values are, monogamy or whatever it is, because you didn't want to be monogamous with me. We ended that when we changed the ground rules. Then I gave up my values and betrayed myself again to stay in a relationship with you. I did that for a month and a half and then I finally decided I couldn't do this anymore. *(Sue starts crying.)* I should have ended it twenty years ago. Through all this process, you have said. "I haven't made a decision," and I believe you when you say you didn't know. I believe you when you say, to a certain extent, that you didn't know that this was having the kind of impact on our relationship that it was. And I don't think I'll ever be able to forgive you for that, at least not now. It's too painful the way it was enacted. It's too painful with what I've been dealing with for the last months, and it continues. So my part is, everything else is a part of that pattern, betrayal of my values, betrayal of my values, betrayal of my values. I knew. You told me. I went into denial to stay in relationship with you. That's my piece in this. I set up the pattern of deceit.

MEDIATOR: Are you saying *you* did?

SUE: I did. I told Brad I don't want to know about it. I don't want to hear about it. Not in my bed. So Brad heard that and didn't tell me.

MEDIATOR: And when did you say that?

SUE: Twenty years ago. And then we changed that and then he was monogamous. It was never discussed that we weren't telling each other the truth. And I didn't need to know about it. But then when we changed the ground rules for the final time in March, then I did want

to know what was going on. But Brad was still withholding information from me. He was under the agreement that we weren't supposed
to talk about it for three months. In my mind that was not...let's do
a check in three months and if we need to talk about something, let's
talk about it.

MEDIATOR: Even before the check-in?

SUE: Even before the check-in. But he didn't understand it that
way.

MEDIATOR: You recognize that he had a different
understanding.

SUE: And that he was operating under the rules that were in place
for twenty years. I believed him when he said that...and also covered
his ass! He didn't have to confront me.

BRAD: I did confront you; it was less than three months later.

SUE: We both understand that. I believe I initiated the
conversation.

MEDIATOR: So before we go into that, Brad, can you reflect
back in your words the acknowledgment you heard Sue make, so she
knows you heard it and because you asked for it?

*The mediator makes a crucial intervention here. I attribute the
distinctly different tone coming from Sue in this session to Brad's taking responsibility for his not being fully honest and explicit with Sue
about how he felt and to Sue hearing it. She now reciprocates in
response to Brad's request. Without an empathic response this can
unravel, and Sue could quickly become accusatory again because acknowledging her part of something that went badly leaves her vulnerable, particularly when negotiating a settlement that involves money
and her quality of life.*

BRAD: So I understand you feel accountable in that you betrayed
yourself when you agreed to enter into a relationship with me back
when Dottie was born, and you described how we've had this pattern of self-betrayal. That in some sense when I made a commitment
to our monogamous relationship–that was also a self-betrayal. And
when you released me from that commitment in March–that was a
self-betrayal for you. And that you finally got to a place where you
just couldn't do that anymore.

Brad has the content accurate, but his tone of voice is pretty flat and without much feeling.

SUE: I hear you saying it. I don't hear the feelings underneath it. I don't let it...I don't see it penetrating within. I hear you're in your head. So I still don't feel heard.

MEDIATOR: Do you know what she's asking for?

BRAD: No, not really. I've noticed this pattern of self-betrayal for...you know, I've been working with it ever since we separated. Cause I've been stuck in the same question. Why did we come to this? I've been working with it in my therapy process. So I know how I've talked to you about how I feel like I betrayed myself as much as I've betrayed you. We talked about that months ago. So I've felt a lot of grief about this for...I'm just sort of wrung out because–

MEDIATOR: *(To Sue)* Do you hear his sincerity?

SUE: I hear his intention. I hear someone who doesn't want to deal with the emotions because it hurts too much.

MEDIATOR: So do you have a picture in your mind of what it would look like if Brad were dealing with his emotions?

SUE: Yes. *(To Brad)* I haven't seen you shed very many tears about the end of our relationship after twenty years. Maybe you're sharing them privately with someone else or with yourself. But I don't see them, so for me it belittles the twenty years we've been together.

This reveals the next level of what Sue needs before she will come to a settlement agreement. Now that Brad has admitted his part in what went wrong, she wants to see him cry as a sign of how important the relationship with her has been. Otherwise, she feels he diminishes the importance of their time together, particularly because Brad does not express his feelings as openly as she does. If he shed tears or had a more feeling tone of voice, she could believe that she had meant something to him.

MEDIATOR: So for you, if Brad isn't shedding tears, then he's not feeling it deeply.

SUE: No, I see the eyes watering up and then I see...or my imagination is that he doesn't want the emotions to come out. When I can't feel that, I don't feel a connection. And maybe that's all he's capable of giving right now.

MEDIATOR: Well the two of you have different ways of expressing yourselves and your emotions.

SUE: Yes, we do.

MEDIATOR: *(To Brad)* Do you think you're feeling empathy for what she said?

BRAD: Yes. I've cried about our relationship so much I'm just kind of tired of crying. I'm sure my therapist would comment that I'm one of her wettest customers. We've been working on this in therapy since last May. Sue made a comment when we first sat down outside about how her grief kind of comes in bursts. And that's what I experience also. That's the way grief works for me and I've had a lot of bursts. On some level, talking about how I feel about all this is just exhausting. *(Brad is tearing here and the mediator hands him a tissue.)* Thank you. So, you know, like I've talked about how I feel about this to friends and to my therapist for months and months and months and I've cried a lot, and I don't feel like I'm here to connect with you *(to Sue)*. I feel like I'm here to communicate with you, but I don't feel I can form the connection that you're asking for. I don't know if I can do that at this point.

SUE: I hear you.

MEDIATOR: So you have felt a lot of grief and shed a lot of tears and you're kind of exhausted from it. And you're obviously not all cried out, but this is not what you've come here to do.

BRAD: Well, that's also true.

MEDIATOR: So, although you're trying to understand Sue here, you're purpose isn't to make a good connection. And in some ways, in order to move forward and do this business part, feeling that connection, for you, might not fit with that.

BRAD: Well, as far as our negotiation and mediation is concerned, it's important to me that we do it cooperatively, but cooperatively is different from being in a connected place.

MEDIATOR: It could be respectful.

BRAD: Yes, certainly respectful.

MEDIATOR: But not necessarily connected.

BRAD: Right.

MEDIATOR: *(To Sue)* Has he basically reflected back accurately what you said? Is there anything else you've said that you want to make sure he heard?

The mediator checks if Sue feels understood because if Sue does not feel understood on this deeper level, she still will not willingly proceed to negotiate the financial settlement.

SUE: *(To Brad)* Are you satisfied with how I responded to your request?

BRAD: I appreciate the fact that you answered my question.

SUE: Is there anything more that you need from me?

BRAD: *(Long pause)* No.

MEDIATOR: Shall we move on to the next issue?

SUE: Do we need to tape this part?

MEDIATOR: No.

The mediator turned the tape recorder off at this point and resumed the financial negotiations that had stalled before she introduced the B-E-A-R Process three sessions ago. Brad began by saying he had consulted an attorney in regard to Sue's earlier settlement proposals and was prepared to respond to those proposals. The mediator remembered that Brad had announced in an earlier session that he planned to do so, but Sue responded with surprise and anger.

Brad voiced that he agreed with nine out of twelve of Sue's proposals and that he had only minor exceptions to the remaining three. Without going into detail on all twelve proposals, Brad's counterproposals agreed with Sue's proposal that they split all of their assets on a fifty-fifty basis even though they had a verbal agreement during their marriage that they would pay for joint expenses on the basis of their incomes which turned out to be a ratio of 5:7 for Brad and 2:7 for Sue.

Brad voiced concern about the amount of spousal support Sue proposed over and above this fifty-fifty split of their joint assets (which included a house, three cars, a stock investment account, three different retirement accounts, a time-share property, furniture, and art objects). After subtracting various post separation expenses they came to a total net amount of joint assets to split fifty-fifty. Brad reluctantly agreed to the fifty-fifty split and also agreed to Sue's proposal that she use her share of the joint assets to buy him out of his portion of the house so she could remain living there. Given the house appraisal, this meant that Sue would owe Brad approximately five thousand dollars over and above her share of the joint assets to buy him out of the house.

What Brad did not agree with was a five thousand dollar amount Sue asked for to make repairs on the house. He also wanted to claim income tax credit on some of his payments following their separation, which Sue had not agreed to. They also both wanted certain pieces of art on which they had not agreed.

Toward the end of the session, Brad offered not only to pay the five thousand for repairs but an additional five thousand so Sue would have some cash after the divorce, if she would agree to give him the tax write-off and a couple of the pieces of artwork they both wanted. This meant that Sue would end up with the house free and clear plus the money she needed to make the repairs. This seemed to surprise Sue in a positive way, but she said she would need to consult her attorney before making any final decision. The session ended there.

What follows summarizes what happened during the final settlement conference. The mediator wrote the following immediately after the final session: "Sue came in a totally different place. The first thing she did was to apologize to Brad and me for her disrespectful behavior at the last few sessions. It was a clean apology. She is still grieving, in pain, and tearing up, but her attitude of attacking victim seems to have subsided. She was more relaxed, less rigid, more real, open, and honest. Brad reiterated that he was shaken that Sue wanted the fifty-fifty split, even though their contribution to joint expenses had been 5:7 to 2:7 all along and that the division of labor around the house had been relatively equal. Nevertheless, he knew the community property law would require the fifty-fifty split anyway if they went to court, so he was resigned to this part of Sue's proposal. He did not agree with the level of spousal support Sue proposed (which was over and above the formula that pertains in their county) but was willing to pay an up-front amount that would enable Sue to stay in the house free and clear plus five thousand dollars for her to make immediate repairs as she wished.

Sue then made a counter proposal, which only differed from this proposal in minor ways, and Brad readily agreed to it for a smooth final negotiation, each giving and taking easily (e.g., Sue wanted an

extra piece of artwork, Brad wanted a little more time to get his be-
longings out of the house). Sue's car had been damaged in an acci-
dent the previous week, and Brad loaned her a car to drive until she
could repair her car. They both voiced appreciation for the work that
had been done with them. They added up the total cost of the divorce
at $9,200, higher than most mediated divorces in the area, and it took
nine sessions, about three more than average. However, they know
how much more they would have spent in the adversarial process.
Each would have had to pay a retainer of five thousand dollars just to
get started. They both left feeling good about how they handled their
divorce and are on their road to healing."

SUMMARY COMMENTS ON THE MEDIATION SESSIONS

The mediator's financial negotiation method seemed to work well, but only after Brad and Sue went through the B-E-A-R Process. The mediator originally suggested the B-E-A-R Process because Brad and Sue reached an impasse after four mediation sessions in which the parties offered proposals and counter proposals to each other. The process totally stalled because Sue felt deeply angered and hurt by what she perceived as a betrayal of her. She continued to make proposals over and above what the law would have required of Brad and refused any of Brad's proposals, even fairly minor ones with no adverse effect on her (*e.g.*, being able to claim certain items as tax deductions).

A party who feels "wronged" often behaves this way. This perception of feeling wronged may or may not reflect reality. Either way, it stalls the collaborative process and often leads the parties to abandon the mediation process for the adversarial route. In the case of Brad and Sue, Sue's belief that Brad had betrayed her and her feelings of hurt and anger blocked any further negotiations. Feeling he would never understand her or take responsibility for what he had done to her, she felt determined to make him pay financially. He felt that no matter what he said she wouldn't believe him and felt hopeless to get a negotiated settlement under those circumstances.

When the mediator suggested another way to dialogue with each other to get through this impasse, they each agreed for a variety of reasons, most obviously that they might prevent spending even more time and money by hiring attorneys to go the adversarial route.

In addition, they would have less control over the final settlement and would likely end up feeling even worse about each other.

It appears that Brad did not want to feel angry or bitter toward Sue. He felt sad about how things turned out, but he felt increasingly clear that his fear of Sue's intense emotionality had aggravated his already hesitant ability to deal directly and honestly with emotional issues. He learned that Sue's allegations that he had not been fully open and honest with her had some truth. Even though he felt strongly that he had not started an affair with another woman as Sue accused him, he began to realize how his silence contributed to Sue's propensity to draw very negative inferences about his behavior. Continuing the mediation even when Sue gave him many angry You-messages enabled him to get some emotional closure with Sue and make reparation. He appeared to have little ill will toward her but did not want to remain married and offered her a proposal that would help her get on with her life.

I believe Sue truly believed Brad had betrayed her, causing her anger and hurt that she attempted to mute by making Brad the bad guy. Sue used accusations to avoid feeling bad about herself. Feeling rejected aggravated her shaky self-esteem, and blame offered her a defense against feeling worse about herself. All of Sue's feelings needed expression and empathy from Brad for her to proceed with the negotiation process. She also needed to hear Brad take responsibility for something before she could agree to anything. Although Brad never took responsibility for having an affair before a particular conversation, he did take responsibility for not being more self-disclosing, open, and honest with Sue, and he apologized for it. In my opinion, this provided a necessary prerequisite for Sue to reengage in the financial negotiations.

Through the B-E-A-R Process Sue came to realize she too played a role in what happened. She began to realize how she had actually betrayed herself and her values long ago by agreeing to Brad's non-monogamy. I believe this proved crucial in her breakthrough. Without her seeing that she had some role in what happened, she would have been less willing to come to an agreement. Just as some people "need their day in court," some "need their day in mediation." Sue needed an arena in which to vent her anger and hurt, to express all of her judgments and feelings of betrayal and rejection and to have them heard and understood. Only after both the mediator and Brad repeatedly empathized with Sue, and Brad acknowledged his contributions to what happened (i.e., his lack of openness and honesty) could Sue even consider her part in the process, let alone verbalize it. The B-E-A-R Process enables the parties to do this in a fair, respectful, safe, and equitable manner. Each stage in the process brings about what each party needs in order to come to a resolution.

I believe this particular mediation process almost broke down at two places. The first breakdown came before we started the taping, when the parties came to an impasse and the mediator proposed they try the B-E-A-R Process. The second near breakdown came toward the end of the first taped session when the dialogue diverged from the B-E-A-R structure. Having it unravel at the end of the session when the mediator had no time to bring things back into alignment with the B-E-A-R Process aggravated this. For the B-E-A-R Process to work, the mediator must keep the parties in the structure. Deviations must remain minor and infrequent for the process to work optimally. But as illustrated in these transcripts, even when the structure bends significantly, it can still work.

More specifically, after a very thorough job of structuring in the beginning of the first transcript, the mediator allowed Sue to move out of the format enough times that the session ended with both participants feeling discouraged. By letting Sue vent, the mediator kept her in the process and, fortunately, Brad could endure the accusations and misinterpretations long enough to allow her finally to hear his and the mediator's empathy.

In addition, these transcripts also demonstrate the power of including the Acknowledge phase of the model. Without Brad taking responsibility for his contribution to the problems in the marriage, the mediation was unlikely to succeed.

I find it as important for mediators to be directive in enforcing the B-E-A-R Process as it is for them to remain neutral about the content of the negotiated agreement. I also believe it important that mediators not take responsibility for the outcome, only take responsibility for helping the parties to communicate clearly and respectfully throughout the B-E-A-R Process, and not promise resolution.

Finally, the method used by the mediator here for the financial negotiation echoes the typical one in which each party offers proposals and counterproposals. As illustrated in this case, this method often does not work well until the parties resolve the more emotional is-sues and achieve mutual understanding. Once the parties have gone through the mutual understanding phases of the B-E-A-R Process, it can work quite well, as this case demonstrates.

However, another method, delineated in the Resolve part of the B-E-A-R Process, can provide even more successful solutions. Once the parties achieve a deeper understanding of what is important to each of them during the mutual understanding stage, the mediator has them brainstorm potential solutions with these underlying issues and meanings for each person in mind, encouraging each party to create potential resolutions that meet as many of the important issues for each of them as possible. This method prevents parties from becom-ing locked into their own preexisting positions and often opens up solutions that neither party would have discovered alone.

For example, Brad and Sue could share what seems most impor-tant to them in resolving what remained in question. Brad could say that he wants to approximate what the law would require of him but not have spousal payments for six or more years that would jeopardize his ability to get back on his feet financially and to move on in his life emotionally. Sue might acknowledge that she finds it most important to have the house for her future financial safety and security.

Given this, the mediator would facilitate a brainstorming session in which they each explore ideas of how to get as much as possible of what both wanted. Having Sue buy off Brad's portion of the house and having Brad pay a smaller amount of spousal support in a lump sum up front, prevents his having spousal support hanging over him in the future and, at the same time, enables Sue to live safe and secure in the house. This solution would meet both of their needs and illus-trates how the process of brainstorming with each person's underlying importance in mind potentially offers a creative and collaborative way to resolve things, rather than going back and forth with proposals and counterproposals.

CONCLUSION

The B-E-A-R Process seeks primarily to achieve clarity of communication, not necessarily resolution of the conflict, although that often happens. Clarity in communication can improve a relationship as well as facilitate a more respectful and less stressful way to end one. In other words, achieving reciprocal sovereignty can mean ending a relationship more respectfully as well as improving it.

If you have a conflict of values with someone who is not physically harming you, honor their sovereignty, even if you don't approve of their actions. Likewise, if you are not harming them, follow what is important to you even in the face of disapproval. Unless what someone does has a tangible adverse effect on you, it is not your business. Unless you are adversely affecting them, it is not their business.

If you have a conflict with someone that tangibly affects you in a negative way, use the B-E-A-R Process while managing your emotions in order to stay in your cortex. If you have learned the skills in this book and use them to the best of your ability, but the other person cannot match your skills, ask if that person is willing to get help in learning these skills. If you cannot control your emotional temperature when in conflict, it indicates that you need help with past traumas now triggered by current conflict (see www.aitherapy.org).

Depending on the degree to which conflicts affect the quality of your life, and the ability of the other person to engage constructively with you or to get help, you might need to consider leaving the relationship. Your freedom to grow and live a happy life may prove more important than a relationship with someone who will not honor your sovereignty and work out mutual differences collaboratively. To the degree that you honor your own sovereignty, you will be able to handle the period of sadness and loneliness that leaving an important relationship can bring.

NEXT STEPS

We have come to the end of the book and the beginning of your journey in the land of reciprocal sovereignty. If you are experiencing a conflict with someone and are having difficulty using the skills delineated in this book, you can contact me through my website www. tonyroffers.com and ask for my help or to give you a referral. I periodically conduct workshops for people who wish to be trained in the B-E-A-R Process. I also conduct couples counseling and mediation sessions in my office.

If you are a professional therapist or relationship coach working with couples and would like further training, I periodically lead professional development workshops in how to use the B-E-A-R Process as a structure for facilitating better conflict resolution skills.

If you are a mediator and would like further training, I periodically lead workshops in how to use the B-E-A-R Process to facilitate mediated divorces, particularly when there is an impasse in the mediation process.

Finally, I also train managers and supervisors in the B-E-A-R Process for resolving conflicts in businesses and other organizational settings.

Contact me through my website www.tonyroffers.com or through my office.

Tony Roffers, PhD

3542 Fruitvale Avenue #218

Oakland, CA 94602

510-531-6730

APPENDIX A

HELPING TO EMPOWER OTHERS

How can we help others in a way that will empower them rather than make them more dependent on us? This appendix explores how to help in a way that honors others' sovereignty and empowers them to greater independence when appropriate.

How do we walk the line between giving unwanted help and failing to respond to others in need of help? We need to wait for others to ask for our help, or ask them if they would like our help before we assume a need. Exceptions to these guidelines occur in an emergency situation in which the person remains unconscious or too debilitated or distracted to answer us, or in the case of small children who cannot yet speak for themselves.

We must be aware that others might not need or want our help. When tempted to help someone, try to clarify your own underlying intention. Are you acting altruistically, or are you trying to make yourself feel better about yourself, trying to appear powerful, or trying to buy the other person's favor?

Many of us try to help in the way we would like help but not in the way the other person wants help. Giving advice before we really know the full situation stands as another common example. Another inappropriate type of helping is when we do something for others when they could learn to do it for themselves. This is called "rescuing."

Effective helping empowers the recipients to help themselves in the future. Although not always possible, anytime you can teach someone how to fish rather than just giving him a fish empowers him. The quadriplegic who has lost his ability to transfer himself from the wheelchair to the toilet is not a candidate for this kind of helping. Some people have such severe limitations that empowerment helping lies out of reach.

In most circumstances, however, even for those severely physically, emotionally, or economically disadvantaged, truly good helping empowers recipients to discover more independence and self-responsibility. Organizations that give small loans to disadvantaged people who want to start their own business provide an excellent example. I have a friend with this empowerment philosophy who goes to countries like India, Nepal, and Tibet once a year with donations from his friends and distributes money directly to people. He gives the seed money to start projects that the local people can continue long after he is gone (see **www.100friends.com**).

What follows are some guidelines for effective helping that emphasize respect for the dignity and sovereignty of the recipients and their capacity to empower themselves by whatever help they receive.

TEACH HOW TO FISH

One of my mentors, Robert Carkhuff, refers to teaching as the preferred mode of helping (see his book *The Art of Helping*).

To return to the example from my own life early in this book, if my friend Joe genuinely wanted to learn how to invest his retirement money, I would start by defining the major concepts involved in the investment world. I would need to teach him how various investments work and why they work that way. He would need to know the basic vocabulary and underlying principles of investing before I showed him how to do it. To empower Joe to invest for himself, I would need to teach him both the investment skills and the knowledge underlying those skills.

STRUCTURING AND CONTRACTING

After clarifying if the recipient really wants help and wants to learn how to do something new *(contracting)*, you need to explain how you will proceed *(structuring)*. Deciding what specifically the recipient wants to learn, when and where you will teach him, and how you each want to proceed can make the difference between success and failure. It also respects the recipient's sovereignty when you invite his input into the learning process.

Structuring constitutes the dialogue between you and the recipient that defines how the two of you will go about the teaching/learning process. Structuring clarifies who does what, where, and when, as well as how you will you go about it. The two of you agreeing to all of this forms the contract. Sometimes structuring and contracting takes a long time and can require quite a formal process. For example, when I consulted with a national association of a medical specialty to revise the training of their medical students and interns, the structuring and contracting phase took months before we agreed on how to proceed.

Using the example of my friend Joe the dialogue could go as follows:

Joe: Hey, Tony, how about showing me that investment system of yours using moving averages that you told me about last Christmas?

Tony: I'd be happy to. What made you think of that now?

Joe: I've been losing a lot of money in my 401(k) and I really don't know what I'm doing. One day I'll hear how the stock market is going up, so I'll call my HR guy and tell him to put my money back in, and then the next week it goes down again. I really don't know what to do.

Tony: I'll be happy to show you what I do. If it makes sense to you, I'll send you the manual that defines all the terms I'll use and a description of the system. After you read it, I'll gladly answer any questions you have. If you're still interested, I'll show you how I actually do it. How does that sound?

Joe: How long will it take?

Tony: I guess it will take you a couple of evenings to read the manual and understand the investment jargon, and then a couple of evenings to show you what I do each week to monitor the plan. Once you get used to doing it, it'll take about fifteen minutes each weekend to follow.

Joe: That sounds okay to me. When can we start?

Tony: I'll overnight the manual tomorrow. When you've had a chance to read it, give me call and we'll get together. I'll show you how I chart moving averages on graph paper. There are also ways to do it on a computer, but I haven't tried that yet.

Joe: Great. Thanks for taking the time!

Had Joe not initiated the process and showed a real willingness to learn, I would have questioned him further about why he wanted to learn my method or spent more time on learning why he wanted to do something different. Had he balked at the amount of time to read the manual or getting together to learn the new monitoring skills, I would have questioned going further. I even hinted at charting something on graph paper, which could have turned him against my method because he often avoids anything that takes that kind of attention to detail at a desk.

The "Get, Give, Merge, Go Model," originally developed by Robert Carkhuff in his book *Sources of Human Productivity* for use in supervisory relationships, provides one way to look at the structuring and contracting phase of helping. This means you *get* the recipient's perception of the help they need, *give* your perception of how you might help, and then *merge* the two together in a way acceptable to you both. Finally, you help them *go* for it by embarking on the helping process that will empower them.

The Merge phase of this model helps to honor your own and your recipient's sovereignty. You don't proceed until you both agree on the what, when, where, and how of the helping endeavor. This prevents a lot of misunderstandings and negative feelings surrounding the helping process. Beginning in this way demonstrates genuine respect for the right of each person to have a say in the helping process.

GET: DEMONSTRATE UNDERSTANDING BEFORE HELPING

When someone asks for your help, directly or indirectly, they usually begin by complaining or telling you about the problem. It seldom proves helpful at this point to jump in from your perspective and offer advice or suggestions. Although it often seems obvious to you, the helper, what the helpee could or should do, the helper must not initiate from his own perspective at this point if he wishes to empower the helpee. Even if you are quite content to "give them a fish" (i.e., give them advice or do it for them), many people take offense because they really don't feel like you understand their problem yet, and you may not, unless you listen longer to their explanation of the problem and what they have already tried to do about it. When someone does not feel understood, they often do not emotionally hire you, the helper, and resist what you have to say (e.g., "Yes, but I already tried that.").

You might better listen to the problem, understand why it's important to them and how they feel about it, and learn what they have already thought about it or tried. When in the Get phase of the helping model, the first thing to do is listen for:

- The problem (what the helpee cannot do for himself)
- The importance of the problem or situation to the helpee
- How the helpee feels

Once you have collected this information, try to put in your own words what you understand. For example, with Joe, I could have said: "You sound frustrated not knowing how to invest your 401(k) money and it's important to make sure you have enough money to live on in your retirement." This goes beyond just repeating verbatim what someone has said to you. You really need to listen for the problem, the importance, and the feeling very carefully and capture them as accurately as you can in your response, although not necessarily in a perfect one-sentence form. The Get phase can take a number of interchanges before the helpee feels understood and before the helper truly understands the helpee's problem.

This skill – empathic listening and responding – serves a number of purposes during the Get phase of the helping model. First, the helpee gets to explore his problem more fully in addition to venting about it. When the helper simply listens attentively and responds empathetically in the effort just to understand what the helpee experiences, the helpee has space to explore the problem and what it really means. Sometimes helpees need only this to come to their own insights or decision about what to do. When this occurs, the helper has empowered the helpee to come to his own resolution of the issue.

Frequently, however, the helpee cannot reach a resolution on his own. The helpee has, however, felt understood and respected, and therefore more likely to open to the helper's ideas or suggestions than if the helper jumped in right away. In essence, the helpee usually opens more to the helper's perspectives and input after feeling listened to and understood.

GIVE: SHARING YOUR PERSPECTIVE

In the simplest form of helping, the helper shares his ideas, views, analysis, or suggestions regarding what might resolve the helpee's problem. For example, I could have said to Joe: "If you're interested, I have an investment system that uses a technical method called 'moving averages' that helps me decide when to get in and when to get out of the market. It isn't perfect, but I've made about 13 percent on my money over the last eleven years and I'd be happy to show you how it works." This gives my idea of how I could help him in a way that would empower him to do his own investing rather than doing it for him. It tells Joe that I have a way that I think might work for him, and if he says yes, we have a Merge and we can proceed to the action or Go stage of helping.

In another simple example, someone may not know how to work an electronic device and you ask if he wants you to show him how to do it. If he says yes, you proceed to demonstrate it slowly in a step-by-step fashion. If he says no, you leave him alone.

Personalizing. More complicated forms of helping include more steps in this phase if you want to maximize the helpee's ability to take personal responsibility for his life. One very powerful skill, called personalizing, is used in psychotherapeutic contexts, but a brief explanation here might prove useful.

To personalize, the helper assists the helpee in seeing (1) what the situation really means to him, and (2) what he wants to do about it.

Our example with Joe illustrates these two steps. Rather than immediately offering to share my method of investing with Joe, which may or may not fit for him, I could have "personalized" with him as follows:

Tony: "What is really important to you about investing in your retirement plan?"

Joe: "Well, I wasn't going to get into it, but I went to my doctor last week because I started getting these strange sensations in my chest. My heart started beating fast and then would slow down and then go faster again. It was frightening. They put some kind of monitor on me for three days and it really made me think about my future. Something could happen to me and I might not be able to work or I might even die and leave Ellen with nothing she could pay the mortgage with. So I'd really like to stop losing money and maybe even make a little bit."

Tony: *"I think I get it. What happened with your heart scared you. And it made you think about what might happen if you couldn't work or if you died. So suddenly investing more wisely in your 401(k) has more importance for you."*

Joe must understand what seems important to him and what he wants to do about it before he can take more personal responsibility for investing in his 401(k) plan. This personalizing stage really helps him to understand what he wants to do and why he wants to do it.

MERGE: EVOLVE AN AGREEMENT ON HOW TO PROCEED

Still using the example of my friend Joe, let's look at how to proceed by merging the process to maintain our mutual sovereignty. Once Joe has explored his problem, understands more deeply why it's important to him, how he feels about it and what he wants to do about it, he becomes more likely both to open to my help and to act on it in a more empowered, self-responsible way.

Joe must willingly and fully participate in the helping process to empower himself. Getting a Merge on what he will do during and after learning the investment method increases his chances for success significantly.

For example, after sharing my plan that monitors mutual funds weekly and keeping some record to see if those funds move above or below a moving average, Joe saw that it required more than he wanted to deal with. As a result, we discussed alternatives such as investing in a bond fund that required monitoring interest rate changes once a month. He decided that investing in a bond fund to get a better interest rate than a money market account and tracking interest rate fluctuation only once a month fit his lifestyle better. We "merged" on that plan.

GO: TAKE ACTION AND EVALUATE

During this stage, you take the action you agreed on in the Merge phase and see how well it works. For example, Joe and I explored how he could choose a bond fund and monitor it. We went through each step of how to select the fund in his 401*(k)*, how to purchase it, and then how to monitor it and decide if and when to sell it.

You effectively help others when they learn to solve their own problems in a way that fits for them, not by making them into clones of yourself. Respecting people's sovereignty helps them in a way that fits for them, not you, and empowers them to more independence.

For example, months later I asked Joe how he was doing with his 401*(k)*. He said that after he understood the difference between an individual stock and a stock fund, and the difference between a stock fund and a bond fund, and the risk level for each, he saw that he should never have been in stock funds and felt quite content with the bond fund he had chosen. He was aware that a bond fund could lose money as interest rates go up, and knew he had to monitor interest rate changes once a month, but it pleased him to get a higher interest rate than a money market account. More important, his increased understanding led him to invest the maximum in his 401*(k)* account, and it built up more steadily than ever before.

SUMMARY

- Leave people alone who do not adversely and tangibly affect you.
- Don't try to help if someone doesn't want it or ask for it.
- Help only those who ask by empowering them, rather than making them more dependent on you, using the "Get, Give, Merge, Go Method."
- Contact me through my website **www.tonyroffers.com** if you wish further training or consultation in this way of helping to empower others.

BIBLIOGRAPHY

Barks, C. (1997). *The essential Rumi.* Edison, NJ: Castle Books.

Carkhuff, R. R. (1983). *Sources of human productivity.* Amherst, MA: HRD Press.

Carkhuff, R. R. (2000). *The art of helping.* Amherst, MA: HRD Press.

Garagnon, F. Unknown source.

Gibran, K. (1963). *The prophet.* New York: Knopf.

Gordon, T. (1970). *Parent effectiveness training.* New York: Wyden.

Gordon, T. (1974). *Teacher effectiveness training.* New York: Wyden.

Gottman, J. M. & Silver, N. (1994). *Why marriages succeed or fail.* New York: Simon & Schuster.

Gottman, J. M. & Silver, N. (1999). *The seven principals for making marriage work.* New York: Crown.

Jung, C. G. (1961). *Memories, dreams, reflections.* New York: Random House.

Tolle, E. (1997). *The power of now.* Vancouver, BC: Namaste.

Tolle, E. (2005), *A new earth.* New York: Penguin.

ABOUT THE AUTHOR

Tony Roffers received his doctorate in counseling psychology from the University of Minnesota. He has served on the faculty at the University of California at Berkeley, San Francisco State University, and Saint Mary's College of California training hundreds of therapists for over two decades.

Dr. Roffers has consulted with a wide variety of professional organizations such as the American Association of Obstetrics and Gynecology where he assisted in developing skill-based clerkships and residency programs in medical schools throughout the country. He has also given guest lectures and workshops at law schools at Stanford University, the University of California at Berkeley and Davis, and at Hastings Law School.

He has taught communication skills and his collaborative conflict resolution model to groups of practicing attorneys and mediators in the U.S. Ninth Circuit Court of Appeals in San Francisco, the Northern California Mediation Association, the American Association of Matrimonial Lawyers, the Alternative Dispute Resolution Section of the Sonoma, San Luis Obispo, and Contra Costa Bar Associations, the Seattle Bar Association, JAMS/Endispute in San Francisco, and the National Institute of Trial Advocacy (NITA).

Dr. Roffers has been trained in many forms of traditional psychotherapy but has more recently focused on the energy therapies. In 1999, he became one of the first professionals trained in Advanced Integrative Therapy (formerly Seemorg Matrix Work) and currently trains therapist in this method. He assisted Dr. Asha Clinton (the founder of AIT) in the design of the training program and currently serves as her educational consultant. His medical history of food and inhalant allergies led him to a study of energy methods for treating allergies and ultimately to the holistic health model he is developing with Dr. Clinton for the physical track in Advanced Integrative Therapy.

He is a licensed psychologist and currently has a private therapy, consulting, training, and mediation practice in Oakland, California. For further information on his training schedule and to request training in the B-E-A-R Process, contact him through his website (www. tonyroffers.com) or at the following address and phone number.

Tony Roffers, PhD

3542 Fruitvale Avenue #218

Oakland, CA 94602

510-531-6730

Made in the USA
Charleston, SC
27 February 2010